**Bonnie Prudden
Shows How You Can B
as You Were in Your T**

There's a widespread revolution in the country—and it isn't on the college campuses. People are getting younger—younger-looking, younger-feeling, and younger inside the skin.

One book that has been both responsive to and greatly responsible for this rejuvenation of the American public is **How to Keep Slender and Fit After Thirty** by Bonnie Prudden. Since the publication of the first edition eight years ago, the book has been a long-term best seller and a classic in its field.

To keep pace with the vigorous new movement, she has written a new revised and enlarged edition of *How to Keep Slender and Fit After Thirty*. While retaining the solid, common-sense fitness program that has made Bonnie Prudden the foremost expert in her field, the revisions reflect all that is new and sound in diet and exercise.

Brand-new chapters specifically discuss the scene today: new developments in exercise techniques, primarily aerobics, jogging, and isometrics; growing threats to our well-being—drugs, smoking, chemical poisons in our foods, and water pollution. The new edition takes all this into consideration in planning a counterattack against the stresses and pace of the seventies.

How to Keep Slender and Fit After Thirty
was originally published by Bernard Geis Associates.

Bonnie Prudden

HOW TO KEEP SLENDER AND FIT AFTER THIRTY

New Revised and Enlarged Edition

PHOTOGRAPHS BY CHARLES STEWART

PUBLISHED BY POCKET BOOKS NEW YORK

HOW TO KEEP SLENDER AND FIT AFTER THIRTY

Bernard Geis edition published October, 1969
Pocket Book edition published October, 1970

**This *Pocket Book* edition includes every word
contained in the original, higher-priced edition.
Pocket Book editions are published by Pocket Books, a division
of Simon & Schuster, Inc., 630 Fifth Avenue, New York, N.Y. 10020.
Trademarks registered in the United States and other countries.**

L

To my daughters Petie and Suzy
—who still believe that nothing is impossible

CHARTS

Contents

Preface to the New Revised and Enlarged Edition

THE GAME OF YOU

I wrote the first edition of this book nine years ago when I was forty-six, and this is the first time in those speeding nine years that I've had the opportunity or taken the trouble to sit down and ask myself what has happened since then. It's been quite an experience—in fact it's almost as though the person who wrote the book is entirely different from the person who is about to rewrite it. Everybody should have a publisher who calls up and says, "Would you please bring the book of your life up to date by the first of next month?" If everyone had to take stock as I've just done, he might uncover some interesting facts and the desire to make some changes. He would find that much change has already occurred, but that much has gone unnoticed and very little came about because of conscious effort.

In looking over the physical changes that of course take place over nine years, I find I am slimmer. Since I was at least as active then as I am now, I have to ask myself why this pleasant surprise. The answer has to be that, due to my research on nutrition for another book, my diet has improved. I'm getting more mileage with fewer calories—and since my body is properly fed, I'm eating less and not even noticing it.

On the negative side, my right leg bothers me. I injured it four years ago and it is still a hindrance. I *think* I can fix it if I'll take the time, but I've been putting it off "because there's so much work to be done." When I think that one over quietly I realize it's a flimsy excuse and that the inefficiency caused by pain actually slows me down much more than would the time taken for repair. I didn't realize until I wrote this down in my Take Stock Chart on page xix that I've let four years go by while I overworked unhurt areas and compounded the original problem. I'd have a fit if one of my students did that.

My hair color is lighter than it used to be because it looks better on TV. I probably have more wrinkles, but as I have never paid much heed to wrinkles, I can't report accurately. I can talk about eyesight, however, because I can't find my glasses without my glasses. The ophthalmologist told me that the reason I had trouble with my eyes as a child was because I needed glasses even then. I feel as though I'd gotten away with something for forty-six years.

Fatigue is the big complaint these days, and I'm happy to report to me that I don't have it. I can still run full-day clinics five days a week, but I don't try to do it all by myself any more—that's how I got hurt four years ago.

Emotionally, I discovered something new when I first started to take stock. I felt as though I were running out of time. As I thought about it I realized that I'd been having this feeling for a long time and that it had been making me impatient and sometimes irritable, especially when things didn't jell at once. I had a few moments of panic until I went back over the section in the chart where I had listed what *had* been accomplished in the last nine years. In a few minutes I felt that sort of relaxing happiness you feel when you find your house keys in another pocket just when you thought you'd have to break a window. Nine years ago I had set myself a tremendous task, and it was a real comfort to find that much of the assignment was already finished. I don't really need a twenty-seven-hour day any more.

In 1960 I knew that the level of physical fitness in the United States was very low. There had to be a way of telling Americans so they would listen and understand that lack of physical fitness would make life less comfortable, less fun—and finally less. I'd done a lot of research on physical fitness in children, and President Eisenhower had authorized the formation of a group called The President's Council on Youth Fitness. Six years had passed since our first report and nothing much had come of it. If anyone was getting "the word," they were filing it. Besides it wasn't just youth that was out of shape, it was everyone. So, with Arlene Francis and Hugh Downs on "The Home Show" and then Dave Garroway on "The Today Show," I tried to catch the people's attention with the *whys* as well as the *hows* of becoming fit.

The weekly TV nudges were a great help and reached thousands of people. Pretty soon I was faced with such letters as, "All right, so physical fitness is important to me—so what's next? How do I get it?"

It never makes sense to complain much about conditions unless you've put your mind to devising ways to change them. Since 1947 we had had pilot studies going, and by then we had a lot of answers, but how do you tell people? A few minutes a week on network TV is an appetite whetter, not an answer. I needed my own show. So in 1963 I made sixty-five half-hour shows for syndication and in 1967 one hundred and thirty more, in color. Right along with them there were appearances on other folks' shows. Some of them were fun and easy to do, such as Art Linkletter's "House Party." Mr. Linkletter is a good sport, and we did some pretty funny things together (a couple were not scripted) and he's just as nice as he seems. One time I did a bit on Groucho Marx's show, and I found that one to be the hardest of all to do—then or any time since, probably because the guest is bound by a script but Groucho isn't. Mike Douglas has been more than generous to physical fitness and to me, and he is the easiest of all to work with. He sits and talks with you for a few minutes before the show (you've already told his people what you want to do) and finds out what's new in *your* field and what *you* want to talk about—and then the sky's the limit. Mike is tremendous fun, and he is also honest and concerned.

My night on "The Tonight Show" was tough for *me*, anyway. I was fully aware that I was getting a crack at that vast audience that only sees TV at night—that huge, tired, often ill, tense group that moves into buildings everywhere soon after daylight, sits at various labors and drags home often after dark to eat meals that often do not nourish, alone or with people who often do not ease, and crawls into bed to watch other people *live,* through TV. It was the same on "The Joey Bishop Show." Think now, if you really cared about people and there they were and you were supposed to make them laugh—how would you say, "Hey fellas, your arteries are clogging, your hearts are getting flabby, your sex appeal and virility are sagging and your blood pressures and tensions are mounting," *without getting caught at it?*

TV was the "sell" all right, but where was the program? All those people couldn't very well come to me—I'd have to go to them. Eight books followed each other, and six records. I started a yearly "crash" course for anyone who wanted to teach physical fitness on *any* level. *Reader's Digest* opened the doors to the national school boards and put my "Fit for Life" program within the reach of thousands and thousands of teenage girls through Girl's Clubs of America. The YMCAs, already involved with my testing and adult programs, began adding "Diaper Gym and Swim" for the six-month-olds. "Toddlers" were put in classes, "Tiny Tots" were toddler graduates, women's classes helped turn "Y"s into family clubs and they even put in co-ed teens and family fitness classes. This year pre- and post-natal classes have moved from the hospital level and can now be found—where? In the YMCA. I began adding equipment and fashions to the physical fitness line—and films.

Most people get the feeling when their children are little that they will be around or at least nearby forever. There is a period when time seems to stand still and is measured only by Sunday school. The more there are in the family, the more it seems to stand still because the last one embodies all the babyhoods that went before and, in some unexplained way, is the same child for a long time. But time doesn't stand still. When I started writing this book I had two daughters still under my wing, though I didn't exactly have them by the hand. One was just out of college and living in New York, and the other was in school in Europe—her father was planning to ski with her in Switzerland over Easter. I'd gone skiing on the morning of New Year's Eve when I was called to the office over the loudspeaker. It was Petie saying unbelievably, "Mommy, Daddy just died of a heart attack." He was forty-seven years old.

Those of you who can share with each other what the children are wittingly or unwittingly—but willy-nilly, nonetheless—going to do when they decide to live their own lives are lucky. It comes like a bolt out of the blue, and one parent shouldn't have to stand alone saying as many do, "What did I do wrong?" One Tuesday evening in the spring of 1962 the phone rang and it was Suzy. She was leaving college to get married and put the boy through school. At a time like that one asks the stupidest questions, like, "When are exams?" I had exactly four days to make the transition from mother with a point of view to mother-in-law with a closed mouth. It's a big step.

A year or so later Petie married and moved to Vermont. They were both on their way. Each had the boy she wanted and the life she wanted and nine-tenths of me was happy for them. One-tenth used to wait for me every evening as I opened the door to the empty apartment. One gets a sort of disembodied feeling that persists for a while. So very recently our house had been full of kids, dogs, cats, white mice, goldfish, muddy boots, and bobby pins. For those of you who stand in just such ghost houses there is a bit of cheer to be found at least on my chart. In the middle guest room now, there is a crib, a high chair, three shelves of toys, and a hobby horse. There's a sled in the garage, and a plastic pool. Your chart goes on, you know.

Addresses are important, because each new one means your life turned a corner. You may, when faced with it, see that you are where you are because you lack both the strength and the courage to get up and git. You may just feel that the next nine years are *not* going to be like the last. Nine years ago I had that apartment in White Plains, New York, and my office apartment at the Institute two blocks away. With the girls away I had stayed more and more often at the Institute. I then called it "an awful lot to do," which was true, but a more honest appraisal made from here and now would be, "I like to hear people moving around till late." Color this section *lonely*.

I had started to build a combination house and Institute in Massachusetts in the fall of 1959. I figured I'd like it and the children would like it and every vacation would be just glorious. It has become the last address on the TSC (Take Stock Chart), but long before it was finished *I* was visiting the *children* instead of the other way around. It's easier to move grandmothers than babies.

There has to be a place on your chart for "future plans," and in mine I have this revision and the finishing of the book *How to Keep Your Child Fit from Six to Twelve*. Then there is the conversion of *Quick Rx for Fitness* to a paperback and, lastly for this chart, a new book for adults, *Keep Fit—Be Happy*. There are two dozen other things I *could* throw into the hopper, but I've learned something from my Take Stock Chart. Don't bite off, even in your mind, too big a chunk. If you do, there's a very good chance that you may get so deeply involved that you forget a very important person in your life—yourself.

When I got to the "Leisure" or "What Do I Do for Me" part of the TSC, I pulled up short. The person I pictured in my mind's eye was not the person on the chart at all, but someone I'd known a long time ago. First I wrote down all the sports and hobbies I have loved in my life, and next to each one I wrote in the number of times I *knew* I'd taken the time to enjoy it recently and the date of the last time I could remember. I'd done a lot of lap swimming to keep in shape last summer, but it had been two years, almost three, since I'd done any skin diving worthy of the name. I'd skied last winter for TV and started the season off with lessons as usual, but after a couple of trips I'd gotten involved with some job or other—and that was it. I have a camper that also pulls a tent trailer. It can go anywhere, but does it? All but a couple of trips have been on business (it's also a TV dressing room), and I've never used the tent at all. I also have a Ski Daddler that I use for ski joring. I used it once last winter. This winter will be different—I have had the word from my own TSC. At the present moment I am sitting in the garden in the Florida house of some very dear friends (my children's grandparents) writing this. Writing in the garden is fine, but *all* the time? Well, the TSC says it quite clearly. You have a dozen hobbies and as many sports and all you do is work. Why?

Everyone but the well-disciplined runs a terrible risk of getting into a rut somewhere along the line. Work is a rut, and I fell into it. We all live as though life will go on forever and there are unlimited supplies of tomorrows. If nine years ago you were in your twenties, you were probably searching. Every ounce of energy was taken up with finding out what you wanted to do with your life and then finding the right job to fit that pattern. You searched for the right mate, the right apartment, the right house on the right street, the right car and furniture—and the right obstetrician. You probably didn't think past how tired you were each night.

If you were in your thirties nine years ago, you were probably climbing the ladder at the job, raising children, going to meetings, running to the orthodontist, seeing teachers and feeding cub scouts. If you were a housewife, you went through "the morass of motherhood" crisis, which made you wonder if feeding, tending, cleaning and clothing was all there was to life. Toward the end of that time there came the second one, the "They're all grown up—now what shall I do with my time?" crisis. Each of these is more painful and harder to take than a good dose of menopause because there isn't a pill—yet.

If you were in the forties you were either on the ladder moving up, or on it moving down—there's no standing still at the office. If you wanted to change jobs it was now or never and you couldn't get that "bird in the hand" phrase out of your mind. If things were just too rugged, a great deal of time was taken up babying your ulcer, low back pain, high blood pressure or tension syndromes (wherever they might be). Some of your friends had died of stroke or heart attacks and you couldn't believe it. The kids had come into their own and gone to college or to work. Some had married with pomp and splendor, some had eloped and some were living in "common loft" marriage, which you find hard to understand—and explain. There have been divorces in your ranks and perhaps you were a casualty. One in ten of your group has been in a mental hospital, there have been one or two mastectomies, and virtually everybody has given up smoking. Menopause flashed its hot little head and who had time for reflection?!

If you were in your fifties (where I am now as I write this), you might have been preparing to retire. *Preparing* to retire is good thinking. The average man dies twenty-two months after he retires mostly because he can't think of anything better to do. If in the fifties you find something that interests you tremendously and you can hardly wait to get at it, that's life insurance that works for *you*. In the fifties men start giving thought to virility and women to wrinkles. At the present moment the best bet for both is physical fitness, and on the horizon scientists are promising a number of benefits for those with the foresight to be around: *(1)* increased sex life (not just in your head); *(2)* a youthful appearance well into what we now consider old age. In the meantime, don't worry too much about wrinkles. Look for signs of warmth, humor, kindness and affection. The worst thing anyone can say to you is, "You haven't changed a bit." If you haven't you are probably psychotic and don't live in the body bearing your name. Rather than wishing for a young face, *work* to build a young body—one that will let you *do* youthful things, not just look as though you'd like to. Make every day count.

If you were in your sixties in the last nine years, you were probably on your way to retirement and if you have lived these last nine years it probably means you know how to eat properly, you enjoy life and you rest when there is nothing more exciting to do at the moment. Perhaps you haven't retired because you didn't want to and nobody was in a position to make you. Well, if work is your pleasure you are fortunate indeed. It will keep you in touch with the things you understand and help you to change *with* the times rather than stand by shaking your head. Whether they want to admit it or not, the younger generation could use the help of a wily old fox who has learned a lot along the way.

Sit down now and do a profile on your life. Answer the questions and add a few of your own. Try to figure out why you repeated the same mistake two or three times . . . how you have spent your time . . . what you want to do now. Do it all honestly and carefully, because you may discover you have been cheating yourself of happiness while time whizzed by in a blinding blur you couldn't see through. This book will tell you *how* to get in shape and stay there. Your TSC may tell you why you *want* to.

TAKE STOCK

This is not a true-false test or a multiple-choice test or a match-the-number-with-a-letter test. When you have finished it you won't have a score that tells you how you stack up next to somebody, or any group of somebodys. Part of it could be called a memory test, some of it could be called an honesty test and most of it could be called an insight test. If you play this little game fairly *with yourself* you may get an entirely different idea *about yourself*—because your answers could only have come from you. If, after you have read over your answers, you feel like saying, "So what?!" don't fight it—but don't throw out the test either. In a month take the same test *without looking at the first version*. Your subconscious may have been very busy the entire time, and you can make changes. Check those changes carefully. A few tries and a pattern will begin to emerge.

Since the discovery of cybernetics (Freud won't have it all his way any more), we know that brains are really computers. They give back the information (or they *can* give back the information) that we have at one time or another put in and stored there. Occasionally we put in some incomplete or erroneous information, a sort of mistake, so to speak—and we find this mistake cropping up over and over. Everyone of us knows the feeling of having goofed. And then goofing again because it seemed the easiest way. A close examination of your last nine

years will give you a good idea of how you have programmed yourself, and it's quite possible that you may
want to erase some of the fouled-up tape and replace
it with something else that will make your *decisions* and
therefore your *life,* easier.

Somebody, and it could have been my mother, my first
arithmetic teacher or even my husband, convinced me
that I knew nothing about business. With this little strip
as backup and along with another bit of erroneous information, namely "there's always tomorrow," I let other
people handle the business part of my work. Eventually I
discovered my error, but it took several bad experiences
plus a Take Stock Chart to find it. There was nothing
the matter with my business sense (other than that part
of the work bored me). Business is mostly common sense,
and I can handle business if I'll take the trouble. Time
has taught me that taking the trouble is a lot less trouble
than the trouble you can get into if you don't take the
trouble. Now ask yourself, "Have *I* got a phony excuse
that makes *me* feel better *and right* when *I* don't want to
do something?"

As you answer the questions, don't make up excuses
and don't ask yourself, "What else could I do?" What you
are looking for is not comfort *at this point.* You are
looking for yourself as you are, not as you think you are.
That person may be from Dullsville, for all you know,
and the real you is exciting and interesting. Incidentally,
if you live around nosy people, don't leave any of your
notes within their reach. If there is the slightest possibility
of others seeing your private thoughts, you'll write those
thoughts differently. You'll write them as though you
expected them to be read. If that's what you want to
have happen, fine, go ahead, but *know you are doing it.*
Then ask yourself why.

It is terrible to be a slave to anything or any one, and
when you are a slave to old mistakes it is not only terrible
but self-destructive. For example, some children have such
terrible lives and the odds against them are so over-
whelming that their only recourse is to run away. Do you
notice how many adults run away and how many ways
there are of running even if one never picks up a foot?

This chart is to help you find errors in your computer. Who *needs* 700 copies of *Time* Magazine a week or seventeen unsatisfactory jobs in a lifetime? Well, that's what can happen when a computer goes wrong. The chart will cover your physical condition, your work, family, friends and leisure. Your answers will become more detailed and revealing as you become better acquainted with yourself.

Chart 1. TAKE STOCK

Details to help you answer the questions are given on pages xx–xxxiv. Copy down the following headings on separate sheets of paper, leaving lots of room for your answers, and follow the instructions carefully.

1. **AGE**
   Now:
   Nine years ago:

2. **YOU**
   Nine years ago:
   Now:

3. **YOUR ADDRESSES**
   Nine years ago:
   Now:

4. **YOUR JOB:**

5. **LEISURE**
   Early childhood (birth to six):
   Middle years (six to twelve):
   Teen years:
   From your twenties till nine years ago:
   Nine years ago:
   Now:

6. **YOUR MARRIAGE PARTNER:**

7. **CHILDREN:**

8. **TALENT:**

9. **EDUCATION:**

10. **THE FUTURE:**

1. *Age*. Write down your present age and the age you were nine years ago. Now for the next ten minutes try to remember all you can about nine years ago. What were you like? What was your appearance? What was uppermost in your thoughts in those days? Picture your house and your relatives and friends and the streets where you walked. Try to remember how you felt about you and those close to you.

2. *You*. Start with yourself and write a brief description about your physical condition nine years ago and then bring yourself up to date on the present.

Mine would run something like this:

Nine Years Ago: Lots of physical activity . . . felt great. Plenty of energy. Hay fever lighter than formerly. Five pounds too heavy for me, thighs as usual. Need reading glasses.

Now: Had flu three times this winter (got up too soon). Muscle tone now miserable but improving with exercise. Not really tired, but not really marvelous either. Writing long hours without shoulder tension, but injured leg hates sitting. Must have gotten mental shot in the arm somewhere, everything interests me and I'm reading as I used to as a kid— everything. Sometimes read all night.

Now take the two descriptions and read them over for all kinds of content. The fact that I had the flu and feel as though I'd had the flu and that there were no pessimistic undertones is a good sign. I could have felt awful and credited my age, or overwork. It there were job or family troubles I might blame them. The flu has short-term aftereffects that were already answering to exercise. I mentioned the overweight and pointed out that "as usual" it was in the thighs. Well, thigh weight is tension weight, and I've had that and gotten rid of it before. The notes indicate I'm all right physically and that my attitude is all right, too. But supposing something were wrong. Supposing I'd gone steadily downhill *without noticing it*— and you can when you are busy.

3. *Your addresses.* Write a brief description of the place where you lived nine years ago. Try to give yourself the mood of the place rather than just its condition. "A shabby little place" tells you very little, but "a shabby little place filled with good talk, warmth and laughter" is something else. So is "a shabby little place—and would you believe it, seven people living there in two rooms!" When you finish, write about any interim places and finally write about today's.

Then read them and see what you get.

4. *Your job.* What about your job? Every job from cleaning the office hall to being chairman of the board counts. Even having no job at all should be noted and the reasons *why* you have no job. Write down what your work was nine years ago and also a quick recall on how you got into it in the first place. The work you were doing nine years ago may have little or nothing to do with its beginnings, say, twenty years ago—or, as in my case, everything, but how you came to where you are is important because it tells whether or not the decisions were yours. Ask yourself about your work and find out why you are in it. Because you like it? Because you are good at it? Because it's *there?* Because the pay is good or the people are nice? Perhaps it's because you'd rather live closer to home even if it means working at that job when you could have a better one in town?

If you don't have a job and don't want it any different, you must be doing *something* that has purpose, even if it is traveling (which gets to be more and more of a job). Why are you doing what you are doing and why aren't you doing anything else? Trace whatever you are up to so that you can trace your own patterns and then predict where all this is going. Sometimes all you will find out is that you are discontented and *must* find more outlet for some part of your personality. If you find that much out about yourself, you are ahead, because when you know for sure that it isn't your ulcer that makes you miserable, but your misery making an ulcer—you change what makes you miserable.

5. *Leisure.* What you do or do not do with spare time can tell you a lot. The ideal life seems to be balanced on three legs: one is work, one is rest and the third is leisure. When one is very young rest *seems* to be overlooked. Actually, children and adolescents will take time for rest when they need it, and they do so more often than is apparent. The danger of too little rest comes in the middle years when the body tolerates pushing if motivation is high enough. Any mother with a seriously ill child has all the motivation needed to stay awake and active for days and nights on end. Any man pinned down by sniper fire in an infiltrated area finds sleep and rest very elusive. Older people learn pace (that's often why they stay alive to be still older) and, having learned more about values and being graduated from child care, wars and business emergencies, they limit themselves to *comfortable* production. Work should be suited to the personality, but the person who puts *all* his life's eggs in a "work" basket runs grave risks.

First, he (or she) can become a colossal bore, since his only topic of conversation is "the job." It becomes harder and harder to find companionship, as boredom is the one thing most people avoid. Then too, a change of pace is necessary to health. You can keep going at a good clip without damage and even without tiring if you constantly switch activities. A hard morning at the office can be erased by a noon workout at the "Y."

Six hours at my typewriter is too long and gives me a backache. However, I can stretch the day to eight hours, six writing and two in physical activity (whatever is in season) and be ready for a pleasant evening at the end of it. Or, since a lot of my work is active and a lot of it even looks and feels like physical recreation, I can work a sixteen-hour stretch and merely feel tired enough to sleep well *if the tasks vary.*

For instance, a press breakfast as a starter followed by a TV appearance. Neither require physical action, and both use up lots of nervous energy. Then a lecture demonstration with a lot of floor exercise. Balance is restored. Lunch at a service club with a half-hour talk (nervous energy again) and then ten minutes of exercise demonstration (balance again). The afternoon often is used for clinics where special exercises for specific needs are demonstrated —that means even the types of movement will vary. There are radio tapings and news interviews intermingled throughout the day. The evening's performance often ends in some socializing for the home team—for me it is usually more talk on the same subject. In the course of the day I probably changed locations six or seven or more times. I changed groups of people as often. I changed activities as often and a lot of it was physical. That means an improvement in strength, a very necessary stretching of muscles and the release of lots of the tension accumulated as I tried to feel out each audience and find the quickest way to reach them.

Lastly, work without a thought to balance can become a death-trap for men when they are forced by the addition of years to retire. A man without direction, without a sense of his own worth other than that which has come from work, doesn't live long after retirement, and that's a pity. Think of the waste of brainpower we suffer because the company has an age limit. Is that really the reason, or can we pin it down to something else? All those driving men who *could* have set up a group to show companies what they are wasting, what are *they* doing? Those men *could* make a hobby of unseating the brash youngsters who take their places. After all, the older fellow still has the contacts, he knows where the bodies are buried and he has lots of know-how. If his body were in shape he would not get into any ruts, for one thing, and if he had at least one all-consuming interest on the outside he wouldn't be riddled and finally paralyzed by fear.

A good look at the way you spend leisure time can be unsettling. Keeping in mind that the brain only gives back what you put in and store, what can you give back if your leisure is lost to sports over TV? Dining used to be very active and stimulating leisure, but dinner in front of TV has numbed thinking and limited the ability to communicate. Before fast cars there used to be leisure just in getting where you were going, shanks' mare or at a slow trot. Today it can be half a day's work to get to a little of what used to be a healthy must. One of the wonderful things about a big city like Denver is that you can see leisure beckoning from the mountains to the west. In Boston and San Francisco and most especially in Sydney, Australia, you can always smell and often see the sea. But what about the middle of a big city in the middle of the Midwest?

Write down all you can remember about your life's leisure activities. Bring the list up to the nine-years-ago point and include your early childhood (birth to six), your middle years (six to twelve), your teens and adult years (twenties to nine years ago). Notice how your activities in childhood have affected your whole life and how you have spent your spare time. Follow these lists with one for nine years ago and one for now—then take stock. Ask yourself if you have a balance. You may find (to your surprise) that you don't. One of the easiest ruts to get into is the "no time for that sort of thing" rut. You just get so busy and so far behind that you soothe a worrying subconscious or perhaps a very conscious mate by saying, "I'll let up just as soon as this is out of the way."

If I were to do a rundown on my leisure history it would read as follows:

Early childhood (birth to six)

Walked in woods and fields and on beaches with mother.
Fished in lakes, streams and sound with father.
Swam at four, in lakes, river, sea and pools.
Rode horseback at six—started on Atlantic City beaches.
Camped out in the backyard alone.
Rowed, poled and paddled boats—was allowed to steer power boats.
Collected wildlife pets and had a dog.
Slept out of doors on a sleeping porch (New York) all year round.
Freedom to roam uncrowded neighborhood with much open play space.
Had a tricycle, Push-Me-Pull-You, skates, swings and a tree house.

Went to dancing school (ballet, "esthetic," tap, acrobatic and folk).

Sang in the choir.

My mother read to me all the time and I could read myself at three.

Middle years (six to twelve)

Hiked at camp and often alone at home. Spent many Saturdays just wandering.

Cooked and camped out in the backyard.

Fished with father and alone.

Had a horse of my own and rode eastern or western as the mood suited.

Swam all summer and went once a week to the YMCA pool in winter.

Started competition swimming and diving at ten.

Good physical education at school—track, dodgeball, gymnastics, tumbling.

Started teaching "setting up exercises in classroom" at age eight.

Dancing school one weekday and all day Saturday. Added elocution.

Went weekly to German gym club (Turnverein).

Started Scouts at ten—was not impressed.

Rode a bike and a scooter.

Rowed, canoed, kayaked, sailed and went aquaplaning.

Went crabbing, clamming and scalloping.

Swam (across the harbor) walked or rode a bike to get places. Rode my horse.

Put on neighborhood plays and was constantly "making things."

Read every book I could get my hands on and was read to by my mother.

Loved movies, theater and music. Played the violin (badly).

Sang in the choir, sketched and painted.

Had a dog (and also her pups).

Was in a convent at ages six and eight—knew every game there is (almost) that takes no equipment and goes on forever.

Went to camp two years at ten and eleven (very boring).

Went on two cruises on old tramp schooners at eleven and twelve (wonderful).

Fell in love with Brooks Everett at twelve.

Perhaps you can't see any reason for my listing and your reading this, but don't stop now. There is a lesson

here for both of us. I got the word when I made the list.
You'll get it in a couple of pages.

Teen years

Hiked and camped and cooked out at every opportunity.
Spent every available minute in or on the water in summer.
Fished alone and with father.
Added water-skiing to other water fun. Thought it a little dull.
Had the cabin job on a thirty-five-foot cruiser of my father's.
  Boat and engine work all day—polishing, painting, scraping
  —no pay (wonderful).
Started to drive at thirteen (all the summer kids on Shelter
  Island did).
Read whenever I sat down.
Became assistant scout leader at fourteen.
Drew, painted, wrote poetry, "stories" and plays. Put on the
  plays.
Lots of amateur dance and theatricals.
Varsity hockey, basketball, swimming and track in school.
  Riding club.
Drama and dance clubs. Art group.
Orchestra, chamber music, choral group and choir. Started
  piano.
Started volunteer work in children's clinics.
Made miniature theaters (fully equipped) as a hobby.
Started studying psychology at Columbia at night while still
  in high school.
Studied anatomy for fun and made hundreds of drawings.
Worked (illegally) on cadavers at night with friends who
  were medical students.
Started dating at sixteen. Loved dancing—hated parties.
Traveled a summer in Europe with my family.
Fell in love several times (some people never give this up as
  a hobby!).
Played bridge with my family (never had the courage to try
  with anyone else.)
Lots of movies, theater and the philharmonic orchestra. Dance
  concerts.
Started mountaineering and skiing.
Worked cattle in Arizona and started breaking horses.
Started studying German (alone) and going to art galleries
  with the boy I married when I reached twenty-one.

My mother hadn't an athletic *skill* to her name. Her father wouldn't permit her to learn, but she certainly saw to it that my sister and I were well supplied. My father passed on his love of the outdoors—and was incredibly patient. Take a look now and see how these things affected my married life and even the selection of a marriage partner.

From my twenties till nine years ago (*twenty-six years*)

Started rock climbing in Switzerland on my honeymoon.*

Continued every summer in the Far West.*

Started figure skating.

Rode a great deal and started the children at age three.*

Hiked with family, camped out often.*

Swam often and started the children very early.

Skied every winter weekend and started the children at three.*

Rock-climbed every summer, spring and fall weekend and started the children at four.*

Took long mountain-climbing weekends and started the children at five.*

Started the children in dancing school and when dissatisfied taught them myself.

Joined the ski patrol and put my anatomy studies to work. Taught teen safety.*

Started the Addlepate Ski School for kids eight and up. First dry ski school in the U.S. (They learned on grass—*before* the season).*

Took on a troop of Brownie Scouts.

Took on a troop of Mariner Scouts for a year. My husband began with Boy Scouts.*

Took on a whole slew of Girl Scouts for modern dance.

Started "conditioning exercise" classes for children so my own would get some.

We grew out of the Scout House and into a public school.

Studied art and piano with good teachers—and Italian alone.

Read a great deal—on a history kick.

Made things for and with the children, knitted everybody into sweaters, tried sewing and needlepoint.

Made shelves, tables and other furniture for the house. Painted it inside and out.

---

* Husband's interests, too.

Had a huge garden (and a yard full of children).

Went to museums, theater, movies, dance concerts and the philharmonic.*

Played touch football and did a lot of partying around our neighborhood.*

Made climbing and ski films.*

Started teen climbing, hiking and ski group.*

Outgrew the school with my conditioning classes and had to go professional.

Put on big shows with hundreds of youngsters each spring.*

Taught First Aid and rounded up blood-bank donors. Worked for Community Chest, set up Red Cross sewing group.

Wrote a book on exercise (not published in original form). Wrote a novel (not published at all) and started choreography for my students.

Climbed in Europe and went to a ranch in Wyoming (children's specialty).*

Looking back (and I never had) I found that my early background prepared me to share the leisure time of my husband. In some cases I changed my specialties (water sports, for instance) for his (climbing and skiing). Many of the things we liked were the same—art, music, camping and theater. Those long lists speak of a variety of *leisure* interests, and in the following you will see how what was once a hobby can enhance work but at the same time *become* your work. This is one of the reasons why some work is more fun than play. You will also see how sneaky work can be when your back is turned. One day you take the trouble to write a list of your leisure activities and it takes *four* lines.

Nine years ago

I had so many weekend clinics I couldn't climb every weekend. When you don't climb every weekend you can't be counted on as a steady climbing partner, and others take your place on the rope. Then too, leading top climbs takes constant practice or you get killed and maybe take a friend along.

---

* Husband's interests, too.

Except for occasional trips on climbs requiring less than expert skills, I quit—and lost an antidote for anxiety and frustration.

I was building a house and lived in it for two years in a partially finished (as to walls and windows!) state. That was camping enough! Camping out, I quit. Instead of getting away from my problems, I settled in with them.

I still hiked and skied when I could, but the desk and tasks were always there. I found it takes habit to go places, and there is always another habit (working) lying in wait.

I read a great deal still, but mostly things that would have some bearing on what I was doing in physical fitness. I drew, but mostly exercises for books. I choreographed, but only exercises for my classes. I listened to music, but with an ear to exercise routines (even with Bach). I put on shows, but they were on TV. I taught groups of all kinds, but as a job. I made films, but for schools. I wrote, but exercise books. I designed clothes and equipment, for exercise. I studied more anatomy—as it applied to exercise. It was almost as if everything I'd ever developed was pointing right down the road to *exercise*. But I had lost the road that led over the hills and away. Look.

Now

I garden (with tractor, etc., and then I put the stuff up).
I play the piano some.
Watch TV.
Read.

Isn't that a shocker? And I truly never noticed, primarily because many of the leisure skills now have a place in my work. That's nice, but it's wrong. It isn't a switch in tempo and it isn't a switch in attitude. It may be exciting, but it isn't restful. It may be fun, but it isn't lighthearted like an afternoon on a glittering slope or a hot sandy beach, or lying face down in a warm sea watching fish through a mask. (I took up skin diving five years ago, but, as I said earlier, I haven't done any worth talking about for a couple of years, so I didn't count it as current.)

As a result of the discoveries I made when I wrote the Take Stock Chart for the first time, I've made some changes. The camper is in action and a Florida night sounds closer there than indoors. The Ski Daddler has been put in order and the ski-joring trails cleared. I'm reading things that have nothing to do with work at least as much as work-related material. This next month I'm snowed under with work, but starting the one after I get a three-day weekend *in the middle of the week* if that's when I want it, I shall combine work with pleasure. And after that I have a two-day job up on the Maine coast, but I'm taking the camper and seven days for it.

What I learned was that I had closed too many windows in the house of my life. I'd done it so gradually I hardly noticed the deepening shadows—and now there is a window-opening job to do. I am more grateful to my parents at this moment than ever before in my life, because only now do I realize what gifts they gave me.

6. *Your marriage partner.* Whom, or—as it is in my case since I married an entire family—what, did you marry? What part has this person or persons played in your life? How did you happen to marry the person you married (if more than one, answer for each, not just the last)? What do you like about your partner and what would you change if you could?

Write down everything you can think of, both the good and not so good about the very beginning, nine years ago and now. Marriage is rarely a breeze, but if you have been successful in adjusting to each other as you were in the beginning, as you grew side by side (not everybody grows at the same rate) and as you are now, there had to be a reason. Can you find the reason for your success? If you had trouble once upon a time, what caused it? If you know anything about yourself now that you didn't know when you needed to know it, what is it?

7. *Children.* If you had children, why did you have them? Many folks think that's the reason people get married, but it isn't so (very often). We are programmed to have children way back when *we* are somebody's children. Even the people (and there are many) who shouldn't have children are programmed—and, sure enough, they too have children.

Write all you can think of that has to do with your children, including the effect they have had on your marriage, how they have changed you and their other parent. Have you enjoyed each other? If not, do you know why not? What have they done with their lives? Has their decision affected your life in any way? Keep in mind, now, that you are writing for yourself, not posterity.

8. *Talent.* Everybody has *some* talent, some people have several talents—and a few are blessed (or cursed) with many talents. Scientists are hard at work on studies that will ultimately lead to the rearrangement of genes. This could conceivably mean that ultimately *everybody* will be so talented they may even disarm the ticking time bomb these same scientists are putting together day by day. In the meantime, find out whether you have used (for your pleasure and satisfaction) all the talents you brought with you into this life.

Very often things get accomplished because several rather modest talents get together at the right moment in time. My work in physical fitness is one of these. The studies were made in the first place because, as an athlete-dancer with an interest in both anatomy and psychology, I knew how a well-coordinated, healthy body *should* move. As a trained observer I knew when it didn't. If you see enough children in a given country sitting, standing, walking and running very poorly—while the children in *every other country you visit are sitting, standing, walking and running very well indeed*—you wonder. Sports, dance, anatomy, sketching, sculpture, rhythm, and psychology all come together to produce observation, comparison and conclusion. My continuing interest in medicine led me into contact with physical medicine and the whys of poor posture, and it didn't take a great deal more observation and pondering to connect the physically under-par human being with insufficient exercise, poor nutrition and an excess of unrelieved tension. That was step number one. Bringing information, especially unpleasant information to people, calls for another talent. There was to be a use after all for those drama club productions, miniature theaters and neighborhood "shows." Putting programs and information down on paper so they can be understood and used brought in not only the writing, but the art work as well. Designing programs and setting them to music on records utilized all the many facets of music from singing (on time) in the choir loft to listening to Schnabel or Casals. No great talent, just a clutter of small ones that fitted together.

Write down every talent you ever had from riding a bike no handed (exceptional balance) to running the department. Next list the uses to which you have put those talents, which ones were not used and why. Is there perhaps a way to tie a few of them into a "clutter" that might open up a whole new world for you?

9. *Education.* Education begins at once (if not sooner). It takes very little time to learn that making a big noise brings help—or a wallop. A few meetings with a Nervous Nellie's hands and the newborn gets very nervous. In the other direction, if you can see, hear, feel or think, your education hasn't stopped. There is a belief that when you get your diploma, your certificate, your Master's or your Doctorate—that does it. Actually, what you have gotten from the type of education offered today is a batch of skills (even thinking takes skill). You really start to put two and two together *after* you get out of school. Of course there are people who don't learn anything much *in* school, and there are those who don't learn *after* school, but if you are reading this book that means you are curious and hopefully discontent—a good combination for learning.

Write down all you can remember about your education, both in and out of school, and list the sources of your education. (I learned all I ever was *taught* about teaching from my gym teacher Mrs. Cook when I was eight and from my gym teachers Miss Gulick and Miss Jones when I was at Horace Mann School for Girls in New York City. I never learned any French while taking it in two schools, but I taught myself quite a bit of German and Italian when I was in love with people who spoke those two languages. Love is a fast teacher because of the desire to please. I did poorly in history at Horace Mann but well with my father-in-law, who loved history and me, too).

Did you get a chance at *all* the things that interested you in school? Is there something you'd like to take up now if only there were time or money or a place where they teach it nearby? What were your reading habits as a child, young person, adult? What are they at this moment? Do you speak or read another language? Have you any "educational" hobbies? Nine years ago, what were you doing with your mind *aside from work?* Have your horizons increased or are you losing ground? What new thing have you learned this day?

10. *The future.* For the past few years "The Future" has looked (and sounded) like a huge dog with a string of cans tied to its tail approaching full speed down a dusty road. There isn't any way to stop it, there's no way of telling how many cans there are, what else might be tied to him and how he'll behave when he gets here. On second look, with all the speed, dust and noise, you can't even be sure that what you see (or think you see) is a huge dog with a string of cans tied to its tail—it could be something quite different. It might be something you should prepare yourself to handle.

Today man is able to tell which sex a baby is before it is born, but in the not-too-distant future he will be able to fertilize human eggs in a test tube and implant those eggs in the human womb. At that time he will also be able to decide whether he wants a boy for Mama or a girl for Papa. It's only a hoot and a holler to the day when he will also be able to decide which characteristics the child shall possess on arrival. Are we *prepared* to make those choices?

We are now transplanting organs with considerable success, and soon we will be able to transplant both organs and limbs not only from man to man but from animal to man. The shocker comes when you realize that we will also be able to transplant from man to animal.

In the near future mind-modifying drugs will be able to assure you of serene contentment, or any of several other "moods"—and there will be regulation of desire (both ways). Scientists are working on a technique to erase unpleasant memories much as today they excise an unwanted growth. After that, the *injection* of memory is a possibility. Won't that shake up the school system! The time of "No more teachers, no more books . . ." will be at hand and I want to be right there to watch.

It would have jiggled the many-faceted mind of Leonardo da Vinci if he were to be shown the world's "progress" since his day. Progress made fairly slow work of it for a long time compared to the speed it has picked up in the last twenty years. From now on, what used to take years will take months—and the Leonardo-jet gap will be narrowed to a step in your lifetime.

I, for one, want to see as much of all of this as I can. I am as curious about the way man is going to handle his new toys as about the toys themselves. To see these changes and to appreciate and perhaps even benefit from them, I have to be here and I have to be fit physically, mentally and emotionally. This chart and the physical tests in this book will help me draw on what I've had, maintain and improve what I have—and ready me for what may come. What is your feeling about the future?

From what you have written and then read about yourself, how well do you think you are prepared—physically, mentally and emotionally—to handle the swiftly approaching changes of the future? Each of the questions was a prime question and will lead to many others. They may also lead to a few uncomfortable moments, some sleepless hours and much soul searching. They cause you to examine the past so that you can *do* something about the future rather than simply be at its mercy.

When you have done your best with your Take Stock Chart, put it away in a safe place, and, from now on, just as you get a yearly physical or a pap test or are checked for cholesterol level, take stock of your life. That way you will always have an up-to-date report on yourself—the most important person in your life.

CHAPTER ONE

Sign here for a new lease on life

Sooner or later everyone gets to be thirty—and then forty. It is a state that is rarely sought after, viewed with despair by a few, resignation by many, and understood by almost nobody.

Youth, as everybody knows, is wasted on young people. Those beautiful idiots, racing around, expending energy as though it were boundless, taking for granted that everyone loves them, waking each morning with fresh mouths tasting of gentle dreams. Young fools with a million years before them. *You* would know what to do with all that energy, that beauty, those endless hours. *You* wouldn't waste them, toss them away oblivious of their value.

All right, supposing you were given two wishes—with strings attached, of course. All bona fide wishes have strings. Wish Number One would grant that you return tomorrow to the youth you once were. You may live your life over again right from the point where you turn back the years. But here are the strings: you must live it the second time *exactly* as you did the first. You must have every fear, say every sentence, make every mistake you made before. Not a single blush less this time.

Think now—would you? Most people, after a few seconds of thought, say firmly, "No thanks, once was enough."

They don't even ask about the second wish. And that's too bad, because the *second* wish is what this book is all about.

1

Wish Number Two is that you regain the looks, energy, desires and drive of a young person, *and know what you know now about life and living*. Now that's quite different, isn't it? To this you'd listen. Certainly there is a string here, too: you'll have to work to achieve it. But if you have lived for forty years more or less, you have already learned that there is no such thing as getting something for nothing—even in a wish. You are well aware that you will have to work for what you get, but you also know that it will be worth it, no matter how much you have to undo and do over.

There are so many reasons why it would be worth your while to turn back the figurative years to the point where you are strong, attractive and functioning at top level. You have a family you wish you weren't too tired to enjoy. Or perhaps you have a family you can't stand, but are afraid to try life alone. You have a great business and you enjoy daily battle. Or perhaps your business is falling apart, but how do you get out of it alive? You would like to be as tough and fearless as ever, but you are afraid that age is slowing you down. Perhaps you belong to a good organization but are crowding sixty and those young fellows may just edge you out. Are you the lady whose husband is doing fine but you feel you aren't much of an advertisement for him? Or perhaps you are still very attractive and full of vitality, but his idea of a big evening is "TV on the Rocks." The kids think you are stuffy—or you think the kids are stuffy. You don't want to retire (and you are right—retirement is too often a jet flight out). You would like to retire, but it is going to take five more years of hard work to provide enough capital for comfort.

Maybe you have fallen in love but you think you're too old for that sort of thing. Or you aren't in love, but you suspect you are missing something and would like to try this business there is so much excitement about— if you could just find someone to give you a long second look.

Perhaps you've become used to the notion that you are less lovely or handsome than you used to be—more listless and apathetic, with no great desire in the world beyond getting through another twelve hours. You hardly remember what it feels like to leap out of bed in the morning, feeling well and eager to meet the challenge of a new day. You face each birthday with gloom, thinking the only way you've grown in the last year is around the waistline. Perhaps your sex life is hardly present. Certainly you don't feel inspired to write a book about it. You may feel old and useless, or you may be clutched by panic, feeling that life is passing you by. Maybe you are just damn tired and bored.

I remember the night before I was married when my mother said: "I guess I must be old. I feel the same as I always did, but if you are grown up, then I must have grown old. All my life I have been waiting for something wonderful to happen. I am still waiting." Perhaps it was because she sounded so lost and sad, when I was feeling so happy, that I filed away her words with a vow that I would never wait for life. Three years later, still waiting for something to happen, my mother died.

There is no area of living that would not be affected by vitality, a strong attractive body, desire and drive. You need to *want,* and then you need the self-confidence to go and get it. Is all this possible at your age? No question about it.

It is not crossing over the border from twenty-nine into the thirties or from thirty-nine to forty and on that has caused you to slow down and to age. What has happened is comparatively simple. As you grew older you did not have the opportunity to move as much as you did as a child. Now you are less inclined to move. The less you move the less you *can* move. The human being who stays in this cycle long enough gets tense and stiff and that is when "age" begins to show. When a sudden effort is made—for example reaching for something or bending over—a twinge of pain is felt. "Getting old," you decide ruefully, "better slow down." So day by day you restrict your physical activity more and more. The less you use your body, the less ability your body has to function well. It is a vicious downward spiral. *But it doesn't have to be.*

As I watch Uncle Charlie, who always played tennis and still does at seventy-five, take over the younger members of his family, or when I try in vain to keep up with an eighty-year-old mountaineer as he takes his daily two-hour "constitutional," I realize that your vitality will generally stay with you—if you refuse to give it up without a struggle. And that goes for almost everything in life.

The first step in our crusade to make your body young is to understand the road you have come, the burdens you have carried and the way in which you have carried them. If you are way over forty, barely forty or approaching forty at a dead run, you have a great advantage that our young Americans are not likely to enjoy. You had it tough as a child. Not very tough for all of you, but tough enough to build a good framework on which to drape a man or woman.

When you were a child, you got out of your crib and down onto the kitchen floor, and if you got in the way of the broom someone "fetched you one." If a sewing box were needed from the third floor, you trotted upstairs to get it. You ran to school or else you were late. If you were late, you stayed after school and sponged blackboards, washed inkwells and "hitched your wagon to a star" one hundred times in rolling Palmer style, with both feet on the floor. You ran home for lunch, because there wasn't time to walk. You sifted ashes, weeded gardens, mowed lawns, washed windows, walked to pick up the groceries at the store, hung up your clothes, shined your shoes and your father's. You walked to the Y, the library, and to choir practice. (That's where you met the kids under the guise of strengthening your character. Oddly enough it did.)

If you didn't do your chores, somebody blistered you. If you got wet, nobody was nervous about it. If you were overheated, you soaked your head. If it snowed, nobody worried that you'd catch cold—you had to dig out the front walk and put down ashes. Girls weren't exempt, remember? And in addition, girls took care of the younger members of the family—and without fringe benefits.

Then there was that Depression. It was awful all right, and nobody in his right mind would want it back, but it toughened the kids. Everybody pitched in and worked for the family, even to the smallest member who brought in his paper-route money. Each had a reason to strive and a reason for pride. If you were a tomboy or ballet dancer in childhood, you are now the kind of woman who can return most easily to an active life. Former tomboys have fallen out of trees, balanced on fences, chased and been chased. In their childhood they built wonderfully hard little bodies which the years may have covered up *but which are still there*. While the dancer's training was different, the self-discipline and body were developed, and it is no trick at all to re-develop them.

The man who delivered newspapers as a boy is the best bet for a quick return to his former physical condition. The boy with the paper route got up at four-thirty, got out his bike and went to his job. While thousands of his less fortunate contemporaries were still in bed, the newsboy was becoming a man with the help of the weather, the hour and the dignity of work. He also learned to finish what he began and to collect that which was his. This training will be most useful in the job you are about to undertake.

Were you an athlete? This will help, too. If you did calisthenics, or trained for any sport, you built a better body right then—and it is never lost.

Did you go in for the outdoor life? You hunters, hikers, climbers and the fishermen who had to walk to get where you wanted to go—all can be grateful for physical money in the bank. Aside from working your body, you developed a liking for the outside of the four walls in which most people live. You know the outdoors is there, which is already a head start. Another thing, you know it is for you, not just for the other fellow. For the sake of the future, even if you haven't done anything about it up to now, you know it is there for your children.

My dad was a wonderful fellow. In his family there were four boys and not two cents to jingle. My dad and his brothers spent their summers roving the countryside with a line, a gun and four healthy, strong bodies. All my young life my dad told me about his wonderful summers. He probably regretted not having sons but he promised me that when "I got sense" he'd buy me a rifle and teach me how to shoot it. I dreamed about that until I was almost grown. But as life got tougher for my father and as he had more worries, he forgot his promise. (I've never let myself believe that it was just because I didn't get sense.) Dad gave up hunting and fishing and grew old. Long before my father finally died, the part of him that enjoyed living died. After I had kids of my own, I decided that this tragedy wasn't going to happen twice. (By the time you have children you begin to appreciate your parents and even to understand them a little.) If you have let one of your own skills fade away, go get it and give it to your young ones. If it is too late, look around for the grandchildren. If there aren't any available, go find some other lost little soul who thinks TV is the all and end of everything and teach him about the world that is outside of walls.

For yourself, you are to get back to it at whatever cost. To do this you will have to take stock and discover what parts of your body and of your life today are working for you, and what parts are working against you. You will also need a long, honest look at the body you live in. You must be as objective as you would be in the appraisal of a new car. Don't fool yourself by sucking in your stomach, sticking out your chest, and then looking in the mirror. That's not the way the world sees you. Women shouldn't think they disguise their flaws by wearing a girdle, either. What's held in at the middle is billowing out at the top and bottom, and the whole thing moves with all the grace of a hippopotamus.

You will need to know where your aches and pains are (as if you didn't!). You will need to know your size and the shape of that size. There isn't much virtue in weighing the same as you did the day you were married if the whole 134 pounds seems to have oozed down into the thighs, leaving you hollow-cheeked and hollow-chested but possessed of a pair of outsized pneumatic legs. It won't do a man any good, either, to maintain the same 185 pounds if most of it has run to his stomach. Would he still look good in his wedding suit?

Another thing you will have to face is function. Do you run any less lightly than you did, or do you run at all? If you throw a baseball, will it go anywhere? Or will the arm go with it? What would happen if you were to get tangled in a fight? Is that old punch still there? When you bend over are you darn careful? Are you afraid to shovel snow? Have you a "trick" back, elbow, knee, neck, rib, wrist, ankle or shoulder? Do you puff on the stairs, have leg cramps in the middle of the night, a pain in the neck at four-thirty in the afternoon and a roaring headache by six? Have you taken to a golf cart or given up singles at tennis?

After you have squarely faced what it is you don't like about your body and your ability to function, you must have the desire to do something about improving them. Because that will be the basis for a new life. You can't change the world or even your part of it until you feel well physically and have the confidence which comes from knowing you look well. How will you do it? Improve your every-day habits of living by putting back into your life the physical activity which our push-button age has taken out. (See the chapter on habits.) Embark on a systematic exercise program, one you can do at home or in the office or on the road (general exercise chapter). Give a critical eye to your present eating habits as compared with what you *should* be eating. (See the chapter on diet.)

Very seldom do wonderful things happen while we wait. We think they happen now and then to others, but if we knew the facts, we would realize that these individuals worked hard to achieve their miracles. If you are determined to have a second chance at living, you, too, must work hard—harder even than the athlete in training. All an Olympic athlete works for is a chance to win medals, fame and honor. *You* want a second chance to live as nature intended you to live, and to enjoy the rest of your life to the hilt.

If you feel that none of this applies to you, because *your* troubles are "psychosomatic," in which the rampant psyche visits destruction on the submissive soma or body, be of good cheer. There is a fifty-fifty chance that your long suffering soma is merely taking revenge on your helpless and miserable psyche. Just which comes first is not important—the main thing is to do something about it. That there is *always* something to be done should be your first rule. The start should be the appraisal. After that, the program. Keep track of your improvement in every area. You are in for some very pleasant surprises.

CHAPTER TWO

Do you like what you see in the mirror?

There are people who never read the directions on the can. These are the same people who put in too much water, not enough turps, forget to clean off the surfaces, and paint themselves into a corner. Before we begin this analysis of your appearance, it is stated here and now in very large caps—READ YOUR DIRECTIONS CARE-FULLY AND *FOLLOW THEM EXACTLY*.

The man who wishes to improve his business, or the lady her home, must take stock of that business or home before a plan of action can be drawn up. If the business involves putting out a wonderful product, and the sales department is too poor to move it there will be no ad-vantage whatever in expanding the line. The product is strong but the sales force is weak. Knowing this, the busi-nessman can draw up an effective plan to remedy the situation without any waste of time or money.

The first step in rebuilding your body is the same as the businessman's first step. Evaluate the present situation. You will have to be your own critic, examiner and tester. You will have to be as severe and as thorough as though your life depended on the outcome of the job. In more than one way it does.

You are used to looking at yourself and others with a more or less critical eye—so let's start with your ap-pearance. Go into a room with a large mirror, strip down and take a good look. If what you see pleases you, great. You can be sure of keeping it from now on. If some things look fine, but you'd rather slide over the rest of it—don't. You've been doing just that for some time anyway, and look where it got you. Don't take the attitude that it is no worse than it has been for years—or even that for your age you don't look so bad. Neither rationalization is legitimate. This is the best time you will ever have to start going uphill.

As you look over yourself, remember that no matter how bad your shape is, no matter what your age and vitality are, no matter how long you have been in this state, all this can be changed. You are never too old or too tired or too broken down. Remember, too, that the closer you are to forty and fifty, the faster all of this can be done because you built yourself well when it counted—in childhood. Today's young people are being robbed of this advantage. They never *have* to move.

Go and get yourself a "little black book," one that can be conveniently hidden in a secret compartment somewhere—no use giving Junior statistics that you wouldn't want the neighborhood to enjoy. Copy the charts as they are set up here and re-check as directed. First, copy Chart 2 and proceed to circle the correct descriptive term for your hair, face, chin, and all the other parts of your body.

But it is not enough to know what is wrong. It isn't even enough to list the problems. It *is* important to do something to correct them. The pages in your little black book will soon contain the answers to your question—"Okay, so I'm not so hot, what do I do now?" In Chapter Five there will be a general exercise program. That you do in any case, but there will also be a section later on in the book given over to special problems. Also you should note which "general exercises" need an extra going-over just for you. As you read on in this book, enter your needs indicated by the charts you fill out, and list the exercises you need.

Chart 2. ANALYZING YOUR APPEARANCE

Look yourself over very carefully and circle the word, or words, that best describe what you see. Check in the index in the back for the exercises you need for your particular problem and add them to your general program.

Hair	Dry Brittle Oily Dull Soft Shining
Face	Firm Sagging Thin Heavy Gaunt Fat Taut Hollow Smooth Lined Florid Pale Tanned Clear Blemished Dry Oily Round
Chin	Firm Sags a little Double chin Jowls Dewlaps
Neck	Firm Fat Thin Dry Wrinkled Good color Poor
Arms	Firm Well muscled Thin Heavy Fat Loose skin
Hands	Strong Weak Thin Slender Fat Smooth Rough
Shoulders	Wide Narrow Round Straight Thin Heavy Sloping Uneven Hollows in front Lump at back of neck Thick
Chest	Well muscled Firm Flabby Fat Thin Deep Small
Breast	Firm Sagging Small Full Flat Over large Lifted
Rib Cage	Wide Narrow Thin Fat Slender
Waist	Small Average Large Outsize Curves in Straight
Abdominals	Firm Flat Hard Soft Fat Sagging Protruding
Hips	Slender Tight Small Hard Protruding Drooping Smooth Lumpy Fat Muscular Skin blemished
Thighs	Slender Firm Heavy Soft Fat Lumpy Hard Muscular Thin
Knees	Smooth Bony Fat Lumpy Strong Weak
Calves	Thin Slender Curved Rounded Straight Well muscled Lumpy Heavy Fat
Ankles	Slender Heavy Swollen Thick Bony Fat
Legs	Straight Well muscled Bowed Knock knees Varicosed Weak Fat Shapeless
Feet	Flat Strong arch Slender Square Well muscled Pigeontoed Turned out Smooth Calloused Corns Bunions Toe deformities Lumpy heels Pronated (wears out heels on inside edge) Tight Relaxed
Skin	Smooth Oily Clammy Dry Scaly Taut Loose Lumpy Tan Colorless Dark Clear Muddy Blemished

Hair

Hair that is dry, brittle, oily or dull often gives the warning sign indicating that something is out of kilter with the entire body. Something may be lacking in your diet. You are pretty much what you eat, you know. Animals that are correctly fed, well exercised, groomed and rested, have good coats—so do people. Check through the chapter on diet as well as the chart on page 127. Some of the answers may be there. Then, too, ask your barber or hairdresser what is suggested for hair that either spends too much time in dry rooms and offices or has been overprocessed—or both.

Face and Neck

The face and neck belong to the body and there is no way of separating them. If the body has tone—the face and neck will have tone. Sagging lines often indicate strain, stress, fatigue, and diet deficiency. It is probable that when tone has returned to the body, circulation improved and excess fat burned away, the face and neck will go along. If nature cannot restore youthful, healthy lines because things had been going wrong too long—there is still an answer. Plastic surgery. No face needs sloppy jowls or swinging dewlaps, and there is no need to endure them. Psychiatry tells us that facial deformities, as well as deformities of the body, inflict emotional harm. Advancement in plastic repair since World War II has made such surgery almost routine.

There is no necessity, either, to feel fear or suffer embarrassment over plastic surgery. There is, however, the need to give Nature every chance to do the job herself— and to put the entire body in top trim before taking such a step. There is little to be gained from taking expensive tucks in material that has not yet become healthy and stable. Allow at least six months for your general program to indicate the rate of facial recovery. After that much honest effort, you can consider surgery in good conscience.

Arms

Arms should be smooth and well muscled. The muscles, if they are in the proper condition, should be loose and pliable when relaxed. In women especially, the upper arm is a target for fibrositis, an unsightly thickening of the tissue which is not only unattractive but painful when pinched even lightly. For the thick, tough arm we must resort first to massage and then exercise.

Hands

Hands are a dead giveaway on many counts. If your work is rough, your hands will reveal it. If you are tense and nervous, twisting fingers will show that also. If you ever bit your fingernails in your life (a sure sign of tension), it will always show by the shortened distance between cuticle and fingertip. The meticulous person gives both hands and nails considerable attention as it is almost impossible to keep hands in pockets forever—especially at meals. Fat hands only appear on a gross body. Poor circulation and any form of fear or uncertainty make hands cold and clammy. General weakness will give them the feel of inadequacy in a handshake. Make no mistake, a handshake is as revealing as a signature—and can do as much good as a smile. Dry, cracked and scaly skin must be attended to with a lubricating cream (yes, men too). Nails call for a manicure, but use good sense when it comes to polish. The truly masculine hand can wear a colorless polish without a qualm in the world. Working ladies will have to leave the bright reds to less active hands unless they have time for daily re-do. The best-looking figure covered by the finest of clothes can be sabotaged by chipped or dirty nail polish.

Shoulders

Shoulder carriage is affected by the way we live, what we think and even what we do not think. It is understandable when architects, dentists, surgeons, or accountants, round their shoulders so often on the job that the shoulders finally bow to habit and remain rounded. However, round shoulders in many people are due to less obvious causes. Most fearless, aggressive people throw their shoulders back—and have since childhood, but youngsters overwhelmed by powerful adults or situations in which they are frustrated and helpless, have a tendency to "pull in" as they try to disappear within themselves. Girls who reach puberty either ahead of their friends, or who feel that sex itself and all its characteristics are not quite nice—round their shoulders in an effort to hide the gentle curve of their young breasts. These girls add insult to injury by making a habit of folding protective arms across their chests whenever they stand still. This adds to the shoulder rounding and starts the breasts on a downward droop. Not only is the line spoiled, but it gives them the look of inadequacy for life.

Technically, when the body is held in this collapsed position the shoulders round because the chest muscles (pectorals) fore-shorten. The constantly overstretched back muscles lose some of their strength and behave like old rubber bands. When you feel like standing straight for a change (or when a parent demands it) the strong counter-pull of the inelastic pectorals quickly tires the back muscles—and the shoulders return to their unattractive sag.

To be round-shouldered, one does not have to be emotionally tense or shy. Just being tall can do the trick. This is particularly true of girls in America. They shoot up, leaving the eighth-grade boys feeling like Max Shulman's "Teen-Age Dwarf." For these girls, the obvious answer is to droop—and they do.

Even athletes suffer from round backs. Watch the shoulders of boxers and basketball players who spend so much time with their hands out front and shoulders closed in. Unless they have really good trainers, they stand like the shy girl with the bust. Then later, when they put on forty pounds, they add the drooping bust as well.

The correction is indicated by the cause. The shortened pectorals must be stretched and the upper back muscles strengthened. If tension plays a part, you will need to prevent recurrence by the constant practice of the tension exercises on page 170.

Poor posture rarely improves without conscious, well directed effort. If your shoulders droop, if they pull forward or are uneven, star them in your black book and put in extra time on all shoulder, chest and upper back exercises.

Chest
When the shoulders are back and straight, the chest is rarely a problem. However, this is a favorite area for fat deposits and the well-muscled youth who worked hard or did weight training often finds that, as the office eats

14

up his workout time, he is growing a bust. Next time you stroll along the beach, take a look at the young American boys we are now producing. You will see that many of them are covered with a layer of lumpy fat. No, it is not puppy fat—it is just plain *fat*. Notice his chest— if it weren't so tragic it would be heartwarming to see that he has a bigger, droopier bust than yours—and far more than his sister. Your fat will have to go—via diet, of course, and exercises for the chest.

Breast

American women (and men) attach singular importance to the size and shape of the breast. Even in countries where it is not considered a national symbol, it is never overlooked. However, there are individual as well as national preferences. The Greeks preferred the small but perfect line. Rubens set the style of opulence. In 1924, American "flappers" tried to outdo even the young Goddess Diana in pre-pubic contour. And today, some of our movie and TV style-setters are vying with each other for munificence past reason, control or good sense. There are some rather unflattering psychiatric explanations for our nation's preoccupation with this emblem of food, love and security—but times will change, and with them, lines.

Much can be done to improve a bust-line. True, exercise will not enlarge the gland itself. That has a mind of its own and is influenced far more by the gyrations of the moon than by any human effort. Nevertheless, remember that the pectorals lie under the glands and that muscles, if they are healthy can be made to grow in size. That is the reason why *all* little girls should have ballet, acrobatics, tumbling, apparatus and gymnastics. If the upper torso is not worked hard, the muscles cannot produce an attractive line. If the opposite problem exists and produces too much of a good thing, one should look first to diet. If there is general obesity, the "general exercise program" will help reduce all parts of the body including the breast area.

If the business of nursing children, inadequate foundation garments during pregnancy, losing weight, or poor muscle tone for too long, has destroyed the last vestiges of curve—or if you are a slim, tiny but overly endowed lady—plastic surgery again comes into the picture. When I was young, my mother's thinking had a great deal to do with my opinions—both when I agreed with her and when I did not. I suspect it is the same with you. Face lifting was once considered foolish vanity for Lady Ponce de Leon and on the same level as men who had "monkey gland" operations. Everyone believed that breasts must never be bumped or cancer was certain. As for tampering with their shape or size, that was unheard of! Times have changed and I, as well as you, will have to change with them.

As we have said, doctors now know that personalities can be crippled by a grossly unbalanced figure. Marriages have been known to suffer—more, I think, from a feeling of inadequacy on the part of the woman than criticism from the man—but never mind who is to blame, the results are the same. The important question is, can the cause of this distress be removed? It can.

Not very long ago a young and unusually beautiful burlesque queen came to the office of a well known plastic surgeon. She had had a baby six months before. (You should be told here and now, if you didn't already know it, that burlesque folk lead pretty prosaic lives off stage—and so do a lot of movie and TV people, never mind what the film magazines report.) This young lady's once perfect breasts had lost not only their ravishing lines, but their content as well. She, the talk of the town, was now as flat as a boy. She admitted it was a small price to pay for her baby, but how could she go back to her old job which paid twice as much as any other job she had been able to find? Four months later she was back at her old job. Had the operation been a success? It certainly had. Before the operation she had been putting on six acrobatic dancing shows a day. After the operation she was paid twice as much just to walk across the stage. Such operations, as well as the correction for over-large or asymmetric breasts, are no more dangerous than any other operation. Try first, however, to do all that you can with diet, exercise and attention to posture. If you do consider an operation, go and talk it over with a good, reputable plastic surgeon—not your mother-in-law or the gal next door. Neighbors and relations have a way of hanging on to old superstitions and half truths long after they have been scientifically proved utter nonsense. At this point I should probably remind you that you, too, may be someone's parent-in-law, blood relation or next-door neighbor— even as I. It is the moment and time to check your facts as well as your prejudices. Progress often forges ahead faster than our sources of information.

The Upper Torso

The upper torso consists of a rib cage which contains some very vital organs. It is covered with muscle, fat and a suit of waterproof skin. When this area is given little opportunity for movement or held in awkward positions and permitted to weaken or grow inflexible through long disuse —all kinds of trouble ensue. It begins to look soggy. It also looks and behaves stiff. It lacks rhythm, and this is odd because inside, it carries the very souls of rhythm— heart and lungs. The front and sides are famous for the accumulation of "rubber tires"—and the back is one of the favorite playgrounds of the tension syndrome.

The fat you see on the *outside* of the upper torso is as nothing to that which is collecting in lethal dollops near the heart, major arteries, around liver, lungs and gall bladder. You can be darn sure that if you *can* see it— it is where you *can't* see it. If the area is too thin, you haven't moved it enough. In either case you need upper-torso exercises.

The Beer Belly

The "beer belly" juts out above the belt and shows up quite often on even the moderately active male. Take a second look at truck drivers, old or professional soldiers and many golfers. The name of this grotesque form of caricature gives one clue to its origin, although the calories need not all be fluid. Another cause comes from the way of life. The "beer belly" never occurs when the whole body is worked well and in harmony—not just in a few isolated areas. Diet is important, but exercises must be directed to the offending area. Results will be speeded by the application of massage (see page 104).

17

Waist

If you are watching TV these evenings, you are sure to see a plaintive, very lumpy lady pointing to her waist and whining, "What do I do about these rolls?" A minute later she is flashed on the screen smiling and very svelte— she is wearing a "long-line foundation garment"—and all her problems are solved. Don't you believe it. Stand behind her and you will see that the whole spongy mass of butter fat has been squeezed in. Well it can't vanish, can it? No. So it simply squirms solidly over the top. If the lady is in decolletage, the effect is disastrous because the glutenous mass is not only in plain sight, it is naked, fish-belly white and shiny. Foundation garments, like make-up, are meant to enhance, not to disguise—and as for doing away with the problem, *only you can do that*.

Massage first as directed on page 104, and then do your exercises. Remember, the slender waist is not the exclusive prerogative of the young, but of the well-exercised of any age.

Abdominals

Abdominals are very important when it comes to appearances. They are the first to deteriorate if the body is not well worked, and they are super-important when it comes to any function worth talking about. They are one of the key posture areas without which one cannot stand or sit properly—and if you can't do either of those with ease, you will tire quickly, which in turn will affect everything else you do.

The newborn baby seems to be all head and tummy. He has spent nine months folded up like a pre-fab water toy. His abdominals have been held in a shortened position and his back stretched. If his life depended on standing up, as it does for calf and foal, he would die in a few hours. The first few months of life will be spent stretching and strengthening the muscles of the torso fore and aft. He will continue to be mostly head and tummy until those key posture muscles become sufficiently strong to pull in and flatten. The healthy active youngster has flat, tight abdominals—and they should stay flat. After a baby or two, the young mother is permitted a *slight* rounding which seems to add to her womanliness, but more than *slight* is neither desirable nor permissible. The healthy active man of the house should remain flat all his life. The way things are going these days, it is sometimes not entirely clear just which parent is going to have—or has just had—the baby.

Most children in America are not active. Most adults, if they were active in childhood, do not remain so. And if they are not active, it is a well known fact that they cannot be healthy. Let me remind you that the person who says, "I'm just fine except for my low back, bunions, nervous tensions and forty extra pounds," is not healthy. Too many babies, trapped in playpens and strollers, form a pattern of inactivity to which they adhere for life. Their tummies remain melon shaped through and past adolescence. During their adult years, they assume the appearance of perpetual mid-pregnancy. A trip to Miami in January will show you the last stage—the return to babyhood, when the human again becomes all head and tummy with spindly after-thought extremities. (Just what *is* it that holds up those swim trunks on older men?) The tragedy is not that this is all too true—but that it need never have happened in the first place.

Hips

The shape and consistency of the seat are worse secret disclosers than a seven-year-old kid brother. The soft, mushy, wiggly behind almost always belongs to the person who is soft, mushy and wiggly elsewhere. The fighter, in ring or office, has the self-preserving tendency to tighten both seat and abdominals. Physical condition will tell you a lot about the person with whom you are dealing. The man or woman of action moves quickly and well. The other kind finds it quite difficult to "get the lead out" for an obvious reason—it is firmly attached. He (or she) has another disadvantage—there is weight where there never was intended to be weight. This forces muscles that are unprepared for such work to overwork. As the weight has also pulled the body out of line, the muscles labor under further handicap. All other things being equal, the mush bottom makes an inadequate sex partner and often feels compelled to hide this fact by boasting of powers he neither possesses nor should make the topic of conversation if he does.

It is sometimes easier for a woman to develop an outsize seat than for a man, but it is no more attractive on her than it is on him. Incidentally, don't ever believe the guy who pats the fanny that looks like the backside of Kelly's barn and says, "I like it just as it is." He's just keeping the peace. During the sack-dress craze, there were three letters by which men (and they'll do it whether anybody approves or not) described the woman who was really entitled to wear one. They were "TLR" for "tight little rear." Pretty explicit. The tight little curve of the well built, thoroughly exercised seat is vastly preferable to a large accumulation of "nervous pudding." And I'd like to remind you again that the girdle does *not* enhance the unenhanceable—it merely changes the consistency. The fat bottom without a girdle is lard on the loose; the fat bottom in a girdle is lard congealed.

The woman who knows she looks well going away has a great psychological advantage, and it can be as disturbing to be a bottomless pole as the other thing. The same exercises that remove fat will also develop a smooth, attractive curve of muscle.

Thighs

Unattractive thighs are more often the unwelcome problem of women than men, but then, since men entertain more cardiac attacks, women probably get the best of the deal. Fat or heavy thighs can show up at any time and often do in early childhood. I knew a perfectly delightful lady who was miserably inhibited and could hardly bring herself to put on an exercise suit even though it was three sizes too big for her and about as revealing as a burnoose. After losing forty pounds and being conned into a leotard and tights, she confessed that all her life she could hear her mother hissing, "Pull your skirts down and cover up your fat legs!" She hadn't even learned to swim because of those "fat legs"—and because of her mother's mistaken idea that you can camouflage fat.

Not only do thighs often run to fat, but like shoulders and upper arms, they are subject to tension and therefore "fibrositis." In this case, the fat will not be soft as it is most of the time around the waist and upper back—but hard and quite painful when pinched. The condition can be so severe that one can hardly get hold of it at all. I have heard women say, "Well my thighs may be big—but they're *hard*." This they say in a tone of triumphant desperation—mistakenly believing that fate—often dealing them raw—was trying to make up for it by making them strong. The prevalence of fibrositic legs among girl athletes is one of the reasons mothers fear athletics for their daughters. "What," they ask, "is an Olympic gold medal compared to a husband?" They've got a point, but it is based on the wrong premise. Athletics do not cause fat, and fibrositis is caused by poor diet and emotional stress. Properly used, athletics develop the most beautiful bodies in the world. If it's beauty the mothers are after, they ought to start their girls exercising the day they are born. The fibrositic thigh is not one bit stronger than the slender one—and it is heavier to carry around, which makes it a handicap at once. Each spring thousands of women, especially the ones who have been under stress during the winter months, get the shock of their lives in department stores. Fully equipped with the latest information on swim suit styles, they go forth to buy. They try on one or two of the newest models, pale visibly, try not to see the rear view and then get the same full-skirted type they have been buying for ten years. Either that or they rush home and launch on a diet. First their cheeks fall in, then their bust falls off—but the thighs remain fat, heavy and unattractive. "It's hopeless," they moan—and start preparing their minds for old age.

Thigh exercises should be preceded by massage. You can do a lot for yourself. If I had that problem (and I do every time I write a book) I would spend part of the household money on a good masseuse. I'd go (and I do) once or twice a week for about six weeks and let a pair of trained hands knead that too, too solid flesh on hips and thighs. I'd cut down on calories and I'd exercise the offending areas to bits and pieces. Find a masseuse who is strong, well trained and merciless. Tell her you don't want to be relaxed and made comfortable. YOU WANT THOSE LUMPS OFF. Go to her in the morning while she is still fresh enough to take you apart. At first she need not be too hard on you, but as the weeks progress, you will mind less and will be able to take more. Don't congratulate yourself—tell her to get tougher. After you come home—or right there if you can—get down on the floor and go through your hip and thigh exercises. No, there is no easy way like lying on a machine, or sitting on a machine, or leaning against a machine. One of the marvelous benefits that go with a good body is a feeling of vitality and power. This comes from effort and self-discipline. Think now, if someone could package it or bottle it or design vitality, wouldn't they have done it and become millionaires long ago?

There are a few people, regrettably few, who have the opposite complaint. Their legs are too thin, and one can see air between them from crotch to ankle. The exercises are the same as for the heavy thigh (page 87), but done with resistance (page 201).

Knees
Knees are highly important and discussed under function, but they do have appearance problems. Just above the joint on the inside of the leg there is a favorite gathering place for fat deposits and fibrositis. Massage to this area should be gentle but thorough. Be sure to follow with exercises for knees and legs.

Calves
Calves can be fat, fibrositic, thin, bulgy or as straight as the legs of a chair. Some of the forms might be called familial, but any form can be modified with effort. The "New England boiled dinner on the back of each leg" so pointedly discussed by the late Queen of Comedians, Fanny Brice, was often caused in childhood by improper ballet training. This need not happen if attention is given to stretching exercise. In the last few years even the dance teacher who knows nothing whatever about muscles, has become convinced that putting children "on the points"

22

too early is futile if not dangerous. If the calves are lumpy, tight or fat, exercise plus massage will help a great deal. It they lack curve and substance do the same exercises, but with resistance.

Ankles
Ankles have almost more to do with the appearance of legs than the shape of the legs themselves. Even a rather heavy leg can appear slim if the ankle is slender. Conversely, the slenderest leg is marred by fat or swollen ankles. Sometimes ankles are heavy due to bone structure, but more often it is fat. If the heaviness is caused when fluid, retained by the body, collects in this area— a consultation with your physician is indicated. Sometimes the simple expedient of using a diuretic solves the problem. This, however, is the time you do not make the decision yourself—leave it to your doctor.

Feet
You have been equipped with ten separate toes, which, if given the chance, are wonderful balancers. Tight shoes compress them into a hoof which is far from efficient. High heels tip the heel upward shortening all the tendons and muscles in the back of the ankles and legs. The range of movement can be so curtailed that both feet and ankles are almost splinted. When they are not used, the foot, ankle and leg muscles deteriorate—and you start to walk "old." *You will need foot exercises whether your feet are fat, thin or perfect.* Massage them even when the feet aren't tired and pay particular attention to the sections on walking and habits. One other thing will help—take off your shoes whenever and wherever you can, and go barefoot. If circumstances preclude that degree of daring, try to wear sandals in lieu of shoes when possible.

Skin
Skin, if brought down to basics, is a waterproof suit that separates the outside from the inside. We are said to get a new suit of skin about every seven years. This is of course oversimplification, but it is true that old skin wears away and is replaced cell by cell. While it is not as

dramatic as the snake's total shedding, it is nice to know that we are overhauled and polished up from time to time. Diet has a lot to do with how we feel, how we behave and the degree of our capabilities. It also affects the skin. Greasy, sugary, creamy, salty, syrupy foods can do more to mar perfectly good skin than a fall from a tree—and the marring knows just where to take place—not the tip of your sheltered shoulder blades—but the tip of your nose.

Diet isn't everything either. There's air, sun and water. For the next week make a list of the time you spend in the house with windows and doors closed. Check office and indoor recreation time and time spent in transportation. Then see how much time you spend out in the air. Now make another list, hours spent in clothes and under bed covers against moments spent as naked as a jay bird. I don't suppose one can revolutionize America overnight, but we might be able to make a few changes here and there. Women will get the best of this one, but in a way, they need it more. Men at least are spared the ultimate discomfort—the girdle. My apartment in New York is said to have a naked slave. I am that slave. Like most New Yorkers, I have a woman who comes in a few days each week and puts things to rights. The rest of the time it's my job. For housework I have found it economical, healthy and comfortable to tear into my chores without benefit or hindrance of housedresses, blue jeans or aprons. If one sits around letting the air get at skin, there is always the chance of draft and chill—if one works, there is neither. Yes, there *is* danger of becoming the talk of the neighborhood—but all that talk will be nothing but conjecture unless you forget, and answer the doorbell.

Sun works for people as it does for plants. If you get too much, you burn and shrivel—if you get too little, you look and feel like something that has lived twenty years under the back porch. Each skin like each plant is different. My father's extraordinary blue eyes looked astonishing set in a dark mahogany face that betrayed an Indian or two in his forest background. The sun was an important part of his well being and twelve hours exposure a day would be just fine. My sister's blonde, gold hair set off a honey tan each summer—but she knew better than to push things. A little at a time added up to incredible beauty, but if you're greedy or negligent, presto—blisters. I am my father's daughter. The sun does many things for me just as it does for many of you. Don't think that you are odd or different, if lying in the sun makes troubles seem unimportant. Don't think there is something the matter with you if rainy, foggy days drive you to distraction—which is burnt away in a hot sun. Everyone needs sun—some more than others and some in greater amounts. Have you ever noticed how skin that is almost blameless everywhere else has a way of breaking out on seats which get less air, sun and water than the rest of the body? Turn that part of you to the sun for a few minutes each of your vacation days and see what happens.

There is something else the sun can do for you. When you have read the chapter on Sexercise and have understood that this is an area where improvement is always possible and acceptable, tack a line on the bottom of your prescription "lie in the sun for at least ten minutes each day." In the northern latitudes this is of course difficult during the winter, but with a little ingenuity, still possible. Buy a couple of reflector panels (or make them out of plywood or heavy cardboard and aluminum foil). Angle them to catch the sun in a sheltered spot of the backyard or rooftop. They will even work in the bedroom with the windows open in midwinter. If the shelter is good and the reflectors aimed correctly you will keep your tan year round and never suffer from that unattractive color (or the lack of color) known as "winter bleach." Notice the wonderful *natural* tan of the weekend skier. The color comes from the sun, but the clear smoothness comes from exercise in the open. Keep that in mind when you do your exercises. If you fail to find a place for such essential but unusual antics in this, our land of diet drinks and filter tips, walk out of doors and fast. You can't be arrested for that.

The Vitamin D provided by the sun must be absorbed through the skin. For this it needs oil—either the natural skin oil, or one you apply. It takes several hours to accomplish this miracle, so don't wash it off so fast. Try to get your sun in the morning with a light covering of oil on your body, then leave it on as long as you can. Incidentally, our skins would do better if oiled regularly anyway—and not just the skin on our faces and necks. If you have been fortunate enough to get a real dose of sun and find your skin drying and scaling—oil it several times every day.

Water is important as everybody knows. Also there can be too much of a good thing. There was a time when people believed that drinking quarts of good clean water was the best cure in the world—for almost anything. Now we know that if you drink enough, you can wash out the essentials as well as the impurities. If you think your thirst (for water) is excessive, check with your doctor.

On the outside of your waterproof skin, water can also do too much of a job. The skin is naturally provided with the lubricating oil it needs to stay smooth and pliable. Don't wash it off so often. When you must shower several times in the course of a single day, replace the oil after the bath and wait a bit before you dress to allow it to be absorbed.

Water has another use. That of forcing the skin to practice a very vital ability, that of adjustment. In Finland people take *saunas*. These are baths in which some steam and much dry heat are used. The bathers go into a tiny (or not so tiny, depending on the size of the family) wooden house. A fire is built in a sauna stove over which have been piled many smooth rounded stones. When the stones are hot—so is the wood in the little house. Water is then poured on the hot stones and clouds of steam fill the air. The hot wood immediately sucks up the water vapor and a very hot dry heat remains. As you know "it's never the heat—it's the humidity"—and in the sauna this principle works too. Sauna bathers can stand much more heat than people steaming in the very wet "turkish baths." After a time in the hot saunas the Finns dive their superheated bodies into icy lakes or new fallen snow. The pores, well exercised since childhood, react with great efficiency and close at once. Colds are rare and chills even more so. I installed one in my first Institute in the United States and failing to have an icy lake or sufficiently reliable snow—put in a *very* cold shower. Through some fault in the plumbing, water turned on anywhere in the building could be heard by a sudden jolt in the pipes. In my office, three flights above the sauna, I and any unsuspecting visitor would hear the thump in the pipes—this was immediately followed by the blood-curdling screeches of Westchester matrons teaching their skins to "adjust." In no time it became the talk of the town. While it was called a health measure (anything I know people will enjoy, but need an excuse to do, I call a health measure) it was probably the greatest single source of sheer delight to all ages. If you wish to install a sauna in your cellar or garage you can buy all the parts right here in America. The stoves are designed for gas, electricity or wood. While the Institute sauna is electric, the one in my country house has a wood stove—because I like wood. Gas and electricity are just as good, save for the fact that they don't crackle, snap and pop.

One word about make-up. American women spend millions on make-up which should be used to enhance smooth, clear, healthy skin and bright, fresh looking eyes. Girdles can't hide fat. The best they can do is give it another form. Well, make-up can't hide sick skin either—or make tired eyes enchanting. Lay the groundwork for beauty with a wonderful suit of healthy skin from sole to scalp—*then* apply the powder, color and lines of accentuating make-up. Instead of the haggard caricature, made more tragic by an accent on shortcomings, you will get the effect you want—health and beauty, youth and chic. You will be in reality what you promise.

CHAPTER THREE

How to test your physical fitness

"I don't want my daughter to have muscles." "Why should my boy exercise, he isn't going to play football—his father and I won't let him." "No, we've passed the stage where people need muscles—life is so wonderfully easy."

Phrases repeated over and over by people who haven't the vaguest notion as to the real nature of muscles or their function. They know nothing of the muscles' magnificent behavior when they are healthy and well treated—and even less about their destructive force when they are not. We worry about obesity, about hearts and lungs. We check eyes and ears and go to the dentist twice a year. In school we are taught that these things are important, but what are we taught about muscles, tendons and nerves, except that they exist and that boys should have them? Girls are rarely mentioned in connection with muscles, babies and grown-ups almost never. Just how important are they?

If you were to peel off your waterproof skin and stand revealed in your muscles, you would be quite a sight, covered by overlapping bands every one of which has some very important function. Each and every move you choose to make depends on a muscle—from the mere suggestion of a wink to carrying the bride over the threshold. The simple business of crossing your knees involves the contraction, relaxation and cooperation of many muscles. Not only are the qualities of your muscles' strength and flexibility of prime importance, but they must function with the proper intensity and in correct timing to give you coordination. Good coordination is that magic quality possessed by the people whose every step and move is made with clean grace and control.

Should you decide to raise a cup of coffee to your lips, for example, you will need the strength of the biceps, but before the contraction of the biceps can go into effect, the triceps that lie along the back of the upper arm, must cooperate and give up contraction. If this relaxation is slow in materializing, a jerky movement will result and you may even get the coffee in your lap. A person who suffers with cerebral palsy cannot count on this kind of cooperation and his efforts to control his short-circuited muscles are terrible to watch.

Just how important are muscles? Their malfunction causes eighty per cent of all the low-back problems. They permit the paunch to appear on even the young and otherwise slender. They are the rack that twists and tortures the hunchback. They are strong enough to break bones and sometimes they do. Muscles make the Olympian or the sloppy slouch in worn-down loafers. Muscles produce the pigeontoed, the round back—and the Gene Kellys. Muscles, not doctors, deliver babies.

Many are the factors that affect muscles. Exercise, habits, stress, work, play and our attitudes toward life. Fear affects muscles and excitement. Drugs and food affect them. Even air, heat or cold. There is a wonderful thing you should know and remember about muscles. They are grateful for attention and you can be absolutely sure of a return on your investment. They love to complain when you overwork them, but in no time they will measure up to demands if you work them sensibly. There is a second thing you should know about muscles and for the sake of your happiness if not your life, you had best remember it. They are like vital women in love. You can strain them, overwork them, ask for the impossible and get it— BUT YOU MUST NEVER IGNORE THEM. Their revenge is sure, and they have a deadly, purposeful patience. Little by little they will fail you. At first with fatigue and then in performance. Finally everything will be an effort. They will have destroyed your will to enjoy the good things and made you a pushover for the bad. One day, when you are faced with the question of survival, you may realize, too late, the most important truth of all—that your heart, too, was a muscle.

To that end, let's find out exactly how you have been behaving toward those all-important muscles. After that, we'll map the plan that will put you back in their good graces.

Copy the function test sheets into your little black book. These tests, beginning with the Kraus-Weber muscle test, will be fully discussed in the balance of this chapter. The Minimum Muscle Test should be rechecked every three months; the other tests every six weeks the first year and every twelve after that. (No, you don't stop testing when you look and feel like a million.) After testing, check your record results with the index on page 298 which will give you the numbers of the exercises you need.

Chart 3. KRAUS-WEBER MINIMUM MUSCLE TEST

(Fitness Tests One through Six)

Date	*A+	A—	P	UB	LB	FBH
First Test						
After 3 months						
After 6 months						
After 9 months						
After a year						

* Names refer to areas rather than specific muscles.

A+ (Abdominal muscle *plus* psoas muscle). Lie supine—hands behind neck and feet held down. *Roll up to a sitting position once.* If you can sit up, put a check under A+. If you fail, enter a zero.

A— (Abdominals minus the help of the psoas area). Same as A+, but with knees bent. Same sit up, and scoring, but under A— in the chart.

P (Psoas area). Lie supine with hands behind neck. Raise legs ten inches above the floor and hold them there for ten seconds. If you pass, enter a check under P. If you fail, enter zero. Count seconds by adding a three-syllable word to the number. For example, one chim-pan-zee, two chim-pan-zees, etc.

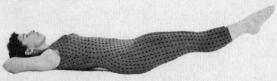

UB (Upper back). Lie over a pillow, hands behind neck and feet held down. Raise the upper body and hold for ten seconds. Pass rates a check under UB. Failure rates zero.

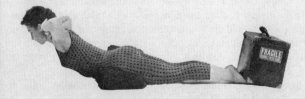

LB (Lower back). Lie over the pillow and using some weight to hold down the upper body, lift straight legs and hold for ten seconds. Score a check under LB if you pass—and zero for failure.

FBH (Flexibility of back and hamstrings). Stand with feet together and knees straight. Lean over *slowly* and see how close you can bring your fingertips to the floor. Hold at lowest point for three seconds. No warm up or bouncing is permitted. Enter T for touch under FBH or record failure by the number of inches between fingertips and floor. A six-inch space would appear as —6″.

If you are one of the legions who wake each morning with a stiff back, you will probably flunk one or more of the first five items in the Kraus-Weber Minimum Muscular Fitness Test. If you do, turn to page 228 and do the Limbering Series for two weeks. If you want to hurry things a bit, repeat the series twice as often as indicated.

Failure of the sixth test is no less important, but since the cause is not just inactivity but tension as well, it will be much harder to repair and will take a longer time. Inflexibility will not prevent the start of a program, however, it will merely hinder its progress. So we will go ahead, inflexible or not—and count on the program to do the job gradually.

Incidentally, failure in Number Six usually falls to men, and it isn't because they are tall and it isn't because their arms are too short. It's because they are under pressure and have insufficient outlet for the tension that builds up daily. Poor coaching can do it too—even if that coaching took place thirty years ago. Mothers will find that they can touch the floor with the palms of their hands while their young daughters cannot even reach it with fingertips. That is tension again—plus insufficient physical outlet. Checks made on children in private schools showed that those students living at home under tension and anxieties they couldn't understand often continued to fail the flexibility test all year. Those away at school, facing up to problems on their own level, improved markedly. After a vacation even as short as Christmas, one could count on a rise in flexibility failure. Weakness is infinitely easier to correct, but flexibility is just as important and often more so. Strong muscles pulling against inflexible muscles cause fatigue. That is one reason why some football teams wear out in the third and fourth quarters while others stay fresh to the end. You aren't going to play football (probably), but the same goes for you.

The results of the Minimum Test are now down on paper. Don't try to figure out what you are supposed to do about it now. We have that all figured out so you can't get all mixed up if you just do as the directions tell you. Let's go on to Optimums. Even if you are in such poor shape that you can't see how you could possibly be taking an Optimum Test after having just failed half of the Minimum, read it anyway and do the tests that are within your reach.

If you passed the Minimum Test with flying colors, give yourself a moment to gloat. That's all it's worth—and let's get on.

The Optimum Tests are a competition against yourself. If you like, you can bring in some friends, but I suggest you also compete on a basis of improvement as well as high score. Prizes are great fun and can be good motivation. The same scoring system suggested for groups such as golf clubs, ski clubs, choral groups, bridge and sewing clubs—in fact any group at all including the much to be admired TOPS Clubs (Take Off Pounds Sensibly) will work for the family as well. Remember, when you get around to the prizes don't overlook a prize for improvement.

Chart 4. OPTIMUM TESTS

Details of the tests are given in this chapter. Follow instructions carefully, and enter the results of each test as you complete it.

	Dates			
Abdominals				
Back and Hamstring flexibility				
Soleus flexibility				
Knees				
Gluteal stretch				
Crotch stretch				
Push-ups				
Chin-ups				
The broad jump				
Shoulder flexibility (down)				
Shoulder flexibility (up)				
Vital capacity				
Constipation				
Sleep				

Test Number Seven: Abdominals

Again we are concerned with the key posture muscles. Let's start with the all-important *abdominals*. This time you want to know just *how* strong they are. There are three ways of doing this. The first requires no equipment, but takes time. The second requires the simplest equipment, but can't be used in group competition unless all the competitors are pretty similar in their fitness levels. The third requires equipment that I think is as important to any household as heat and light. The equipment is called "weight bags." They will be used by every member of the family once you realize their value, so one might as well go ahead and invest in them. In case this investment in time and effort is likely to hold up the testing, use one of the alternatives.

Take the position you used in Test Number Two for Abdominals Minus Psoas. If you are going to use the first alternative, just do as many held-down, bent knee sit-ups as you can. Be sure to keep your hands locked behind your head. If you are very good at this, I suggest you sit on a small, soft pillow to avoid wearing the skin off your tail bone (coccyx). If you are thin, you should do this anyway. Enter your best effort in Chart 4 next to *Abdominals*. Don't be surprised if you can't cough or sit up in bed the next day without feeling ruptured. You're not. Your neglected muscles have merely said "Hmph! So it's you!" To improve your score, do half your optimum number twice daily.

The second alternative will cut down on time. Pick out a book that looks like a reasonable weight you could hold in your hands behind your neck while you sit up. Make it just as heavy as you think you can manage. Father may need the encyclopedia and mother, Shelley's poems. Incidentally, if the needs are reversed, the lady will test herself while the husband is at the office. No sense in ruining the whole thing at the outset. Now do as many sit-ups as you can. The added weight will cut down the repeats considerably. Use the same method for improvement—do one-half your optimum lifts twice daily.

The third way is by far the best and involves the use of weight bags. You should have these anyway since you'll need them for almost all your exercise as you improve and don't wish to increase the time you allot each day.

The minimum number of bags for a good, rounded program is ten. Four five-pounders, four two-pounders and two ones. This certainly is sufficient for any weight reduction program and it is really enough for almost all pre-season sport training. You will probably clean up enough on your improved golf swing to pay for the whole shooting match in one afternoon. If there is an ex-athlete involved, better add two ten-pound bags. Weight lifters return to full strength very fast at any age—and need the challenge. For information about where they can be purchased, write The Bonnie Prudden Institute, Stockbridge, Mass. 01262.

Do your first sit-up free without any weight added.

On the second sit-up, carry one pound in your hands behind your head. On the next make it two. Add a pound with each sit-up until you can no longer raise yourself. Enter the weight you are carrying for the last successful sit-up next to *Abdominals* in Chart 4. Don't forget to note the date. If you managed to get up to ten pounds enter it. It may not sound impressive, but you will have lifted fifty-five pounds, and I'll bet it didn't take more than a minute and a half. To improve your score, lift one half of your optimum lift ten times twice daily. If you are scoring the first alternative just enter the number of sit-ups. If it is the second, list the number and also write the name of the book in the margin so that you will always work with the same weight.

Test Number Eight: Back and Hamstring Flexibility
This time you will not be content just to touch the floor and let it go at that. Stand on the stair or a box and reach downward as you did on the minimum test. Press down as far as you can go. Measure the number of inches your fingers go down the side
of the box or stair and enter
the result next to Back and
Hamstring Flexibility in plus
inches. If you just manage to
touch, enter T. If you were
shy of touching, enter the results in minus inches. To
improve your score in this
test, stand on the edge of the
stair each day holding a
heavy book or object in your
hands. Lean over and bounce
twenty times allowing the
weight to pull you down toward the floor.

Test Number Nine: Soleus Flexibility
Stand facing a wall with feet parallel and toes about three inches away. *Heels flat on the floor.* Bend first the left knee and then the right. See if you can touch the wall

with the bent knees but be sure to keep the heels on the floor. If you can't, move your feet nearer the wall until you can. Both feet may have the same measurements, but if you have injured one or the other, the distance for that one may be shorter. No matter what the measurements show, they will need improving. If one leg has an edge, get after the other with a vengeance, as you are only as good as your weakest part. Enter the measurements in the two spaces for left and right feet after soleus flexibility.

Test Number Ten: Knees
It is always the aching joint that seems most important at the time, but I think that of all the joints that can make you miserable and curtail your activity, the knees have it. Pretty soon not only the troublesome knee is complaining, but the other one that must bear the burden. Then the ankle and hip of the uninjured side set up a chorus not to be ignored. Even if there is no pain involved, but merely a "trick knee," one never feels completely secure and at ease whether the game be tennis, baseball, or getting across Main Street against the light.

There is nothing so disquieting as the tall, handsome ex-athlete who can't bend down to tie a shoelace lest a knee "go out." Basketball and football account for many of the male knee problems and as the number of skiers increases we will find that the knee injuries also increase.

For most of these problems insufficient activity was the original culprit and the best way to take care of it is to set up a competition, not among friends, but among knees. Get the bathroom scale and a small stack of books. Pile the books beside the scale until the surfaces of scale and book top are even. Place one foot on the books and the other on the scale. Bend both knees until you are all the way down, then rise up one quarter of the distance. Look down at the scale and note the weight carried on the foot on the scale. Do the same for the other foot and enter the two weights in the two boxes next to knees. This information is highly important for all athletes, in fact for everyone, because if one knee is not doing its share, the other will be overburdened and the weak one further weakened. The day you need to make a strong, quick move with one of those legs you may not have a chance to choose the one you want to represent you.

Test Number Eleven: Gluteal Stretch
Did you ever notice how old folks who have let themselves go seem to putter along? You have the feeling that if they had to take one side step they might end in a heap. You are almost right. People who only move forward—and that very slowly—lose their ability to shift weight, for one thing, and they get tighter and tighter all over. If they fall, instead of giving, they break. Sit on the floor with your tape measure close at hand. Place the soles of your feet against each other, letting the knees fall open. Now, holding tight to the feet, pull the *top of your head* to rest on your insteps. If it touches easily, enter "T" for Touch. If you can't make it, measure the distance from head top to instep and enter in minus inches.

Test Number Twelve: Crotch Stretch
This area is highly important to all action. Those interested in the chapter on Sexercise will recognize it as a must for both sexes. Sit with the soles together as in the previous test and grasp the ankles firmly. Allow your elbows to rest on your knees. Now press downward with the elbows forcing the knees closer to the floor. Touch is entered as "T." Failure, in the distance between the knees and the floor. Don't tip for a better score, who's fooling who?

Test Number Thirteen: Push-ups
This is not the moment for the ladies to withdraw. Only the mistaken ideas visited on this generation of physical educators by theorists who had very little contact with athletics for girls—or with girls themselves—have prevented the distaff side from using this very profitable exercise for keeping bust-lines up and upper arms down. Start with the top of the push-up and be sure that your body is held rigid in a perfectly straight line. Let yourself slowly down, counting three seconds (three chim-pan-zees) before touching the floor. Rest for a second. Swing

both hands around over your back to touch them together. Then do push-up number one. After reaching the top of the rise, descend slowly again. Repeat as often as you can without losing either the straight line or the slow *three second* descent. Enter the number of the last correctly performed push-up on your test sheet. If you can't even do number one, don't be either surprised or dismayed. Enter a zero and get after it. Anybody can improve if they work.

Test Number Fourteen: Chin-ups
(Also for women—flabby arms, back and chest muscles not withstanding.) If we all had done chin-ups over the years, there would be less of all three—and fewer dowager's humps and pains in the neck. For this you are going to need a chinning bar—but there should be one in your home anyway. Choose a door that is used often by the entire family and one that is passed through most of the time empty handed. The bathroom is a good one. If you buy one of those expanding bars with suction cups on each end, have the man of the house put a bit of bracing under each side. They have been known to come unstuck and end exercise programs with a frightening flop to the floor. I am not happy with door sills either, they can break and fingers can slip. I once watched my peppery five-foot-four neighbor challenge his football-halfback six-foot son to a chinning race. Son could do three, father five. He was on his way up for six but one hand came off the sill and he hit with a fracturing crash. The incapacitation might have stopped a lesser man but two weeks later, cast and all, he was showing his nurse how he busted his leg by climbing on a hospital water pipe. Hang with palms facing away from the body and *feet off the floor*—you are not to have the advantage of a push, however small. Pull up until your chin is just over the bar. Then let yourself *slowly* down, taking three seconds to reach full stretch. Drop down to the floor and stretch both arms straight down *hard*. Do the second pull up immediately, but this time reverse the direction of the hands. Lower yourself again, taking three full seconds. Get down, stretch arms and repeat as often as possible,

alternating hand direction each time. If you can't do a single chin-up, don't worry, you will. Reverse the procedure by climbing on a chair and letting your body hang free with the chin just above the bar. Then let yourself down slowly, trying to increase the number of seconds used in the descent to ten. When you can do three in this manner you will be able to chin-up once.

Test Number Fifteen: The Broad Jump

How far can you jump? Go and get your sneakers, and if you don't have any, buy a pair. Don't get those double-barrel, non-skid snow treads that basketball players use. Get the thin-skinned ones that let you feel the ground under your feet. Remember, this is a new way of life, and not a flash in the pan. It doesn't matter if you are eighty-four, have bunions and can only take one small step at a time. That's precisely what you want to know— just how small is that small step?

Choose a place in the yard, living room, bedroom, kitchen or garage that has the length of space you will need. If you are an ex-varsity high jumper you will need more room than those whose last jump was taken to avoid an irate parental swat on the rump. Apartments *are* small, but there is always a hall and it might be good for some of your sedentary neighbors to see some constructive physical action. Place a strip of Scotch tape at one end of the space. If the area permits you to leave the marker as a reminder to practice, use adhesive tape and mark it *"Start."* It can be great entertainment at cocktail parties, but be sure the guests remove shoes and socks or stockings. Skin has more traction. Put down strips every six inches starting one foot on the near side of the distance you think you can make with ease. The distances will be different for the eighty-four-year-old who is going to take one step and the fellow who will fly seven feet, but you are the best judge of that. Caution: *take it easy.* It's better to get off to a non-impressive start and improve enormously, than spring something during the first blast-off. Incidentally, clear away any scatter rugs and other impedimenta that might scatter *you*. Stand behind the starting tape and jump forward as far as you can safely—with both feet.

Measure the distance from the tape to the heel that is nearest the tape. If you *must* fall, fall forward—and be sure there is room for such a mishap. In a year, you'll need no help for this sort of thing—but at first try, bring in a friend to spot you. Enter results next to "Broad Jump."

Those who have let their feet, backs and balance deteriorate too far to take off into the air with both feet, even for a few inches—will have to start with a step. Start with both feet behind the starting tape and take the longest *safe* step you can, first with one foot and then with the other. Add the results and divide by two. Enter the result with "M" for modified.

Test Number Sixteen: Shoulder Flexibility
Ideally you should have no difficulty putting the left hand down your back to meet the right one coming up—or vice versa. Shoulders do take quite a beating over the years so your test results may be less than ideal. Reach down the back with each hand and have someone mark the reaches. Almost always, one reaches farther than the other. Enter the winner's initial with the difference in reaches. For example, R + one and one-half inches would mean that the right hand could go one and one-half inches farther down the back than the left. Now do the same reaching upward and enter the winner.

Test Number Seventeen: Vital Capacity
The better your lungs behave the better you will feel. More oxygen is available for your body and therefore you can accomplish more with far less fatigue. Lungs like everything else improve or deteriorate according to use. Riding in an automobile, even with the windows open, doesn't do much for your lungs. Climbing five flights of stairs, even with the windows closed, will. If you have had any unpleasant surprises lately when you had to dash to catch a bus or take the stairs two at a time it is not due to age. It is due to disuse. There is just a bare possibility that *misuse* also enters into the picture somewhere. I can't talk about this first hand as I gave up smoking when I was eleven and got on the swimming

41

team. Then as an athlete I had so much status (those were the old days when athletics rather than wheel power made you important), that I didn't have to smoke to impress my friends and I've never taken it up again. However, as a mountain climber, I have had an opportunity to compare the reactions of both my smoking and non-smoking friends to altitude. The smokers suffer torments at fourteen thousand feet and the non-smokers don't even notice it. No, I know you aren't planning an Everest expedition—but what shows up in extremes also counts on lower levels and you must admit you probably aren't in the shape those climbers are in either. You may just notice a lower deficiency even at sea level. One other thing to take into account: Stand off from the city and notice what hangs overhead. The smoke, fog and smog aren't exactly harmless either. So when you can—get far away from it—far far away.

As soon as you start your exercise program, your body is going to demand more fuel and your lungs will have to get with it. They won't be any more cooperative at first than your muscles—but they too can be had. As your vital capacity improves, you will notice the years falling away like leaves in autumn. At first one or two—then a crowd.

Put a tape measure around your chest and exhale completely. Measure. Now take a deep breath and measure the size of your chest again. Subtract the first measurement from the second and enter it under vital capacity in your chart. Singers and mountaineers expand up to five and six inches. Today's children, trapped in playpens and strollers, may net as little as one-half inch expansion. It really doesn't matter how poor you are at the start—improvement is what you are looking for.

Test Number Eighteen: Elimination
It is said that America is the greatest nation of physickers in the world and there is no doubt about it. Forty is given as the age when you become dependent upon the various nostrums which spelled backward are not more necessary than those spelled forward. *Age is not the cause of constipation.* Bowels don't move because people don't

move. Various forms of stress can influence bowels to either extremes of activity *but even stress gives way when sufficient physical outlet is present.* The average human being need depend on nothing but himself for regulation. What gets a person started on physics?

My mother took five little brown pills every night of her life. At some time, long before I was around or observant, she didn't take any. The first dose became a habit and then had to be doubled. Then she added and added, until she was taking so much that, given to a "beginner," it would have acted like a blasting cap. There were two reasons for such unreasonable behavior. My mother led a comparatively sedentary existence which made her feel sluggish and certainly inhibited proper elimination. Also, she believed the ads. "A good cleaning out" they said. "Improve your breath and complexion" they said. "Get rid of that headachy feeling"—"that logy feeling—"don't be tired all the time"—"TAKE WORROMOT (tomorrow spelled backwards) AND HAVE A LOVELY DAY." A lovely day, that is, after you hang around the house all morning waiting for the cramping results.

My mother used to capture my sister and me every Saturday night and ram the stuff babies are supposed to hanker after down our unwilling throats. If ever there was trauma, that was it. I would spend all evening gnashing perfectly healthy teeth and hating my mother for the indignity she had visited on my perfectly healthy, beautifully functioning insides—and loathing tomorrow in advance. When a morning stomach ache woke me I would race for the bathroom where my insulted innards, twisting and writhing, would produce anything but a normal stool. Then I'd hate my mother some more—and add my father because he didn't save me. I still distrust Sunday morning and when I wake up depressed, I have to remind myself that it's been thirty-four years since I had a physic. My two daughters have never had one. *Moving* people don't need them—nor will you.

If this is one of your habits, it won't give you up easily. Physicking is not one bit different from addiction of any other kind. After you have developed a physical life, however, and your body has changed—let your mind play ball. More than half the time it's fear that keeps you at things you have long outgrown. Keep track of the number of times you felt it necessary to take some form of medicine for this problem. (Prune juice and bran cereals don't count.)

Sleep is covered later in the book, but here is where you keep score. The greater your physical outlet, the less tension you will have—and tension murders sleep. Enter a letter in your black book describing your sleep now and keep doing it in the future. (E for excellent, g—good, p—poor, d—disturbed, i—insomnia.)

Test Number Nineteen: Heart Action

Healthy hearts don't suffer from exercise—they suffer when they don't get it. Let's check yours now and watch it improve as the rest of you gets into shape. I imagine that of all the parts of you that would benefit from your efforts, your heart will top the list. Less weight means less strain. Better muscle tone all over means better muscle tone of the heart. More exercise means better circulation which will take some of the load off that poor faithful (up to a point) organ. For instance, leg muscles that have an active union card can be counted on to squeeze blood along the veins back up to where it has to go. The folks with varicose veins ought to keep this in mind. While exercise cannot cure such a condition, it can help keep legs healthy, then should operation be necessary, results are good and incapacitation-time cut to a minimum. No surgeon is ever happy when he looks down at a section of skin prepared for his scalpel and notices a soft, loose, saggy mass. His glance toward the anesthetist may contain more than the question "Shall we start?" It may also hold, "I hope we make it." The anesthetist is under no illusions. His instruments tell him quite clearly what the flabby heart is doing. When I look at people I think of their hearts—when I think of hearts, I think of them being like people. Just which of your friends would you like to have pounding away inside your chest? A fat, wheezy Mr. Colt who scratches his bulging stomach while warm beer collects on his sweaty chin—or lean tough Bob Mathias, Olympic decathlon gold medalist—whose skin is firm over hard muscles and who has every reason to want to live? Your heart may look like neither of these but it will be better for you by far if you draw away from Mr. Colt and nearer Mr. Mathias.

Incidentally that old bogy about "athlete's heart" has been unfrocked. The "enlarged" heart of the athlete is more to be envied than anything else. It got that way working—the same as your biceps can. The athlete's efficient heart needs to work far less to accomplish far more, so it usually beats more slowly than the so-called normal heart. After extreme effort, it quiets down more rapidly. Studies show that athletes have the edge on longevity and those fellows you read about who drop dead on golf courses had their heart problems long before they ever got to the locker room. There *are* enlarged hearts that are unhealthy—there are big arms, too, but that doesn't mean the biceps are firm and strong. So don't confuse the two.

Incidentally, if the man in your life wants to go golfing more than you like (the term "golf widow" wasn't invented by men)—let him. Go and find something vigorous *you* like to do. There is nothing in the world like a beautiful new body and a mysterious air (no you don't have to earn it, just wear it) to make a man wonder what the lady he thought he knew so well is up to. Besides you'll feel better, and who knows what you may find to be up to. It certainly beats sitting home being sorry for yourself.

Chart 5.   HEART ACTION TEST

(Record here the results of your heart action, as described under Test Number 19 in the text.)

Date	Rest	Standing	Action	After 1 min.	After 5 min.

Lie down comfortably for ten minutes. Don't get up for anything. Then take your own pulse and write down the results under "Rest" in Chart 4. Should you never have had occasion to take your own pulse, rest the right hand palm upward on your knee. Place the fingers of your left hand in the soft hollow of your right wrist between the right outside edge and what feels like two strong cords running into the hand. Place your thumb under your wrist. Now press gently with your fingers until you feel your pulse.

Count the beats while the sweep hand of your watch registers a full minute. Enter the number of beats under "Rest." Stand up and immediately take your pulse for another minute and enter in the space under "Standing." Now stand in front of a stair or a box about eight or nine inches high. Using that old second counter "one-chim-pan-zee, two-chim-pan-zees" (after twelve it has to change to thir-teen-pan-zees)—step up. It will consume one full second to get both feet up there. Then step down. It will take a full second or one-chim-pan-zee to get you down again. If you are in pretty good shape, take this "going nowhere walk" for sixty chimpanzees or one full minute. If you aren't, go for thirty. Then enter your pulse rate under "Action." Sit down and rest for one full minute and then enter the pulse rate taken after it has passed under "one full minute." Then rest five more minutes and take it again. The results go under "After Five Minutes." Notice that you take this test every three months. If you are ill even with so unimportant a disease as a cold, don't take it. The results will be inconclusive. There is no use, either, in comparing the test you have just taken with the "step tests" used by various athletes. The conditions for theirs were different. This is yours to chart progress, not compete with a four minute miler.

CHAPTER FOUR

Facts and fat

Fat is the great concern of the day, and with good reason. But just how fat is fat? That "well, at my age" answer is still illegitimate. There's no truth in it. Neither is the "too far gone" phrase or the "I like it this way" phrase. You don't and you know it, or you wouldn't be bothering to read this. Bodies were never meant to be fat, and that goes for every age.

Aside from ruining your appearance—which makes you embarrassed and lacking in confidence—obesity brings a host of other ills we can all very nicely do without. You constantly feel tired. Why wouldn't you, carrying all those extra pounds around every time you take a step? As your energy and vitality decrease, so do your activities. You withdraw more and more from life because you feel too listless, and you're too self-conscious about your ugly shape to participate in living. You also feel guilty and rather stupid to have gotten yourself into such a mess. Don't believe that myth about fat people being jolly. They're miserable.

Then there's the matter of health. Being overweight puts an undue strain on your entire body, particularly on your heart. Each extra pound makes you that much more susceptible to a heart attack. Dr. Wilhelm Raab, a cardiologist of wide renown, does five hundred half knee-bends daily. He claims this will work his heart to the point where it will stay strong, instead of going soft as so many underworked muscles do.

You might say that your waistline is a direct clue to your life line. As the waist expands, chances for a long life diminish. The American male has less chance of making it from forty to fifty than the men of ten other nations. His expectations of reaching sixty are less than men of fifteen other countries. (Twenty-four per cent less than an Italian and fifty-five per cent less than a Swede.)

The main reason for American obesity, ironically enough, is our vaunted high standard of living, which permits us to eat more and expend less physical energy than people in other lands. Also, we have a tradition, along with other countries, in which food and hospitality tend to be synonymous, thus putting a premium on overeating. And in our country's early days, plumpness was a visible sign of prosperity; with some of us, the idea dies hard.

The average American who is fifteen to twenty pounds overweight often eats too much because of emotional problems: boredom, restlessness, compensation for some deprivation in his life, or anxiety during some emotional crisis. All of us are guilty of this kind of stuffing occasionally, and some of us are guilty of it constantly.

Whatever the reason for obesity—and it is generally *not* glandular or hereditary—the important thing is to do something to correct it, for your happiness and for your health. And despite all the pills, appetite depressants, liquid diets and what have you, the only safe and sure method for taking off weight *and keeping it off*, is to eat less and exercise more.

To lose weight you must have patience and perseverance, not to mention will power. But most of all, you must realize that you have to change your eating and exercising habits *for life*. There is no percentage in seesawing back and forth, gaining back what you lose, and then losing it again. Furthermore, this practice raises the very devil with your system which cannot adjust so quickly and so often to a new you.

As if it weren't hard enough to lose weight, many of us have the added problem of the reaction to our efforts of family and friends. Sometimes I suspect it is due to an unconscious jealousy or dog-in-the-manger feeling. They wish they had the guts to do something about their weight problem, so that when you start facing yours, it upsets them, and they find all kinds of fault with what you are doing. "You're losing too fast" . . . "Wrong diet" . . . "Your skin will sag," are some of their helpful comments. The only course for the reducer is to ignore these comments.

One woman wrote me a letter that made me wish I could personally tell off each member of her family. She said: "I'm a mess. You probably wouldn't even speak to me, if you met me. But I want so much to do something about myself. Would you write to my family and tell them that it's all right for me to exercise and take walks? Would you tell them that I can't eat the way we used to and *they* still want to? I hate to say it, but they make fun of me, and my daughter tells me to act my age and stop embarrassing her. You said it could be done even at fifty or sixty when you weigh two hundred. Well, I weigh two hundred, but I'm only thirty-eight."

I didn't bother to write to the family. You can't change attitudes like that by mail. I did write to the woman, since she obviously wanted to do something about herself, and we set up a program that she put through on the q.t.

Since she was the cook, she had it in her power to feed her family more low-calorie foods. She lived on the bus route, but there was nothing to prevent her from walking a mile or two and then taking the bus.

Her daughter was in school till four-thirty, so all activity took place before then. The real problem was an aunt who lived with them and reported everything that went on. With reporting aunts there are several alternatives: (1) get rid of them; (2) threaten them (our woman couldn't have threatened a flea at this point); (3) bribe them. We used the third. The eighty-two-year-old aunt was just waiting around to die and could not understand the terrible and wonderful desire to live that filled her monstrous-sized and easily intimidated niece.

It took a year for the woman to lose fifty pounds, and a second year to get rid of the last twenty-five. At about one hundred and forty pounds she started helping out at the "Y," and every day she was able to add about three hours of hard work on a gym floor to her surreptitious program. That broke the back of the problem. She looked wonderful, felt wonderful, and her daughter was too heavy to borrow from her very trim wardrobe. The last I heard was a brief note: "Nobody steps on me any more. Thank you."

If your family is sympathetic to your efforts to lose weight, you can steel your will power by making a boast to them, or getting the other overweight members to reduce along with you. Fear of failure and competition are great motivators. At my Institute for Physical Fitness, we instituted a "Skinny Club." Every month, each member of the club would bet on the weight he intended to lose. He wrote this down on a slip of paper, with a dollar bill to back up the boast. If the members of the club did what they said they would, their dollar was returned. If not, the kitty got it, and the money was divided among the successful.

A class of thirty overweight men and women set up a different kind of betting program. They chipped in two dollars per person, the winner to have an evening for two in New York. One young man and his wife, the least likely looking people in the class, set out to win. And they won.

But that wasn't the biggest surprise. It was what was revealed as the layers of fat came off and the bodies learned how to move. Their personalities changed. Confidence showed first as a flickering spark, then it began to glow. At first it was a little thing—the girl who had been puffy, heavy and shy found herself leading the class across the floor in an easy run. Five weeks earlier she hadn't even been able to run; now she was out in front. About ten pounds lighter, and with hours and hours of exercise to music behind her, a new body was emerging. As she moved, her face changed. From being a nothing, she now knew in every part of her that she was something. As if her husband's face weren't enough, the silent class broke into spontaneous applause, and she started to cry. Something wonderful had happened to her—and it can happen to anyone who works for it.

The experts say that clinical studies on overweight people show that exercise *does* help you lose weight and does *not* increase your appetite (unless done strenuously or for a long period of time). And although it does indeed take seven hours of woodsplitting to lose one pound, if you do it for half an hour every day you will have lost a pound in two weeks and twenty-six pounds in a year. Even the small difference in energy expended when typing on an electric rather than a manual typewriter can add up to pounds gained or lost during a year.

Another benefit of exercising while you are reducing is that it keeps your muscles and skin toned, so that you don't end up as a slim but sagging creature full of floops and droops that hang like Kipling's Rhino Skin, itchy with cracker crumbs. Exercise will also redistribute the weight where you want it to be. (You can lose the necessary number of pounds and still have a paunch, if your abdominal muscles are weak.)

Another aid in reshaping your body, in addition to diet and exercise, is "do it yourself" massage. You don't have to go to an expensive salon to get the benefits of it. Take a roll of fat at your waist or on your thighs and gently knead it with your fingers. This breaks down the fat so that it can be carried away by the bloodstream.

Chart 6. WEIGHT

Weigh in every week on the same day and preferably at the same hour (Monday is always discouraging—Friday is better). If you are deadly serious (as I have to be in this matter) weigh in every morning. If you find you are up, go light on food and do extra exercise.

Date	Weight	Date	Weight

Chart 7. MEASUREMENT

Measure the upper arms at their fullest, but do not contract the muscle. The chest and waist areas are not hard to find. The midriff measurement should be taken halfway between the chest and the waist levels. When you measure your waist, don't pull in, just stay relaxed. Take the abdominal check just below the navel at its most protuberant point. Hips 1 can be found easily if you stand with hands on hips, fingers pointing down. Slide the hands about two inches toward the back. The lumps under your hands are hips 1. Measure for hips 2 at the largest part of the hips. Thighs are measured at their widest point, but unweight the leg before you start. The knee measurement is taken about two inches above the kneecap. Calf and ankle are easy to find. Be sure the leg is unweighted. Enter your findings and check every six weeks.

Dates

Neck					
R. arm					
L. arm					
Chest					
Midriff					
Waist					
Abdominals					
Hips 1.					
Hips 2.					
R. thigh					
R. knee					
R. calf					
R. ankle					
L. thigh					
L. knee					
L. calf					
L. ankle					

Fat has a way of setting up depots in places it finds comfortable. Unless one is terribly fat all over, there will be far less fat on often used hands than seldom used waist and upper arms. Even people who are quite acceptable to themselves in most areas can be made miserable by fat deposits on hips, thighs and abdominals. As we have mentioned before, the hard-packed fat that is associated with fibrositis is just as unattractive as roly-poly mushy fat— and it's no more useful. Locate these fat-happy spots and get rid of them. The Spot Obesity Chart shows the usual fat depots and lists by number the exercises which will work these areas. Enter these numbers in your little black book. Some of them may be there already for other problems. In order to note your progress, however, you may want to take inventory of the fat you have on hand from time to time. Six week intervals will show considerable change if you are doing as the directions tell you.

How can you measure your fat loss? For this you will need a tape measure and a pair of scissors. (No, you are not going to remove it that way.) A better instrument for measuring fat is a pair of calipers, but do you have a pair? No, then with care, you can substitute a pair of scissors. Turn to a new page in your little black book and draw Chart 8 which is to track fat loss and muscle gain. As you follow through on your exercise program, the fat which does not belong will come off. The "too thin" areas will gain in muscle and curve outwards. If you do as you are told, there is no chance of "putting on" where you want to "take off"—or vice versa.

If the scissors are sharp (they never are if you are trying to cut something, but they might be if you are trying not to) cover the cutting edge for one inch up from the point with Scotch or adhesive tape. Take the fat blob you wish to measure into a tight roll with the fingers. Holding it firmly, measure the thickness of the roll with the points of the scissors. Then measure the width between the points with your tape and enter it on your Spot Obesity Chart. You will not wish or need to measure all the spots on the chart. Note only those that are important to you. (You will need help with the arm, shoulder and upper back.)

Note on the chart which way you should roll the fat for measurement. It will be along the bone of arms and legs, horizontally at midriff, waist and abdominals.

Chart 8. SPOT OBESITY

To locate fat spots on yourself take out your scissor-calipers and tape measure. Pinch the flesh of the check spot between thumb and fingers and measure the size of the roll between the points of the scissors. Measure the distance between the scissor points and enter the results on your chart.

Arms. Pinch the fat on the back of the upper arms close to the armpit. *Upper back.* Pinch just below the shoulder blade on either side. *Midriff.* Pinch the spot halfway between armpit and waist and halfway between your exact center line and the outer point of your side. *Waist.* Pinch at the waist three inches to the right or left of center. *Abdominals.* One inch to the right or left just below the navel. *Hips 1.* Pinch the lump just below the waist and just back of the side line. *Thigh.* Sit down and grasp the flesh at the top of the thigh about three inches below the point where the leg joins the torso.

Dates				
R. arm				
L. arm				
Upper back				
Midriff				
Waist				
Abdominals				
Hips 1.				
Thighs				

Once you have determined your "problem areas," the exercises demonstrated in Chapter Five will go far toward helping you reach your desired weight and measurements. But this is only half the story. No chapter on "facts and fat" can be complete without some discussion of diets.

The cynic used to say that death and taxes were the only certainties in life. Today he could add a third—dieting. To be "with it" today, you have to diet. People who know virtually nothing about food, know *all* about diets: low cholesterol, high protein, crash, liquid, banana, steak, cheese, all-meat, no-meat, cooked, raw, ten-day, thirty-day, pills, tablets, wafers, all-fluid, no-fluid mush. There are diets for losing and diets for gaining. Ulcer diets and diets for diabetes, colitis, gastritis, arthritis, and what have you. Name it, there's a diet. It may not be correct, in fact it may be downright harmful, but it's there.

Not only are people confused about which diet to choose, but even more so about "how to." I have known people who have manfully tried to insert their diets into spaces between meals. Others gave up all but diet foods, of which they consumed such an abundance that they gained ten extra pounds. "Diets just don't work for me," was their eternal reply from then on. They are seconded by those who lose, and gain, two hundred and sixty pounds each year—ten off, and the same ten back on every two weeks. These people, of course, are convinced that "there is a level below which I simply can't go."

There are the headachy dieters and the heart palpitators. These "just know that eating too little is bad for the digestion." When their stomachs are empty, they insist that "the stomach juices begin to dissolve the stomach walls." There was a time, and I thought it was past, when people believed that idle hands and stomach juices got going on devil's work. To this end, they kept the stomach overworked all day and ate a large bowl of porridge at night, so that no damage could happen while they slept.

Today we know that proper diet means what you eat, how much you eat and when you eat it. I also think that it is important to list one more concern—*with whom you eat*. To give you the most in enjoyment and physical benefit, a meal must be eaten in a pleasant and tranquil atmosphere. If that means eating alone, then by all means eat alone. Most people, however, prefer eating with a congenial companion.

I have a powerful, well cared for and reliable Oldsmobile. Into it I put high-test gas recommended by my mechanic. (Mechanics may ignore their own bodies and those of their families, but they are meticulous in the care of their machinery.) I use the best grade oil and grease, and the water that goes into the radiator is clean. In return, I expect top performance, and I get it. If I were to let the gas gauge drop to zero, my car would stop. If I were to let the oil run low or get mucky, I'd be in trouble.

People, too, need decent care and fuel. Their actions are just as dependent as a car's on the food they consume. Inferior food—inferior action. Then, too, balance is important. All the good gas in the world won't keep a car greased, and quarts of milk cannot balance out absent fruits and vegetables, no matter how many vitamin pills you take.

Balance in timing shouldn't be overlooked either. Eating on Monday and starving on Tuesday is the last word in stupidity. My car, given half a gallon of gas at 8 A.M., cannot run till noon, even if I promise it ten gallons of high-test to be delivered at 12 sharp. Nor can people.

To look and feel our best, we should all eat a "balanced diet," whether we want to lose, maintain or gain weight. You and I both know what a balanced diet is. Any tenth grader can tell you: meat, fish, cheese, milk, eggs, vegetables and fruit, whole grain cereals or bread. We full-grown and more or less educated adults often forget that list, as we plunk down fifty cents for a grease-soaked, machine-pressed, bread-extended, third-grade hamburger patty, lying in a mess of ketchup between two sides of an air-filled, nutritionally valueless, white roll.

If you want to lose weight it takes will power. The method is devastatingly simple—eat less (but eat a balanced diet) and exercise more. If you take in two thousand calories a day in food and drink, and then use up that two thousand in energy, you will maintain your weight, whatever it is. If you only use fifteen hundred, you will store the extra five hundred. Do that for a year, and you will have accumulated quite a dividend—about fifty pounds. By the same token, if you use twenty-five hundred, you will be drawing on your bank account of stored fat, and you will lose weight.

A real calorie trap for the unwary are tasty snacks—

potato chips, nuts, cheese bits, crackers, dips, pretzels, and a thousand other beautifully packaged, conspicuously displayed, useless delights. They contain, besides many calories, fat, salt—and the habit. Like the alcoholic who can't stop with one drink, the potato chipper, popcorn popper and nut nibbler can't quit after one bite. One always leads to another, and another, and so on up to two and even three thousand calories. To compound the problem, snacks usually go with cocktails and are designed to tempt you past the one-drink stage into two. Why else do you suppose bars provide you with all those goodies? It's called "casting peanuts on the waters." After a while there's very little room left for mixed salad, steak, fish or liver. Oh, you may eat them just because they're there, or because you don't want to insult the cook, or you always "clean up your plate," but you neither want more food nor feel you need it.

Now what, precisely, have you done? You have filled your quota of calories (that number which you can eat without putting on weight) with food that is inferior for energy production, body building and repair. Then you either forego the good food because you are stuffed, or you exceed your quota by eating both, and so you store fat.

Each year in the summer months I teach a number of courses in physical fitness. The first day I tell the students a few things about food. I list the foods that I call "dead." These are the devitalized foods manufactured with an eye to "shelf life" rather than food value. Then we go over the "enriched" variety. Processing has removed much of their minerals and vitamins, and a token of these have been replaced artificially to enrich them. I point out the lard-ladlers: French fries, onion rings, hamburgers, hot dogs. The pimple producers: pies, cakes, cookies and doughnuts. And the tooth decayers: soft drinks and candy bars. I suggest that they lunch on fruit salad, cottage cheese, bran or whole wheat muffins and skimmed milk. Sounds pretty grim, doesn't it? But these people will be on a gym floor at least eight hours a day. They'll be hot, sweaty and full of aches. In those all too short days, the heavy ones must lose weight, the flabby ones must tighten up, the weak ones must grow strong and the tense ones work out their tensions. They couldn't do it if they were too tired because they used fuel that left them hungry although stuffed all day.

Breakfast shouldn't be hurried, if you can avoid it. It should be a good breakfast. Not big, *good*. Citrus fruit or juice and whole grain bread or cereal. I usually add two tablespoons of wheat germ to my cereal. If I know that lunch will be sketchy, I have an egg, either boiled or poached. If I have the egg, I don't have the cereal. No use being a pig about it. I like coffee, but sometimes tea suits me better. Most people's systems tell them what's good for them, but too many people don't listen. Watch a dog eat grass and learn something.

A dieting lunch is hard to find for people who work. I try to stick to fresh fruit salad and cottage cheese. If that's not available, shrimp salad or shrimp cocktail usually is. I can't eat at diners, except breakfast, which is their best meal anyway. But there is no law that says you can't have breakfast for lunch sometimes.

For supper I try to have lean meat or fish, with a vegetable and salad. If I have one cocktail and no bread and butter, I can have a dessert. If I'm at L'Aiglon in New York, I have to have rum cake, and if it's the Log Cabin in the Berkshires, it's pecan pie. Most other desserts leave me cold and with a couple hundred free calories to spend on another drink. It's all a matter of balance.

There are some foods I have given up for life. That doesn't mean that if I happen to get a plate of them at a barbecue, I'm going to have a fit. I'm going to eat them like everyone else, when it's a matter of courtesy. On my own, I will never eat again: mayonnaise, oleomargarine, butter (most of the time), fat on meat, white bread, fried foods, potatoes (not because they aren't good for you, but I love them running with butter or sour cream, and you know what *that* does), doughnuts, Danish pastry, flapjacks, corn (except right out of the garden in season), limas and peas (most of the time). I gave up some of these because the price in calories was far too high. Others I use as helps in the balance game. There are fewer calories in asparagus or carrots than in limas, for instance. It's the same with ginger ale—a passion with me. It gives way to club soda, which is also cold, wet and bubbly, but has no calories to ginger ale's one hundred. (There are ginger ales made with artificial sweeteners, but I prefer club soda.) These small sacrifices don't seem very great when I consider the penalty of overindulgence—I feel heavy, awkward and ugly. My clothes get too tight, and I get too loose. I know better, and I hate myself.

There are certain quirks to dieting, which I first thought applied only to me. But as interviews pile up year after year with people who come to me to lose weight, I find that many of us share these peculiarities. For instance, I know that if circumstances force me to have a big lunch, I'll be starving by dinner time and have to eat heavily again. It isn't logical, but it's a fact and has to be faced.

Another version of this I call "off to a bad start." If I start the day eating "junk"—coffee and a doughnut, pancakes or Danish pastry—by eleven I'm hungry and find myself hunting for lunch. That day fruit, cottage cheese and yogurt won't do. I keep on with the junk all day, because I have set the pattern in the morning. The vitamins and minerals I need are missing, so I still keep hunting for food. By four o'clock all I can think about is a hot pastrami on rye with a big pickle. I'm not through after supper, either. Ten o'clock finds me furtively buying potato chips to go with the beer and pretzels which I know will give me two extra pounds by a week from Friday.

There is another trick that nature pulls to confuse you. I call it "My God, what happened to Joe?" Every once in a while, I go on a tear, eating what, when and where I please and as often as I please. This usually accompanies an emotional problem, but whatever the reason, off I go. After about three weeks of this I get nervous and weigh myself. To my utter joy, I find I don't weigh an ounce more. Then, being human, I'm off again the next time someone passes the peanuts. For four weeks, and sometimes as long as six, I'll get away with my sins, particularly if I was in very good shape when I started. But Dorian Gray has nothing on me, and the picture is being painted all the same. Suddenly one day I weigh not one ounce or one pound more, but *six pounds*. I've been caught, and I begin to sweat.

For some reason, we are all very much like the "one hoss shay." When we go to pot, it shows all at once, but the undermining has been going on for a long time. It's shocking though, when it suddenly shows. That's when they say: "My God, what happened to Joe?"

Now when this happens, you have to go after yourself with a vengeance. What shows of the damage is bad enough, but what doesn't show is worse. Go on like that too long, and you slip into the chronic stage which is hard to pull out of. That's when you start getting fringe "benefits" such as constant fatigue, an unsatisfying sex life, a loss of courage, or the feeling that you are growing old.

So many people go on diets, suffer miseries the first week, get on the scale, and not a darned thing has happened. They feel there is only one thing left—shoot themselves. So they go out and eat a sundae, a way of thumbing their nose at fate. Then there is the person who does beautifully for three weeks, and along comes an occasion. "Off with the diet, on with the party, we only live once." At the end of the week, they are right back where they started. What's to do? Shoot yourself? Fortunately there is a simple answer to this. Occasions should never be missed. You are right, life is short, and who knows when the opportunity will come again.

When I was on Dave Garroway's television show, "Today," I had about ten minutes each week to get across to Dave's seven million viewers that they should move around a little, exercise to music, and build themselves up to enjoy life. A new reducing pill had just come on the market, and I wanted to prove I could take off weight without pills. The idea was right, but my timing was awful. It was two weeks before Christmas. There I stood in my leotard in front of seven million Americans of whom about six million, nine hundred thousand were in need of what I was about to show them. I got on the scale, and the needle popped up to one hundred thirty-two. Even I was a bit surprised. "There," I rallied with all the assurance in the world, "one hundred thirty-two, and if I can do it, you can do it. One pound a week for six weeks. No diet, I'll just eat less, no desserts and exercise fifteen minutes a day."

I was very conscientious that week. I did everything Bonnie Prudden says to do. I walked whenever I could, watched my food intake and did my exercises. It was no hardship, and it was kind of fun. The next week I tipped the scales at one hundred thirty. I was flying. "See how easy it is?" I told my audience. (And I really believed me, too.)

Then came the week before Christmas. The first party was on Tuesday, there were three on Wednesday, Thursday was Christmas, and I went on the air on Friday. "There's no use my getting on the scale, folks," I confessed. "I'm right back where I started—one hundred thirty-two pounds." I was shocked, chagrined and more than a little embarrassed that I hadn't delivered as promised. As I filled in the mark of my failure on the very large graph (see below) we kept for charting my progress, I wrote above the shameful rise, "Christmas."

Chart 9. WEIGHT GRAPH ON THE "TODAY" SHOW

On Dave Garroway's "TODAY" show, I learned that a rise in weight due to an Occasion is not the end of the world—or the program. Draw up your own chart similar to this one, and enter the cause for any sudden gain (there's *always* a cause, we don't really live on either love or air) above the spike on the chart. Then you'll know *why* you got out of control.

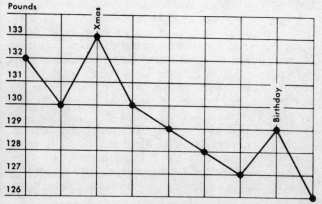

Chart 10. DAILY EAT SHEET

The best way to control calories is to know exactly what you have eaten each day in the week. If you lose weight on your diet—don't worry. If you gain, glance over last week's Eat Sheet and cut out the high calorie items. Remember—it takes time before improvement shows, so don't get discouraged.

	SUN.	MON.	TUES.	WED.	THURS.	FRI.	SAT.
Breakfast							
Break							
Lunch							
Cocktails							
Dinner							
Evening							
Snacks							

People are really nice. They wrote me consoling cards, and I learned another lesson, which may help you. One woman wrote: "I'm so sorry you gained all that weight, but secretly I'm glad, because I did, too. It makes me feel less of a fool to know I'm not the only one." I had said that my only excuse was that it had been Christmas and my kids were home. One man wrote that his kids were home, too, and wasn't it wonderful to have them. As I said, people are really nice.

I went at it again all right, with determination. New Year's morning, when I suspect almost everybody was where I was wishing I were—in bed—I turned in a score of one hundred thirty. It hadn't been too difficult. But I learned something you should know. When weight comes off fast, it can go back on in a hurry, so don't believe any of those ads which claim to work the miracle of seven pounds off in seven days by taking pills. Just don't get discouraged if it takes a while. You took years to get it. Would you say twenty? Well, figure that it will come off at about the rate of one month for each year.

Each week after that I lost one pound until January 29, when my birthday rolled around. Again my audience was understanding. Again I was forced to make public the results of a wonderful occasion. One week later I finally hit one hundred twenty-six and stayed there (until I started writing this book).

What about food faddists? There are many now, and there always have been. There are people who eat nothing but "health foods" and others who wouldn't touch them. Both are faddists. Some people feel undressed until they've taken their morning vitamin pills, some eat yeast, molasses, figs, prunes, apricots, raisins, nuts, honey, vinegar, sunflower seeds and liver. There are others who scream "garbage" at the mention of yogurt. Actually, there is value in all of these foods, *as long as the tail does not wag the dog.*

My first brush with differences of opinion about food came when my daughter, Suzy, then eleven, went to the North Country School in Lake Placid, New York. They grew their food organically. That means that they used only natural fertilizer, such as manure, mulch and ploughed-under crops. Even fallen trees were allowed to rot and go back to the earth. The cattle, pigs and chickens eaten at the school were raised on land organically enriched. No poison sprays were used on fruits or vegetables. Since the school disapproved of additives, all citrus fruits were ordered undyed from Florida and sent up in shipments at regular intervals. They were dull in color but met the school's standards. Candy, white sugar and soft drinks were outlawed. The school made its own maple syrup, and honey was plentiful. Snacks were fruit juices, raw vegetables and whole grain cookies or muffins. Milk was not homogenized. Bread was made from stone-ground flour, and their cereal was freshly ground each day.

When Suzy first started at school, there were a few weak wails about chocolate bars, but they were replaced by the excitement of getting in potatoes before frost, going nutting and picking chickens. My first surprise came at Christmas vacation, when the dentist proclaimed Suzy free of cavities. For the two years she remained at that school there were no cavities.

Then her usual severe winter head cold failed to develop. The school had a cheerful infirmary, but the only person I ever saw in it was a small boy who had brought back a case of measles from vacation. When Suzy reached adolescence she grew three inches, but added hardly any weight. There were no pimples, her hair glistened, and she was straight as a Balinese. She even escaped the traditional ill humor and moodiness of the adolescent. Except for feeling "wonderfully sad" sometimes, there were no moods.

Then she left North Country and entered another school nearer home. This school was less concerned about food for the body than food for the mind. The food was tasty enough and typical of the kind I remembered from school days. By Christmas Suzy had gained ten pounds and developed five cavities. She was back in the world, so to speak.

A Word about Organic Foods

When the Breens ask me to dinner, I always go. First of all I like them. They are charming, attractive, intelligent, well informed and fun. Also, they are all slender and this fascinates me. I'm not fascinated particularly because they aren't fat, although I must say it's more pleasurable to admire faces with fine lines and taut skin. Their slenderness fascinates me because they eat so much and so well.

"Mater" is Mrs. Breen's mother and she won't tell anyone her age. Old she is and wise and spry as a cricket. She is also the very best cook in my acquaintance. When I had learned the lesson of Suzy's diet at North Country, I started to watch what the people around me ate—both those who lacked vitality and those who had it in abundance. Since the Breens have it in great abundance—as well as the look of health and the rare quality of being relaxed and happy—that's the family I'll tell you about.

They grow most of what they eat. No, they aren't farmers—Robert Breen is a movie producer. But they bought a country place in the Berkshires, bought some cows and then belled them so that you think you are in a high Swiss village when you walk around the grounds. They planted a few vegetables and "Mater" took over. I asked her for her secret and it's really very simple: "I pick it after the water is boiling and I don't cook it more than it needs."

A few vegetables led to a few more and pretty soon, what started as fun, turned into a full blown hobby. Paul, Mater's grandson, found that the old farm was running over with grapes. An ancient book from the Lenox library started him on winemaking. The wine you get at the Breens can't even be discussed in the same breath with commercial wines, nor can the liqueurs.

I was just beginning to see the possibilities in the Breen arrangements for good food when I heard Dr. Ernst Winter, professor of Political Science at Iona University, speak in Watkins Glen, New York. He, too, was slender, as were his two young sons. (I hear there are three or four more young ones at home.) He began gardening on a window sill, became interested in erosion and history and fell in love with an American girl. "We decided to marry and start homesteading," he said, "so we bought three and a half acres in West Nyack." Well, West Nyack was home-steaded, if ever, about two hundred and fifty years ago. Now it's pretty much suburbia, I thought.

"Oh yes, to some extent," Dr. Winter assured me, "but we manage. First we built a greenhouse, then a barn and finally a house. That is the proper order. We grow farm animals, food and children. We raise seventy-two per cent of all we need." (I'll bet that family rarely needs a doctor.) There was only one disturbing thought that occurred to me. Dr. Winter was telling his audience that his life had begun in Vienna, in the heart of the city, that he never dreamed he would find his way to a "homestead" in West Nyack. He said he had been afraid of the dark as a child, and that animals had frightened him. He had had many fears and uncertainties. Not so his kids. If a job had to be done at the barn even the littlest went down in the dead of night without a qualm. His sons talked to animals and for all he knew, the animals talked back. Anyway they understood each other and nobody was afraid of anything. These boys, he said with disarming sincerity, may be the new Americans. Boys who have their feet on the ground and learn about life and work and dignity so early that it has become a part of them long before there are over-whelming problems to face. Then I thought of the Breens who have balanced their hectic lives with peace and the expert production of all the necessities. Were they, too, the new American family? It is to be hoped that many of us will pick up such rewarding hobbies, but let us examine these two successful families—successful in ways that are very rare. Are they new? No. These are the *old* American ways that built this land and fed its people well, demanded toil for benefit and honored honest work from the youngest to the oldest.

This is not a book on diet. There are a few tips here that work, but you will have to start studying the problem for yourself and if you do get the "homesteading" bug, I'll be glad to swap farm news with you, for as of this year, I've started mine like Dr. Winter—on my window sill.

CHAPTER FIVE

Exercises to trim the figure

And now we come to the moment of truth—the moment when you begin to *do* something rather than just read or talk about it. There are a number of questions which are always raised by my audiences when I discuss exercise. The first and probably most frequent is "When is the best time to exercise?"

There is no best time. You take whatever time you can get. Naturally, if the morning hours are free you are probably freshest then, but on the other hand when you come home in the evening beat-up and dog-tired, that is probably when you need it most.

Not for the sake of the body but for the sake of yourself and your habits, try to find the same time each day. If you are a housewife, wait until the children are off to school and your husband to the office. When no one is likely to disturb you, you can go through your exercise program without interruption. Many of my friends exercise from nine-thirty to ten in the morning. They have informed their friends and relatives that they are not available at that time. They do not answer telephones or doorbells; they simply work as though they were not at home.

The professional person who must be at the office will find that the end of the day crowds around his ears and he had better, if he can, get his ten minutes in first thing in the morning before he leaves the house. Then if he has time for ten or fifteen minutes later in the day so much the better, but at least he has had his ten minutes.

The next question that is raised is "What is the minimum amount of time I should spend on exercise?" The minimum would be about fifteen minutes a day. This will not net any tremendous dividends but when you add it up, it's over an hour a week. If you can manage to get in a half hour a day you will find that it really pays off.

The third question is "How long should I exercise at any one time?" There is no real limit to an exercise period as long as you keep rotating the exercises. I never spend more than fifteen seconds on any one exercise and then I move on to another area. I may return to the first area again and again but never longer than fifteen or, at the most, twenty seconds at one time. If you are in wonderful condition you can go on as my summer physical fitness classes do for hours and hours and hours. If you are in poor condition you should start with about five minutes. Later in the day, add another five and still later another. This way you can get in a half hour without ever tiring yourself. The trick, of course, is to rotate the areas you are exercising.

The next question is "Where should I exercise?" This is usually followed by a sigh and the remark that there is so little space. Most of the exercises in this book have been designed for a small place. A bedroom, living room or even the bathroom should suffice for most of them. Chapter Six, on habits, is designed to show you how to use the world around you to supplement your exercise program.

The fifth question (and this is almost always asked by women) is "What do I wear?" I do not approve of shorts. In the first place, they usually inhibit motion whenever you try to pull a leg into a bent knee position. In the second place, they are not attractive looking when you move and they do not cling close enough to warm the muscles as you work. I suggest that you get a pair of my Bonnie Prudden exercise tights and a leotard. You may feel that you are too outsized for this, but believe me, they improve the line of any figure no matter how far it has gone in any direction. When you look down at yourself in a pair of tight-fitting tights you can see every bulge. If your abdomen protrudes, you will pull it in because you cannot bear the sight. The tights will not impede any motion, and they will keep you comfortable as you work. It is always important to look dressed for any occasion, and exercising in bathing suit or pajamas is certainly out of place.

Then comes the question about music. (I will keep saying "Use music" throughout the entire exercise program.) There are many different tastes in music, and some people will enjoy Grieg while others will work best to the latest in pop sound. The important point to make here is that you should exercise to music with a good rhythm. I personally have always enjoyed Leroy Anderson's and Les Baxter's records, and they can be purchased almost anywhere. I've put out several records myself (see the list in front). For forty-plus minutes I yell at you to very good exercise music. Exercise to music you enjoy—music that has a beat which you can follow.

Then comes the question whether you should wear shoes. Not if you can avoid it. However, if you cannot avoid it, pick up a pair of the Bonnie Prudden fitness slippers. While they are non-skid on the bottom, the top is so gently fitted to the foot that you will not realize you are wearing a covering at all.

So, armed with your little black book, music (whether it be radio or record), comfortable, attractive clothing, your test sheets and determination—set sail. If you can manage to get through the first session, the first step will have been taken. The next step, if you have worked hard, is a *hot* bath. Tomorrow you will hate me. You will be stiff and sore and convinced that a pin has fallen out of at least one hinge. The cure of course is another hot bath— the limbering series on page 228 as a warm-up for the warm-up—then more exercise. You hope this will pass, and it will. But don't count on it the next day because that is the day it will be worse. By the third day you may notice a return to a semblance of normal. "Hah!" you will say, "I had to go through all of that just to feel almost the same as I did before I started." The answer is no, you will *not* feel the same as before. The absence of pain will be the same, but this time there will be a feeling far more positive. Day by day you will notice new things you are able to do—things you had given up and almost forgotten about.

So for the record, since this is your private study, save a page in the back of your little book and head it "Surprises." On that page you list the changes as you note them. You don't believe it, but this is your birthday—you have accepted the second wish.

Chart 11.   SAMPLE DAILY WORK SHEET

Copy this work sheet into your black book. Keep track of everything you do so that you can check improvement against work. Should an area lag, you will see why right here.

Problem	Exercises	Sun.	Mon.	Tues.	Wed.	Thurs.	Fri.	Sat.

Your exercise program should never be a hit or miss affair—whether you plan to devote ten minutes or two full hours. If it is, you won't get results and will be discouraged. At first, before you learn how, you will have to give quite a bit of attention to what you are about. Later it becomes second nature and you do it without thinking or consciously planning.

Should you be fortunate enough to have an hour to devote to yourself, you could use the daily exercise schedule.

Chart 12. YOUR DAILY EXERCISE SCHEDULE

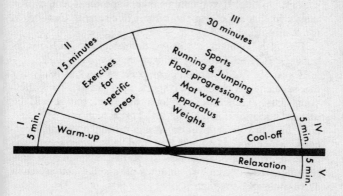

Divide your hour into five segments. The first is the most important and while you may omit any other segment, *never omit this one.* Warm-up exercises prepare your muscles for the heavier work to follow. They protect against injury, and since warm muscles are twenty per cent more efficient than cold muscles, the warm-up determines your performance. *No extreme stretching or spike exercise such as running or jumping should ever be done without warm-up.*

The second segment should be given over to your special exercise needs which have been determined by the tests on page 54. Precede your special flexibility exercises with your exercises for strength whenever possible as they will give you added ability and protection.

The third segment becomes more important as your ability improves and you are able to widen your activity horizons. By the time you reach this area, you are ready for anything and it is a rare muscle that gives you trouble if you have worked it well to this point. If you can spend more than a half hour on your exercise program, add those extra minutes to this segment. Sports of all kinds, mat work, apparatus, floor progressions (page 91), swimming, diving, weight training, all are made more fun and more beneficial if you precede them with correct exercise.

The fourth segment is given over to Cool-off. These five

minutes of easy exercises let your heart simmer down, but prevent chilling. If you cannot take a shower, spend a little longer in this area. Use the same exercises for Cool-off as for Warm-up.

The fifth segment is always desirable, but not always possible. It is set aside for relaxation.

If you are limited in time, or perhaps not yet ready for the segment given over to sports and heavier activities, your activity schedule will look different, but it will be just as important. Divide it into three sections. The first and third are given over to Warm-up and Cool-off exercises, which are identical. The middle section should be used for your special needs. Right in the middle of this section, spend one or two minutes on a spike activity such as running or jumping.

If you are starting at the very bottom and are able to exercise only a few minutes at a time, start with a few minutes of Warm-ups and save one minute for one of your special needs. *Always add the relaxation section if you belong in this group.* Don't be satisfied with these few moments however. Later in the day repeat the Warm-ups and work on a different "special." Keep track of what you have done so you will not overlook any area that needs attention.

1 The Swim

Stand with feet well apart for balance. Keeping the legs straight, bend forward from the hips. Use an over-arm swim stroke. Do eight strokes

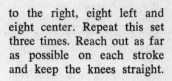

to the right, eight left and eight center. Repeat this set three times. Reach out as far as possible on each stroke and keep the knees straight.

2 Thigh Shift

Stand with feet far apart and *somewhat* turned out. Keeping both heels flat on the floor, bend the right knee. Return to the erect position and then bend the left knee, shifting the weight to the left thigh. Alternate legs for eight shifts.

3 Waist Twist

Stand with feet well apart and extend the arms to the sides. Twist the upper body all the way around to the right and then to the left. Start with sixteen twists and work up to thirty. By following the backward flung hand with your eyes, you will also improve your neck and chin line.

4 Torso Shift

Stand with feet apart and arms extended to the sides. Pretend you are standing between two walls that are about six inches beyond your reach. Keep the hips absolutely still and the shoulders level. Reach with the right hand to touch the imaginary wall, then shift the upper body to touch the left wall. Start with eight shifts done slowly and work up to thirty at the lively tempo.

5 Lateral Stretch

Stand with feet apart and place the right hand on the right thigh and the left straight overhead. Lean upper body and raised arm to the right as you slide the right arm down the leg to knee level. Holding this position, bounce the upper body downward in four short, easy bounces, then do the same to

the other side. Repeat for four sets. Do not let the upper body lean forward at any time.

6 Snap and Swing

Start with feet apart and bent elbows held at shoulder level. *Snap* the elbows back for a count of one. Then return to the starting position for the count of two. *Swing* the arms open and back for the count of three and return to the starting position for the count of four. Be sure to keep the arms above shoulder level at all times. Do eight sets.

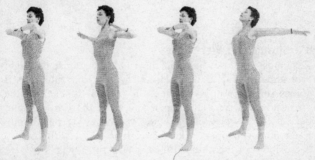

7 Hip Twist

Turn the right foot inward as far as possible. Bring the hip around as well. Then twist the foot, leg and hip outward. Repeat the rotation eight times with each leg slowly, pressing open and closed as hard as you can. After eight slow rotations, double your time and do sixteen to each side.

8   Shoulder Twist

Rest most of the weight on the right foot, twist the right arm under as far as possible, and watch your thumb as it comes round. You should feel the pull in the back of the arm and shoulder. Then open and twist the arm out and back as far as possible, keeping your eyes on the thumb. Each time you open, take a breath in. Start with four to each side and then eight together. Do three sets.

9   Right Angle Twist

Feet well apart and the upper body held at right angles to the floor. Keep the head still so that the upper body may twist against the two set ends of the spinal column. Swing the left arm open and up allowing the bent right arm to follow part way. Then swing back to the opposite side. Start with twenty and work up to fifty.

10   Back Stroke

Place the back of the left hand on your left cheek, pressing the elbow back as far as it will go. Hold the elbow in the stretched position and swing the hand back and down to complete a circle. Keep the shoulders facing front. Alternate eight each side.

11   Descending Hip Wag

Start by swinging the hips from side to side but keep the upper body free from any *lateral* motion. When the hips are moving freely, lower the upper body slowly toward the floor, taking eight full counts before the hands touch and eight before you are standing erect. Do two sets.

12   Knee Bends

Stand with legs together and feet parallel. Rise to the toes for a count of one and bring your arms forward for balance. Tighten your seat, abdominals, thigh muscles and

knees. This will keep you from teetering. Keep your back straight and lower yourself into a deep knee bend. Don't let the *knees open*. Rise again to the toe position and then lower yourself to your heels. Do this exercise to a count of four. Those who can, start with five and work up to fifty daily. They need not all be done at one time.

13 Walk-outs

Start in the standing position with feet apart and heels on the floor. Without bending the knees, lean forward from the hips and place a hand on the floor. Walk the hands forward for three counts but do not move the feet. On the fourth count when the body is stretched all out, press the pelvis down with a sharp movement, but do not bend the arms. Walk the hands back for two counts and allow the last two for standing straight. Do two at the start and work up to eight.

EXERCISES TO HELP YOU PASS THE MINIMUM FITNESS TESTS

If you failed any one of the Minimum Tests (page 30), this is where you start your special exercise program. These exercises should be done as often as you can fit them into your day, since until you are proficient with these, all others will be difficult.

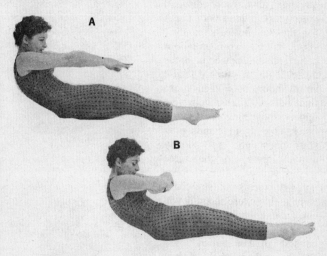

A

B

14 Abdominals

(A) Sit on the floor with feet and arms stretched straight out in front of you. Drop your head, round your back and roll *slowly* down until you are at rest. *If you can,* come up the same way. If not, then get up with the help of your hands. Do this exercise at least ten times twice daily. After a while you will build enough strength as you fight gravity in the descent, to enable you to sit up with arms outstretched. (B) When

C – D

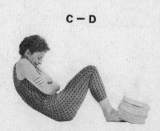

you can sit up with arms outstretched, start your roll down with arms across your chest and come up with outstretched arms. Work for the time you can do the roll up with folded arms. When you can sit up with folded arms, advance to a more difficult exercise. (C) Bend your knees for the roll out. By bending your knees, you cut out help from the powerful psoas muscles and are forced to use your abdominals even more than before. Thrust your feet under something or somebody, cross your hands over your chest and roll slowly down. Come up the same way if you can. If not, come up with arms outstretched. Repeat this exercise until you can come up with arms folded, then advance to the hardest in the series. (D) Place your hands behind your head while in the knee bent, held down position. Roll slow-

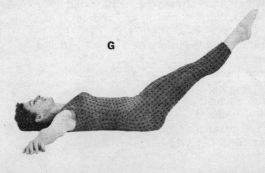

ly down and as slowly up again. If you can't come up with your hands behind your neck, come up with them across your chest. Do the roll downs until you have the strength to come up with hands behind your head. At this point you pass the Minimum Abdominal test. That doesn't mean stop there. That means continue doing ten advanced roll downs twice daily for the rest of your life.

If you were unable to pass test number three, either had difficulty in holding your legs up for the full ten seconds, or found that your back was unduly arched, the following exercise will correct the condition: (E) Lie on your back with knees bent and resting. You will feel that your spine is pressed flat to the floor. *Keep the spine flat to the floor at all times.* (F) Raise legs straight into the air. At this point you will still be able to keep the spine down. Drop the legs back to the rest position. (G) The second time you extend your legs, lower them about six inches nearer the floor. Retract to the rest position. Keep extending and retracting until you can no longer keep the spine down. At that point, go back to the angle of extension when you still had full control over the spine and do ten. This exercise should be done twice daily. Ultimately you will be able to extend the legs an inch or two above the floor while maintaining a perfectly flat back.

(H) If you failed Test Four, lie prone on the floor with arms and legs outstretched. Raise first the right arm and then the left, being careful not to roll the upper body from side to side. Do eight with each arm and proceed to the double arm lift. (I) Lift both arms and chest from the floor and then lie back and *rest* for three seconds and repeat. Do eight. Do three sets of prone arm raises each day.

H

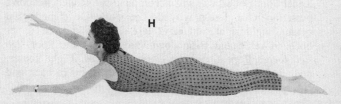

I

(J) If you failed Test Five, lie prone on the floor and raise the right leg as high as possible while keeping the knee straight. Alternate with the left for eight lifts each leg. If this exercise is difficult or causes discomfort, place a pillow under the hips to prevent hyper-extension. Do three sets of prone leg lifts each day but do not do them all at one time unless you alternate with a standing exercise.

J

To pass Test Six, place the feet wide apart and be sure to keep the legs straight. Place your hands behind your back and keeping your head up, lean forward from the hips. Bounce the upper body downward *in short easy bounces*. Repetition, not strain, will accomplish the stretch, so don't push too hard. Let gravity do the work. Do eight to the center, eight right and eight left. Then allow the upper body to relax and hang downward toward the floor. *Do not force*. Repeat the same easy bounces. Eight center, eight right and eight left. Remember, tightness in back and hamstrings is aggravated by stress. The more tension your day holds, the more you will need this exercise. Just as rain clouds warn you that an umbrella is indicated, a difficult day should tell you to do back and hamstring stretches. You usually do not wait until drenched to use rain protection. Don't wait for the backache before exercising.

K

L

Keep in mind that neither a loose seat nor a fat seat nor even a nonexistent seat is attractive. Not only should the appearance of this area concern you, but a seat that is not functioning well will age you faster than baldness or white hair. Before doing the following exercises, check with massage on page 104.

15 Knee to Nose Stretch

Get down on all fours and bring the right knee as close to your nose as you can. Then stretch the leg back and up; at the same time raise your head. Try not to bend your arms at any time. Do eight to each side four times. This exercise stretches the back

muscles and improves the line and strength of both the gluteals (seat) and abdominals. A must on your program. Alternate with an erect exercise.

16 Back Leg Swing

Start on all fours. Carry the left leg across in back of the right foot and set the ball of the foot firmly on the floor. Keeping the leg absolutely straight, swing it around and place the foot *flat* on the floor in front of the left hand. Do four complete swings and then alternate with the other foot. *This is not an easy exercise.* If you can do one at the start, you are doing well. Work up to the point where you

can do two sets of four. This exercise strengthens the whole lower body and stretches both legs and feet. The waist, too, comes in for considerable action.

17 The Hydrant

Start on all fours. Raise the right leg to the side, keeping the knee bent. Stretch the leg straight out to the side. Don't change the position of the upper leg at all, but bend the knee again. To rest the muscles, carry the leg straight back as in the second position of the knee to nose kick. Then repeat the Hydrant. Start with two to each side, but work up to eight. The Hydrant works "Hips One," those two bumps on the outside of the hips that are both prominent and hard to lose. It strengthens the lower back and gluteals and stretches leg muscles.

18 The Table

Lie across a bench or a table. Grasp one side with both hands and hang over the side with bent knees. Slowly extend the legs until the body is stretched straight out. Hold for a slow count of three and bring in the legs. Rest for the same count and extend again. Start with four and work up to ten. At this point the time element can be helped by cutting the number back to five and hanging two or three pound weight bags across the ankles. This is a must for all sports.

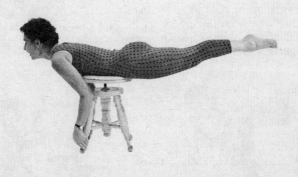

THIG THINNING

Strong thighs are not synonymous with big thighs. Before you do these exercises, if your thighs are over size spend a few minutes with the fibrositis massage on page 104 and *then* do the exercises.

19 Side Bend and Stretch

Rest on your right side. Be sure you are on your side and not leaning back comfortably on your hip. Stretch your body out straight and point your toes. Rest your upper body on your right hand, *not the elbow*. This stretches the upper part of you while you are busy with the lower. Bring the left knee behind the left shoulder and *keep it as close to the shoulder as you can,* then straighten the leg. Bend the knee again and stretch it back to the starting position. Do four on each side and do four sets.

20 Supine Hip Twist

Lie relaxed on your back and rotate the left foot outward as far as you can. Hold the foot in this position and raise the leg until it is almost at right angles to your body. At the peak of the lift, rotate the foot all the way in. Hold the foot rotated inward and lower the leg. Do not relax the foot or leg when you lower the leg, merely touch the floor with the foot and keeping it in its rotated position, raise it over head again. At the peak of the lift, rotate the foot outward. Lower the leg in the rotated position to the floor.

Alternate legs three sets each side. This is excellent for heavy thighs, insufficiently used hips, and for leg stretch.

21 Lateral Leg Lift

Lie on your right side resting on your elbow. Stretch your body long and point your toes. Lift the left leg only as far as you can without rotating your body to lean back on your hips. You will not be able to lift very high—the hip joint will limit the lift. Bend the knee close to the body. Stretch and then extend it. Do eight bend and extend movements on each side for three sets. This exercise im-

proves leg control, and therefore helps your walk. It works the hip joint which gets very little lateral exercise in our way of life.

22 Leg Twist, Sitting

Sit on the floor leaning back to rest on either hands or elbows. Cross the left leg over the right and twist the leg until the big toe touches the floor. Keep the leg crossed and try to rotate the foot so that the toes point to the ceiling. After the foot is rotated carry the left leg back to a spread leg position and try to rotate the foot so that the *little* toe touches the floor. Hold the leg open and rotate the foot inward until the toes point to the ceiling and repeat. Do this exercise four times with each leg. This reduces and strengthens thighs and increases the range of hip and ankle joints.

PROGRESSION EXERCISES

Start your progressions across the floor with these exercises. You really don't need much space and even if you are only able to take ten steps, it is enough for a good beginning. *Always walk back to your starting corner.* This gives your tightened muscles a chance to stretch and the tired ones a chance to rest. Constantly vary the exercises to prevent both fatigue and boredom.

23 Toe Walk

Rise high on the toes, tighten legs, hips, and abdominals, lift your chest but press the shoulders back and down. Relax your arms. Go across the room in this manner, but walk back flat-footed. Yes, this exercise is for men too. (If you are curious enough to risk discomfort to find out how much you need this work, try fifty steps in this position and then try to walk upstairs the next day.) Return to the starting corner and go on to the next exercise.

24 Toes In

Turn the toes all the way in and walk pigeon-toed across the floor. Walk back relaxed and with a normal step.

25 Finger Drag

Lean forward until the fingers drag as you progress across the floor. Lead each step with the heel. This exercise stretches the back and heel cords and strengthens the back.

26 Hip Twister

Take each step forward, turning the foot way in and bringing the hip around. Forget the arms except to get them out to the side. As you improve, they will naturally move against the feet to increase the twist. Excellent for all sports as it increases control over the upper and lower torso as separate units.

27   Side to Side Jump

Stand on one foot as though you were standing on one rail of a narrow gauge railroad. Jump over to the other rail with the other foot. Cross the floor jumping from side to side. Forget the shoulders at first, later you will find you can exaggerate their natural lift and this will exercise them as well. This strengthens feet and legs and waist. It is particularly good for sports calling for quick changes of direction, such as basketball and tennis.

28   Knee Lifts

As you cross the floor, lift each knee until it is at right angles to the floor. Be sure the toe is pointed as this stretches the muscles of the lower legs and increases the range of the ankle joint. The stand leg should be absolutely straight and the heel flat to the floor. This exercise increases balance and control, stretches leg muscles and strengthens feet and thighs. As soon as you feel you can do it with ease, try running in the knee lift position.

29 Stiff Leg Runs
Run across the floor at a good quick pace and extend the legs with each step. As in the foregoing exercise, point the toes and bring the heels to the floor.

30 Skips
You used to skip once, you should again. In fact you always should. If you would feel silly skipping down street, I could understand. But you'd feel sillier if one day you found your bones had grown old and brittle from disuse. First try it frontwards, then back. Then skip from side to side. Put on a good waltz rhythm and skip twice around the room. If it will make you feel any better, draw the blinds—but skip.

GENERAL EXERCISES

This series should only be done after considerable warm up. It works for strength, flexibility and coordination of the entire body and is excellent preparation for *all* sports.

31 Monkey Walk

Keep the legs straight, palms flat on the floor and the feet as close to the hands as possible. This forces the weight onto the arms and stretches the back and hamstrings. In this position, walk across the floor. If it is difficult, start with four steps and work up to twenty. *Always alternate this progression with one in which the body is held in the erect position.*

32 Horse Kick

Cross the floor on all fours, kicking each leg high in the air.

33 Hop Frog

Stand with feet together. Lean over and place both hands in front of the feet. Jump both feet close to the hands. Repeat across the floor. Start with four and work up to twenty. *Alternate with erect exercises.*

34 Hand Walk—
Foot Jump

Prepare for this exercise by standing erect with feet apart.

Jump in place until you are certain of the rhythm, then stoop down and pound the same beat with alternating hands on the floor. Follow this by combining both hand and foot action. Walk the hands and jump the feet across the floor. Keep the legs straight as in the Monkey Walk. *Alternate with erect exercises.*

35 Zig Zag Foot Jump

Keeping the same beat with both hands and feet, walk the hands but jump both feet from side to side. In this exercise the knees should bend on landing and straighten in the air. *Alternate with erect exercises.*

36 Seat Lift

This exercise throws considerable weight on the arms and shoulders. It prepares for cartwheels and hand stands. Stand erect at the start. Lean down to place both hands on the floor. As a continuation of the same motion, thrust the seat into the air *letting straight legs hang down.* When you drop back to your feet, stand erect and take one step forward and repeat the exercise.

37 One Arm Seat Lift

Place the right hand on the floor and jump both legs to the left. Allow the legs to bend so that you end the jump in a stooped position. Then place the left hand on the floor and jump both legs to the right. Alternate in this manner as you cross the floor. Lifting the unweighted arm high in the air facilitates the jump.

FOOT MASSAGES
AND EXERCISES

I. MASSAGE

Frequent foot massage should be a must for everyone, especially in cold weather or when fatigue has set in. It need not take long and is most beneficial.

38 The Arch
Place the fingers of the right hand flat over the toes of the left foot. The thumb goes under the instep. Press the toes down to increase the arch of the foot. Alternate this with the Press-up.

39 The Press-up
Place both hands under the ball of the left foot and pull up as far as possible. Do four sets wherein you alternate the Arch with the Press-up. This improves foot and ankle flexibility.

40 The Twist-out
Place the left foot on top of the right knee. (If this calls for more flexibility than you can muster at first, place the foot on the floor as close to your body as possible.) Twist the foot so that the sole faces up. With the left hand on top and the right underneath, rotate the foot inward as far as possible. Alternate this with the Twist-in.

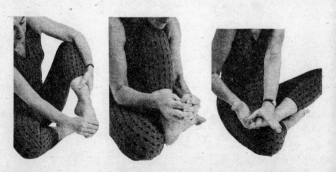

41   The Twist-in

Grasp the left foot in the right hand by placing the
thumb on top and the fingers underneath. Rotate the foot
inward. Alternate these two exercises for three sets. Improves foot and ankle flexibility.

42   Toe Spread

Grasp the left foot with both hands placing the thumbs on
top and fingers underneath. First spread the toes wide and
then, as if your toes were webbed, try to continue the
separation between the toes by pressing your thumbs to
meet your fingers through the flesh of the foot between
the bones of the toes. Spend about one minute on each
foot in this manner.

43   Ball Press

Place the fingers of the hands on the upper surface of the
foot and the thumbs on the ball. Press the thumbs hard
against the ball of the foot in small circles as though you
were trying to loosen the bones in the foot. Spend at least
one or even two minutes on each foot in this manner.

44   Heel Cord Relaxer

Tight heel cords lead to fatigue and an old, inflexible
walk. Place the fingers on one side of the heel cords and
the thumb on the other. Start at the heel and move the
cords back and forth from side to side as you slowly move
your hand up the leg. Repeat this action four or five times
trying to relax the foot and ankle consciously as well as
manually.

After using the foot massage you will find that your feet feel warm and flexible. This is because you have worked over and warmed the muscles—which improves circulation and readies your feet for the exercises to follow.

II. EXERCISE

When your feet are allowed to deteriorate either through a lack of use or because of misuse, trouble is inevitable. If this is your weak area, be sure to spend considerable time on both massage and these exercises.

45 Soleus or Heel Cord Stretch
Stand with feet parallel and heels flat on the floor. Keeping the seat tucked under, bend the knees as far as they will go while the heels are still down. At that point, jog in short easy bounces trying to stretch the heel cords a little at a time. Bounce ten times, go on to another exercise and then return to this one.

46 Heel Cord Stretch (continued)
Stand on a book, box or stair with the insteps and heels free in the air. Press the heels down in short bounces, ten bounces to a set. Alternate this exercise with another exercise and return to it later in the exercise period.

47 Instep Stretch
Rest on hands and knees with insteps flat on the floor. Rise up onto the tops of the toes thus increasing the arch.

100

Go back to the knee rest position. Repeat four or five times. After this becomes easy go up onto the insteps and bounce gently three times before coming to rest. This exercise gives more flexibility to the ankles.

48 Roll-out

Start with feet parallel and flat on the floor. Roll onto the outer edges of the feet and curl the toes under. Be sure that both the toes touch in front and the heels in back. Roll back to the flat-foot position. Alternate this exercise with the Toe Lift.

49 Toe Lift

From the flat-foot position, raise the toes but be sure to keep the ball of the foot flat on the floor. Do six sets of the Toe Lift afternating with six of the Roll-outs. These exercises increase both strength and flexibility of the feet and ankles.

50 Edging

Start with feet parallel and flat to the floor. Bend both knees keeping the pelvis tucked under. Shift both knees to the right so that the feet roll over onto the right edges. Without straightening the legs, shift the knees to the left and roll onto the left edges. Do eight shifts to a set and do three sets. This is for increased ankle flexibility.

51 Heel Lifts

Start with feet parallel and flat. Raise the right heel but keep the ball of the foot and the toes on the floor. Return

the right heel to the floor and raise the left. At first, make these separate movements and do them very slowly, always trying to force the knee farther and farther forward over the toes. After you can do it easily, change feet at the same time, raising one foot as you replace the other. Start with twenty changes and work up to fifty. Good for strength, flexibility, balance and control.

52 Toe Rises

Start with feet flat and parallel. Tighten abdominal, seat and thigh muscles and rise slowly to the toes. Lower slowly. The first time you rise, count one and one for the descent. The second time, take two counts to reach the peak and two to drop back to the floor. The third time, take three counts and so on for eight. Then go back down with seven, six, and so forth. Increases strength, control and balance.

53 Toe Rises (continued)

Start as before but when you rise to the toes, behave as you would if your head were against a roof. Do not let the body go any higher as you lift, but press the knees and hips forward into a pelvic tilt. This increases abdominal strength as well as gluteal, feet and leg strength. Do four.

102

"BREAK UP" MASSAGE

54 Shoulders

Tense shoulders usually become hard and painful. The first object of the massage *is not relaxation* . . . you will have to break up the stiff painful areas. This is sometimes called "pinching massage" and it is exactly that. Take a fold of the flesh between thumb and fingers and knead it. You can be gentle at first, but as you find you can tolerate the discomfort more easily be less gentle. Don't stay too long in one area. Start at the shoulder edge and work toward and then up the neck. Three minutes every other day is a good start. Follow this massage with the shrug exercises on page 170.

55 The Arms

Tension attacks the arms too, and causes them to look fat and often lumpy. Make a mitten of your hand and reach around to the back of the arm. Squeeze and knead. Start your pinching action down near the elbow and work your way up the arm. Be gentle at first, but not too long. There is nothing in the medical literature that says you can cause damage with this sort of work. If you are in terrible shape, you may bring out a bruise or two, but then you'd bruise after any massage. Spend about one minute on each arm every other day.

56 Mid-Section

Take hold of that spare tire with both hands. Roll it first down and then up. As pain lessens, be more unkind to yourself and don't overlook any fat depot. If they are in front, they are in back, too, and they are just as unsightly as the ones you can see. Follow five minutes of massage to the mid-section with the waist exercises listed in the index.

57 Hips I

This is the hardest of all to do alone. If you can't find a second person to help, place your leg out to the side, or if standing, place it on the edge of the bathtub. This relaxes the side hip roll so that you can grasp it. Tension takes its toll here and the area is often subject to pain. Like the other tension-thickened areas, it must be broken up. Spend about one minute on each side after your bath or shower. The heat has a tendency to loosen the flesh and make it less tender. After the massage do hip exercises.

58 Thighs

This is one of the favorite tension spots—and one of the hardest to control. The whole thigh may be stiff and hard, or there may be isolated

areas. The most painful seems to be inside the thigh just above the knee and on the outside about halfway between hip and knee. Use the same rolling action where you can. Remember that the prime purpose of this massage is the break-up of the stiff tissue so that it will be soft and pliable. (If you have varicose veins ask your doctor if there is any reason why you should not massage the thighs in this manner.) Spend two minutes on each leg and then do knee bends and hip exercises.

A BONUS EXERCISE PROGRAM

THE THREE-WAY STRETCH

Everyone knows that without strength a body is indeed at a disadvantage. A lack of flexibility can be just as damaging and we should keep in mind both that tension often causes inflexibility and that inflexibility can contribute to tension and to pain. Exercises to correct this lack must be done often throughout the day in order to have noticeable or lasting effects. The first exercise follows.

59   Hamstring Stretch

Sit spread legged on the floor and grasp the right leg at the ankle and just under the knee. *Keeping the head up,* the back flat and the legs straight, try to pull the chest down onto the thigh in short bounces. Bounce eight times to the right and then eight to the left. Grasp both ankles with both hands and try to pull the chest toward the floor for eight bounces. *Keep the head up.* Do three sefs.

60   Back Stretch

Sit spread legged on the floor and grasp the right leg at the ankle and just under the knee. Keeping the legs straight, drop the upper body over the leg and try to touch it with the right ear. Bounce eight times right and eight left. Then grasping both ankles with both hands, try to bring the head close to the floor. Do three sets.

61 Gluteal Stretch

Bring the right foot close to the body and bending the left leg, carry the left foot to the back. Clasp hands behind back and try to bring the chest close to the front leg. Do eight bounces and alternate feet. Do three sets. This exercise stretches the outside seat muscles and the low back.

THE THREAD NEEDLES

62 Thread Needle Kneeling

(A) Start on hands and knees, and swing the left hand over head. (B) Bring it down through the space between the weighted right hand and the knees. Try to put your shoulder *and ear* on the floor. Do eight with each arm, then four, then two and alternate for eight. This exercise develops flexibility of the torso, especially the waist, chest, shoulders and neck. It also strengthens the arms.

A

B

63 Thread Needle Standing

Do this exercise exactly as you did the Thread Needle Kneeling except that this time you are on your feet instead of your knees. This is considerably more difficult and must be taken in smaller doses. Start with four and work up to eight on each side before you try the diminishing sequence.

64 Heel Pull

Lie down resting on the left elbow. (A) Bend the right knee and place the right hand *inside* the right leg and under the right heel. (B) Holding the heel, straighten the leg. Repeat this stretch four times and then alternate with the other leg. Do two sets. This stretches the backs of the legs, arms and shoulders.

A

B

65 Back Arch

(A) Lie prone resting on elbows. Bend the knees and tip the head back. Try to bring the head close to the feet. (B) Hold the arched position for a count of three and relax in the prone position for a count of three. Repeat three times. This is excellent for back flexibility.

66 Knee to Nose Supine

(A) Lie supine resting on elbows. Bring the left knee close to the nose. Try to point the toes and keep lower leg parallel with the floor. (B) *Keep the knee as close to the nose as possible,* then straighten the leg. Do eight with each leg. This exercise stretches the backs of the thighs.

67 Prone Leg Crossover

Lie prone with arms slightly bent and out to the sides. Spread legs wide. (A) Lift the right leg out of the hip without bending the knee *or moving the hands from their places on the floor.* (B) When the leg is at its peak lift, bend the knee and try to bring the right foot to touch the left hand. Replace the right leg and alternate with the left. Start with three to each side and work up to six. This exercise builds strength in back and seat muscles and stretches the muscles of the torso and the front of the upper leg.

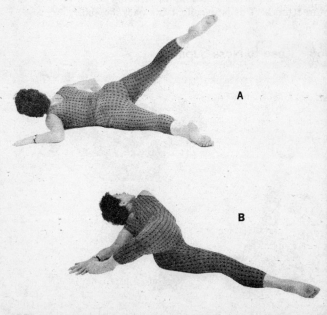

A

B

68   Balanced Leg Stretch

Balance on the seat grasping the ankles in both hands. Press the legs outward to full stretch. Hold for a count of three and resume bent knee position. As you improve, lengthen the time the stretched position is held. Excellent for leg stretch, abdominal strength and balance.

69   The Cat, Table and Old Horse

(A) Start on hands and knees. (B) Drop head, and hump the back like an angry cat. Pull in the abdomen. Hold for a count of five and then allow the body to assume the

A

B

starting position in which the back was level as a table.
Do five. IF THE BACK IS INFLEXIBLE AND STIFF
instead of leveling off after the humping, drop the back
in a sag like the back of a sway-backed old horse (C).
This exercise strengthens the abdomen and at the same
time stretches the back muscles.

70 The Bicycle

(A) Lie supine resting on elbows. Do a *slow* bicycle action with the legs for eight counts. (B) Roll the lower
body over onto the right hip *but keep both elbows tight to*

A

B

C

the floor. This will work both hips and waistline. Do eight bicycle rotations in this position and alternate with eight to the left. Do three sets. When you have improved considerably try the no-handed bicycle the same way. (C) Eight center, eight right and eight left.

71 Twisted Sit-up
Lie supine with knees apart and bent, feet held down. (A) Place hands behind neck and roll over onto the right shoulder. (B) *Stay in the rotated position* and roll up to a sitting position. Slide the left elbow *outside* the right knee. Maintain the rotated position and roll slowly down

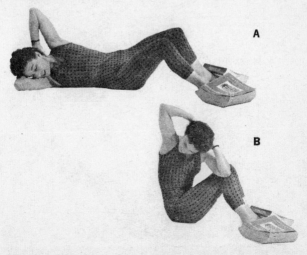

A

B

again. Without stopping the motion, roll over onto the left shoulder and come up with the right elbow leading. Alternate in this manner for four on each side. As you improve, hold weights behind your neck to make the exercise difficult.

72 Leg Extensions—Sitting

(A) Lean back on your hands with fingers pointing forward and knees bent. Extend the right leg and then change with the left eight times. (B) Sit up and extend arms to the side. Do the same leg extensions. After you have improved, extend both arms and legs at the same time and hold for gradually increasing periods of time starting with three seconds (C).

A

B

C

73 Push-ups

Start prone on the floor with hands flat just outside the shoulders. Spread legs wide and curl the toes under. *Keeping the body absolutely rigid,* press up into a straight arm Push-up. From the top of the Push-up, let yourself *slowly down to the floor.* Rest the arms by bringing them to touch each other above the waist. Repeat just as long as you can maintain rigidity. If you cannot do even one Push-up, do a Let-down. Assume top of Push-up position and let yourself down, counting slowly to five.

74 Upper Back Lift

Lie prone, hands resting on the floor. Raise upper back and open arms to stretch chest muscles. Do five. This strengthens the upper back.

75 Upper Back Lift over Bench

(A) Lie over a table or bench with feet held down. Drop the upper body until the head and arms come to rest on the floor. (If the table is high the arms may hang

A

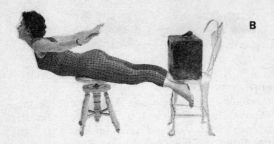

free.) (B) Lift upper torso until the body is at least level. At first carry the arms back and out, but as strength improves, stretch them forward to increase the weight the back muscles must lift. Start with three lifts and work up to ten. Later use weights held in the hands so that overloading will continue, but there will be no added time needed.

76   Bent and Spread Leg Lifts

(A) Lie prone. Bend the right knee and lift the leg from the hip. Replace and stretch leg. Alternate with the left leg, eight on each side. (B) Lie prone with legs spread. Anchor the hands in an outstretched position. Lift first one straight leg and then the other. Eight each side.

77 Side Extensions

Start resting on side, feet a little apart with the right in front. Lean on the extended right arm. Raise the body and lift the left hand overhead. Hold for a slow count of three. Roll over and do the same lift on the left side. Start with two to a side and work up to four.

78 Prone-Supine Twist

(A) Lie prone with the right arm extended and the left supporting action close to the body. Lift the left leg straight as possible. (B) *Keeping* the leg in the air, roll the body back onto the right hip and raise the leg still higher. Roll back to the starting position but keep the leg in the air. Do four on each side.

A

79 Side Drops

Start sitting with legs outspread. (A) Drop first to the right side resting on the right elbow which is placed on the floor *above* the shoulder. This stretches chest, shoulder and under the arm. Swing back to the sitting position, (which calls for strength of the torso muscles). Lean far forward (touch the toes if possible as you swing past) and (B) drop to the other side. That forward lean stretched the back muscles. Do eight Side Drops.

80 Leg Walk-up

(A) Lie supine with arms outstretched and leg raised overhead. (B) Swing up to grasp the leg with either hand and walk up hand over hand to the foot. The swing up

A

B

strengthened the abdominals, the walk up stretched the back and hamstrings. Do four with each leg. As you improve, try to grasp higher and higher on the leg until you can go right up to the ankle without intermediate steps.

81 Roll-out Jackknife

(A) Lie supine with legs spread wide and arms overhead. Stretch as long as possible. (B) Roll up to a sitting position and drop the upper body to the left letting the left ear touch the knee of the outstretched left leg. Roll back and swing up to the right. Alternate in this manner for eight

A

roll outs. The abdominals are strengthened as you roll up and the back and hamstrings stretched on the lean toward the straight leg. The shoulders and arms are stretched on the roll out.

B

82   The Peanut Push

(A) Start on hands and knees with insteps flat on the floor. Sit back until the seat is as close to the feet as possible, the arms outstretched, the chest pressed between spread knees. (B) Keeping the chin close to the floor as though you were about to push a peanut across the floor, press the upper body forward. (C) When you have gone forward until the thighs are lying against the floor,

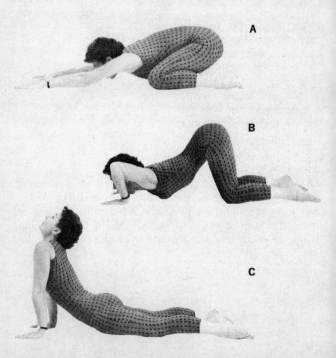

A

B

C

D

straighten your arms and throw the head back. (D) Then
arch the back, letting the head drop down and pulling
the abdominals in. Do six. The first position stretches
instep, arms, chest and shoulder girdle. The forward
thrust strengthens arms, shoulders, chest and upper back
while working for back arch. The extended position
further arches the back and the humped position stretches
the back and strengthens the abdominals.

83 Heel-down Knee Bend

Stand straight with feet together and heels flat on the floor.
(A) Go down into a deep knee bend thrusting the arms
forward to maintain balance. (B) Keeping the head at the
low level, straighten the legs, grasp the backs of the thighs
and lean forward. Prevent falling by holding onto the
thighs. Straighten and repeat six times. The heel-down
knee bend stretches the soleus as it strengthens the thigh
muscles. The effort to maintain the squat position without

A

B

toppling over backward strengthens the muscles at the front of the lower leg (anterior tibialis which is important for people with flat feet). Straightening the legs while keeping the head down stretches the hamstrings and back while strengthening the thighs. Standing erect strengthens the back.

84 Stretch-outs

(A) Start by standing with feet apart. Bend over from the hips and, keeping the knees straight, walk the body out on the hands to the stretched out position. (B) Then, keeping the feet facing straight forward, press the heels back flat on the floor and press the head down between the shoulders in an effort to rest the chin on the chest. Repeat this action six to ten times. The walkout strengthens the arms, shoulders and chest, the press back stretches the hamstrings, soleus, arms, shoulders, chest, neck and upper back.

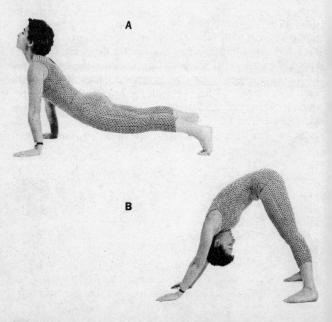

A

B

CHAPTER SIX

Brush the cobwebs out of your habits

If you do it often enough, it becomes a habit. Tension is forever seeking outlets and finds them in nail biting, lip chewing and hair twirling. The habit of daily bathing, imposed by higher-ups in the beginning and willingly undertaken during the mating stage, stays with us not only because it is more comfortable to be clean than dirty but because we can't imagine anything else. Rising with the sun can be a habit and so can breakfast in the afternoon. Hanging up clothes is a habit, as is undressing by gravity. A friend of mine once asked her son, after he had repeated the same minor misdemeanor for the twentieth time, "Dickie, why must you always leave your bicycle there?" His answer was sure, confident and definite, "Because I always."

Get out that little black book again and make a list of the things you *always* do. For example, you may always get up at the same time even on the days you could sleep till noon. Perhaps you always take a shower, perhaps a bath. Do you always have orange juice for breakfast no matter what else is available? And when you dress do you put on your make-up or your clothes first? Some men shave dressed only in a towel. Others wait until they have gotten into pants, shoes and undershirt.

Do you always listen to the news or read the paper at breakfast? Do you have a second cup of coffee? When you go for your train are you the one who catches it with not a second to spare or have you been waiting ten minutes? Do you lean one elbow out the car window?

Where is your left foot when the right is on the gas pedal? When you sit on one foot, which foot is it? Do you carry a suitcase in the left or right hand . . . put your feet on your desk? When you come home, do you kiss your wife on the left or right cheek, the forehead or her mouth? Do you KISS her or aim at her?

Do you stop what you're doing when he comes home, get up and meet him at the door and then *look* at him? I mean really look, checking his face for disappointment, discouragement or exhaustion? It is terribly sad how few people really see each other. Friends of mine have several very beautiful pictures. Any one of them could hang with credit in a museum. They don't hang them all at one time however. One group is always hidden away from sight. Every few weeks they change not only the groups, but the usual place for each masterpiece. They tell me that the unaccustomed is more demanding of attention, for one thing, and also that it is more fun to meet an old friend in an unexpected place. These people have learned to *look*.

One can't change partners every few weeks of course— although there are those who try. So rather than permit partners to become a habit, one has to make a habit of giving full and purposeful attention to the changes in that partner. You know yourself that you are at least ten different people depending on the hour, the place and the company.

American women have lovely hair and by twelve-thirty as they trot off to the luncheon meeting, it will be soft, sleek and shining, but you ought to see it at breakfast! I will never understand what makes a woman feel that she can wear a head full of disfiguring armour in the presence of the man who makes love to her, and often in the bed where that love is being made. Marriage was never meant to guarantee insensitivity either to beauty— or the lack of it.

I am similarly amazed at the man who hurries home, showers, shaves and puts on a clean shirt to have dinner with the Joneses but who shuffles into the bedroom wearing a clear case of eleven-thirty shadow, the day's grime, not to mention sweat (albeit dried) and a pair of pajamas

124

his mother would have used for waxing floors. Write down every habit, good, bad and the ones that don't matter either way. After the good ones put a plus. After the ones you could do very well without, put a minus. Ignore the others. What's the score?

Pay special attention to the habits you have when it comes to making love. Think back to the beginning when there were never two evenings alike. Remember how you started thinking about it at about four in the afternoon and if you happened to see some swinging little figure on your lunch hour, you started planning at noon? How about it now, is it, God forbid, a habit and nothing more? On my honeymoon in Europe, I met a delightful, very vivacious opera singer who told me in her charming accent, "I am divorcing my 'usban because 'e makes love wiz me on Tuesdays." I was somewhat startled. Tuesday seemed as good a day for love as any of the other six. My face betrayed my confusion and my friend broke into uproarious laughter at the stupidity of the young in love. *Only* Tuesdays, darling," she explained, and I got my first glimpse of what can happen when the great moments of life become a habit.

Do you read in bed, or in the bathroom? Do you stop by the icebox on the way upstairs? Do you pick your teeth, or your nose, scratch your head or your ears? How do you sit in a chair and how do you stand? How do you lie when you rest? I have a friend I like to telephone just to hear him answer. It's exactly like opening the door onto a brisk, shining, autumn morning, and it's never any different.

How do you look at people? Usually I like to look at them and if one has a smile hovering around waiting for an excuse to break out, I usually provide the excuse with a smile of my own. One week I was tired, disgruntled and in a hurry as I approached a receptionist's desk. Instead of looking at her and checking for signs of humor, I snapped briskly, "Bonnie Prudden to see Miss Harrick." Her head came up immediately and a smile spread across it that shocked me right out of my ill humor. "Oh hello, Miss Prudden. I've been waiting almost a year to tell you that those neck exercises worked and I haven't had a tension headache since you were last here." She was so enthusiastic that I felt terribly ashamed of my gloomy approach. We must have smiled together a year before and she must have felt she could ask me about the exercises and why would she have remembered me out of all the thousands she has to see in a year? I'm back on the look-pleasant routine again.

You will be changing some very fundamental things about yourself so you can expect some surface changes too. However, don't try to do it all at once or you'll look as though you are suffering from amnesia. Just take a few at a time—the most important—and keep after those few. After a while they will become part of you and you won't have to think about them. And if there were some you had to put a watch on, you'll be able to forget about it, because they'll be gone.

To see what your habits do—or do not do—for your body, check yourself out on Chart 13.

It Always Pays to Get Out of Bed

The habit of getting up in the morning is already established. Here's where you make it pay off. After the alarm clock has been shut off and before you open your eyes, roll over flat on your back and start this series of six morning warm-ups.

85 Morning Warm-ups

1. Stretch your whole body long. Reach with arms over head, stretch your legs and even point your toes (unless that makes your feet cramp). Grow longer and longer until you are at full stretch, then count ten slowly while you hold it. Relax and repeat the supine stretch once more.
2. Spread your legs wide and anchor one foot in each corner at the bottom of the bed. Twist your upper body to the right and reach the left hand across your chest to touch the right side of the bed. Repeat with the other hand to the other side of the bed. Do this four times.

3. Lie back flat and then reach toward the foot of the bed with both hands. Roll *slowly* up to a sitting position, roll down and then up once more.
4. Push both legs over the side of the bed with knees apart as though you were about to get up. Place your hands on your knees and lean forward until your head hangs down between them. Then bounce downward gently six times.
5. Stand up by pressing hands on your knees. Keep the pelvis tilted under and halfway up, hold the tilted position, tightening every muscle you can find for a slow count of five.
6. Stand straight and press both arms back hard—then drop them to your sides. Do three slow circles with your shoulders, pressing them up, back, down and forward for each circle.

Chart 13.   IT'S ALL IN A DAY

Take stock of your life for a week, and then total the hours you spend in rest, inactivity and doing something that will build a good body. Enter the number of hours spent in each category and if you find your inactive hours are far in excess of the active hours, embark on a specific activity project.

	SUN.	MON.	TUES.	WED.	THURS.	FRI.	SAT.
SLEEPING							
At night							
Day naps							
SITTING							
Meals							
Travel							
Work							
Telephone							
Passive entertainment							

STANDING							
Work							
Travel							
MOVING							
Walking							
Work							
Recreation							
Exercise							

THIS WEEK'S TOTAL SLEEPING TIME _____

THIS WEEK'S PASSIVE HOURS _____

THIS WEEK'S ACTIVE HOURS _____

A stall shower is a fine piece of apparatus. The potential round back (and that's everybody) should place a hand on either side of the doorway at shoulder level, stand back two or three feet depending on your height, and let the upper body drop through the door to stretch the pectorals or chest muscles. Press further for two sharp bounces, then stand back and drop your arms downward and shake them loose. Repeat the same thing once more.

Hot water is a good muscle warmer. As it plays on your lower back, lean over with legs spread and knees straight. Bounce the upper body downward five times. If you have fat spots, the shower is a good time to knead them gently—and not so gently—especially the areas referred to before as "Hips 1." Take hold of the fixtures (Caution: Don't turn them or you may find you are more athletic than you think as you try to escape live steam). Do five knee bends, either half or full, depending on your condition. Finally, don't forget that ten-second cold shower which will keep your thermostat in good order.

The procedure of drying the toes should be used exactly as the ballet dancer uses a barre. Instead of sitting down and leaning over to dry them, put one foot up on the toilet seat and rest it on the heel. Dry the toes carefully and change feet. After a few weeks promote yourself to the basin for toe drying. At first you may have to lift your leg by hand to get your foot up onto the basin edge. I do, too, after I've had a strenuous workout following a period of inactivity. After a while, it will swing up very nicely. As you may have guessed, toe drying is of secondary importance. What we are really after is crotch stretch. Clothing that inhibits movement as well as our way of life offers few opportunities for this activity. Result—inflexibility just where you can't afford it.

86 The Towel Exercise

After your shower, towels are useful for resistance exercise. Your skin needs a brisk going over, not only to get rid of grime but to vanquish the scaly bits of skin that have not been worn off. Don't swipe the water away or, worse yet, mop it away. Rub vigorously. When you dry your back, pull one end of the towel against the other, *hard*. (A, B and C) This will be very good for the upper arms as you saw back and forth. Then, hold both ends of the towel firmly, letting the center droop toward the floor. (D)

A   B

C

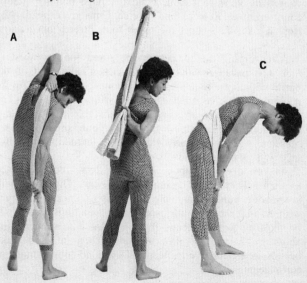

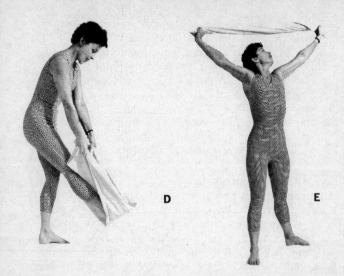

D   E

Step one foot into the towel, pressing it to the floor. Pull
as hard as you can with both hands but keep the resistance
caused by your foot firm. Hold the hard pull for a slow
count of five. Release and stretch arms over head. (E)
Repeat the pull against the other foot. Stretch once more.

After drying the toes, turn the stand foot outward so
that it is parallel with the basin edge. Take hold of the
basin with both hands and pull your pelvic area toward
it. Do about five such stretches with each side. (The
further away from the basin you are able to place your
stand foot, the greater will be the pull on the crotch
muscles. Age should not deter you—I learned this from a
seventy-six-year-old lady.)

As you dry fatty spots with your towel don't be nice
to them. They aren't being nice to you. The towel will
keep your hands from slipping as you knead the spots
with considerable enthusiasm. When you finish they will
be glowing, which means that the blood is busy moving
about in there. The hitherto undisturbed fat globs, like
beetles under an overturned rock, are no longer quite so
complacent.

When you brush your teeth, incorporate two other actions. Tighten both abdominal and seat muscles and rise to the very top of your toes.

If you don't have to wear socks or stockings till later in the day, then by all means don't do it. When you finish your shower you should put a little oil on your skin—all over—not just the face. Then if you are out of doors for a minute, you can let the sun at your uncovered legs. Even a few minutes here and there will help you to get some of that coveted Vitamin D. Also, tan legs are better looking than pale white ones. When you do have to put on socks or stockings, stand on one foot and bring the other up toward your hands holding the garment. Perhaps you will have to lean against a wall for balance at first, and your back may be in such poor condition that you cannot lift one foot at a time. When mine was bad, that's how I judged my progress. The better I became, the easier to lift that foot up. On days when I had lost ground, I was as helpless as though both feet were stuck in cement. If you are in this category check the limbering exercises on page 228.

Break-fast

Going downstairs to breakfast—or in fact any time you go down a flight of stairs—start at the top by tightening your abdominals. Lifting your chest up, get the shoulders back and DOWN. Lift your head up—you know where those stairs are. If you are worried, hold on to the banister. Now go down slowly so that you feel every muscle in your legs working.

Breakfast can be delightful or pure misery. Remember —if you can't eat in peace with the people who inhabit your house, get out and eat somewhere else. If you must prepare food for people who disturb you, find some excuse to eat your solid food later. A cup of hot tea taken for appearance's sake won't hurt.

When I was a little girl my mother was ill. She was never at our breakfast table. When we had maids, which was off and on, I guess I ate breakfast. Left to my own devices, which was most of the time, I grabbed what was handy and ran. Too many people do exactly that all their lives because it became a habit long ago. In our complacent world, breakfast is pronounced "brkfst"—and means as much. Say the word slowly in its proper form: break-fast. That's what it means. You break the fast of the long night. Also the family is gathered together (or should be) before it sets out to face the world. A friend of mine who survived the Warsaw Ghetto told me that he never leaves his breakfast table without a long wonderful look at each member of his second family. He straightens David's tie (his first son died in a gas chamber). He just likes to look at Marianne (his little twin girls were carried off one night by soldiers in a truck and were never heard of again). His second wife is American and knows nothing of these things—other than that they happened. What she does know is that she married the gentlest, most considerate man in the world. She told me he just looks at them all a hundred times a day with what might be called the true understanding of our mortality—and gratitude for every hour that can be shared with those he loves.

If you haven't bothered to look much at each other lately, breakfast is the best of all possible times. Men always look and smell wonderful after sleep, shower and shave. Women who are crisp and efficient give both men and children the feeling as they leave that the house and all they hold dear will be there when they return. Dressing gowns are pretty dangerous attire. They are meant for evening and bedrooms, and they have a way of reminding older men of a Marie Dressler character in the last act—and younger men that the chipper little miss he married is "getting on." You are better off any morning in a shirt and shorts or slacks if the figure will stand it. If not, a cute house dress emphasizes the fact that you are ready for the day and not just around between naps.

Check with the section on diet so you will know what constitutes a good breakfast. "Coffee and Danish" do not. Children will eat what they are trained to eat, and try to remember that the day of the Junior King is fast disappearing. The small fry are not to be feared and obeyed any longer. It's the other way around—they should be afraid of *your* displeasure and they should obey *you*. They should be at the table on time, eat what you eat and listen to what you are talking about (so it better be worth listening to). They should be a pleasure to have around and they should not be tolerated at the table until they are. You can't change them with words, but you can with example. Start by looking at each other and at them. Johnny isn't just a clumsy kid who always knocks over the milk. He's your son and today he may save some kid from being hit by a car—or he may be hit by that car himself. Jennifer has to face the principal because she cut school yesterday and got caught at it. She's nervous, that's why she's poking her egg. You're sorry she has an unpleasant moment or two in store, but you'll be home to hear about it when she gets home. Dad has a red-hot deal going and it will benefit the whole family if he swings it. How many fathers take the time to explain either the deal or what it will mean to the family?

You are leaving the house. It will take a short time to walk a mile at 120 steps to the minute. A mile may be too much for a starter. Try a half mile—or even a quarter. School kids walking a half mile there and back over nine months would take off (or prevent the accumulation of) six ugly pounds of fat and the whole trip would amount to a few minutes a day—just long enough to memorize five of the six verbs they need for tomorrow. Men who go to work forty-eight weeks out of the year would do the same with eight pounds. Naturally you can't build your house exactly one mile from school and station, but you can pick up the bus a half mile along the way and you can park the car a half mile this side of your destination. If your wife drives you to the train you can even set a good example and set her thinking about you seriously by having her drop you the half mile away.

A Mop Is a Mop—And That's All
Housework will not keep you fit or beautiful. If you think it will, go and take a walk in an area that is full of housewives. Your observations will put to flight any such ideas as, "I get enough exercise as it is." My best thought on housework is, do it well, do it quickly and get on to some-

thing else as fast as you can. Housework is a job and, as a job, it has to be done, but it is not without occupational hazards. These hazards are both physical and mental. A muscle must be worked to stay in tone and ready for action, and so must a mind. Housework is repetitious and works only a few muscles. Today many women are married to men who do jobs that have the same hazards so they can count on parallel deterioration. Their bodies will become thick and unattractive even as their wives and they, too, will be capable of spending all their leisure hours at spectator entertainment. Not so with everybody, however. These are days when good help is hard to find, housework is not quite the drudgery it used to be and many are the wives of thinking men who are doing their own. If they don't exercise their minds, they won't be able to keep up with husbands who must fight a battle of wits five days a week and over thirty-six holes on Saturday. Haven't you seen them at club affairs all sitting around together? Everybody talking, nobody saying anything. When you meet the man in town on business and he expresses himself clearly, has a wonderful sense of humor, some very sound political ideas and floors you with a discussion of philosophy, you get a disturbing picture. Any muscle exercised properly will grow and so will a mind, but if you are forever washing, scrubbing and polishing, you will find few intelligent conversations that interest you or to which you can contribute anything at all. You'll have what your mother told you was a very good excuse— "your home." Not to mention "the children"—WHO DO NOT NEED YOU AND SHOULD NOT HAVE YOU MORE THAN A FEW HOURS A DAY. But you won't have your husband. There are ways of making the housework routine pay off physically, but just don't count on it for everything.

Making beds is always a bore and if it makes your back ache, check the exercises on page 228. However, if you take huge stretches and reaches instead of comfortable short ones, you can do your muscles a lot of good. I used to hate the mattress turning bit, but good as it may be for the mattress, it's a lot better for you. Every heavy thing you have to lift all your life is good for you just so long as you are strong enough to do it. Since you don't always have a choice as to whether you will or will not lift—you'd better stay strong enough.

When objects slide under chairs, don't take the easy way and lift the chair out of the way. Go under after it. Sounds active and unnecessary, I know, but consider the actions of children. They use the floor as chair, bed and playground. Old folks stay as far from it as their height will allow. The more contact you have with the floor and the more practice in stooping and crawling, the younger your body will stay.

When you dust, reach again. Plant your feet at one end of the piano and reach all the way to the other end if you can. The short steps will get the job done easier, but they arc the badge of age. Only the young body stretches *and it stretches just as long as it is forced daily to stretch*.

When you mop and lean down to slide it under furniture, keep your back and knees straight and your feet apart as in Exercise 87. If you have to lift furniture, remember that it is a form of weight lifting and weight lifting is being used by every good coach in the country to get his teams into shape. Speaking of lifting things, I feel something should be said about children lifting things. If their hearts are healthy, *they cannot be injured by heavy activity* Once upon a time, a man had sons to help him and a woman had her girls. Wealth could be reckoned by how many pairs of hands would be available. Whatever else those young people felt, there was no confusion as to their right to eat the fruits of the family's labor since theirs had been a part of it. Once I saw a woman with her two children at a grocery store. She was a nice-looking person and her children were clean and well mannered. The boy, about thirteen, taller than his mother already and with the mid-section of a man of fifty, was choosing the kind of cookies he preferred. His mother hefted both the grocery bags, took the heaviest herself, and the little girl staggered out with the other. The overfed parasite at the cookie counter never even noticed. He finally joined them clutching his dozen molasses cookies. God help the girl who marries that boy, but who should really take the blame? The nice-looking lady who is stealing his manhood bit by bit as she has stolen away his right to eat at the family table. Children's characters, as well as their muscles, grow when they are allowed to lift and carry burdens —whether those burdens be physical or emotional. Only one perequisite: they should be strong enough. So prepare them from the beginning.

87 The Magic Mop

A. Whenever you have to mop under furniture, bend from the hips and keep the knees straight. This increases the flexibility of back and hamstrings.

B. After you have finished mopping a room, grasp the handle in both hands and step through the space between your hands—first with one foot and then the other. Then step back again. This keeps the back limber and strong.

C. After you have shaken out the mop, hold it in front of you with both hands. Raise the mop overhead with stiff arms and press back, trying to bring it down to touch your hips. Start with hands wide apart, but work them closer together as you improve. A great posture aid, this mop-exercise stretches chest and arms.

D. Place the mop back of your upper back and then twist as far as possible to the left. Keeping the feet wide apart and the legs stiff, twist all the way to the right. Start with twenty twists and work up to fifty. (It will slim your waist and midriff.)

E. Start sitting on the floor with the mop handle held in both hands, which are six inches apart. Bend the left knee and place your foot on the handle. Press the foot out until the leg is straight. Return to bent knee position and repeat four times with each leg. This stretches arms, back, shoulders and hamstrings. To increase difficulty, merely hold the hands a little further apart.

F. Lie on your back holding the mop over head with one hand, bend your knees and place both feet wide apart on the mop handle. Stretch both legs straight and return to bent knee position. Do four and then change hands. To increase difficulty, draw the feet closer together. This stretches arms, shoulders, back and hamstrings.

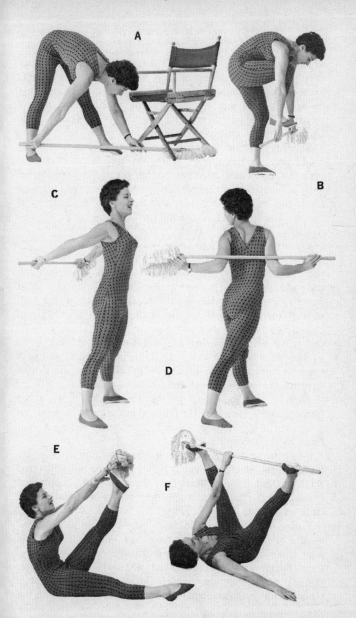

Remember, as you try to scrub the soccer field out of the children's wool socks, that you are keeping your arm muscles strong. And don't forget arm massage. When you squeeze the water out of woolens, you use finger muscles, and hands, too, must be used if they are not to become stiff and knotty. As you wring water out of anything, you will find that you always twist the same way, so try to alternate directions.

Should you find yourself standing at a sink or ironing board, rise to the top of your toes and lower slowly as you lay out each garment to be pressed. Also, dishes can be rinsed on tip-toe. The more often you change level, the less tired the feet will be—and the exercise of changing will strengthen them further.

Stairs Are an Apparatus

You hate the cellar stairs? So did I until I learned what they could do for me. Stairs are not an inconvenience, they are an apparatus. Use them. Put whatever you must carry in one hand, then go down sideways using the wall or rail for balance. Face the wall on the left side and step down the first step with the right foot. Then, keeping the pelvis straight, bring the left foot across and down to the step below exactly as though you were doing a tango. Continue down in this manner and on the return trip use the opposite wall going up.

Stop to get clothes out of the washer and if it's a top opener, don't just lift the clothes out—make a habit of lifting them high in the air and carrying them above your head to the folding table.

After these things become habits, you forget you are doing them—so maybe you'd better warn your friends and relatives that these actions have been carefully cultivated for a good purpose. Otherwise they may worry about your state of mental health.

Going back upstairs—in fact going upstairs at any time —can be very useful. Have you ever noticed a poor old soul climbing slowly upward—seat out-thrust, feet flat and wide apart? If you were asked where her trouble was, you'd probably say "her back." Oddly enough, while back strain is showing, inadequate feet are probably causing the awkward compensating position she has assumed. She does not place the ball of her foot on the edge of the stair, but the whole foot—and turned out besides. Try, yourself, to climb a flight in that position and you'll find your seat sticking out, too. If you climb that way be sure to start the foot exercises on page 98 at once. Here are some ways of climbing stairs that are as good as a gym class. In fact they *are* a gym class.

1. Place the entire right foot on stair number one. Then place your weight on the foot and rise until you are standing straight with the leg stiff. Then rise high on the toes. There should be a one-two-three rhythm which could be spoken as "step-straighten-rise." Go on to the next step with the left foot. A slow waltz record can be used to good effect. As long as you are doing it to music, you might as well come back down. Don't turn around, simply reverse the dance step. Step down onto the toes of the right foot for the count of one. Drop down to the heel for the count of two. On the three count, thrust the left leg out back in preparation for the next step down. On the count of one, bend the knee. If you keep the foot facing straight as you bend the knee, you will feel a good stretch in the heel tendons. Keep each movement clean and don't let them run together.

2. Try going upstairs as babies do, one foot leading the whole way. Easy, you say? Do it fast and feel those quadriceps burn. Remember you have two legs, always alternate an exercise.

3. Many people run upstairs two at a time. It's good for you and should be done whenever you can. Now go up two at a time *slowly*. You'll be surprised. It's much harder. Try coming down backwards the same way. If I could, I'd make every other stair in homes out of bounds. In schools only every third step should be used by anyone over seven. We would probably cut our muscle-failure rate in half the first year.

4. If you can jump both feet up the first stair, do so. Then go on about your business. The following week jump the first stair and add on the second. Keep adding week by

week until you can bounce right to the top. In two months you'll be so agile the neighbors will wonder what elixir you are taking.

5. Spraddle climbing is good too. Notice how almost all locomotion is done straight forward or back. Hip joints need angle workouts as well. Step the left foot into the left corner of the first stair and the right into the right corner of the next. The stairs in my friend's house are seven feet wide. I trust she will know where to use sense rather than my directions. Continue this spraddle climb to the top and come down backwards the same way. If you wish to take the time (and you ought to), complicate things by *backing up* and coming down frontward. NEVER JUST GO UPSTAIRS.

6. The cross-over comes when you are pretty advanced in the art of stair climbing. Place the right foot in the left corner of stair number one. Then the left foot in the right corner of stair number two. This, too, can be complicated by backing up and coming down frontward. Needless to say, you hang onto the banisters for dear life.

7. One-legged hops are for experts. Hop up one stair on one foot. Change feet and hop up the next. After a week, try hopping the first and second stair on the same foot and the third and fourth on the other. Add a stair at a time as you find you can. Sooner or later you'll make the whole flight on one foot. Two to one, the kids won't be able to match you.

A word about banisters. If there's one around and you can get away with it, slide down occasionally. You always wanted to, anyway. It won't do much for your muscles, but the seventy-year-old lady who told me to include it says it does a lot to keep your perspective out of moth balls.

No matter how you take the stairs, you do your heart, lungs and legs a good turn. Think of them not as isolated trips you wish you didn't have to make but as a program specifically designed to make you better looking, more efficient and feeling younger. Let's see what my office stairs do for me. The office is on the fifth floor and there are sixty-eight steps which I take at the rate of two steps a second, counting the usual one-chim-pan-zee, two-chim-pan-zees fashion. So it takes thirty-four seconds to arrive. (You can stand in the lower hall as many as four minutes, waiting for an elevator.) One burns up about 7.3 calories going up and about 5.2 going down for a full minute. Let's say I average three trips a day, five days a week, forty-eight weeks a year. That would add up to about eight hundred and sixteen minutes just walking up and down stairs. I counted the minutes I waited for elevators one week and it averaged out to two minutes a trip or twelve minutes a day. My eight hundred sixteen minutes of walking stairs at the rate of 12.5 calories a minute permit me thirty-four chocolate bars or seventy-nine extra extra-dry martinis—without a pang of conscience. Incidentally, I saved myself forty-eight hours that I would have spent standing still, waiting for and riding in elevators. Since waiting irritates me, especially when I'm in a hurry— which is all the time—and since crowds in close quarters are great bug spreaders, I probably prevented thirty-four hours' worth of accumulated tension and possibly a cold in the head.

Traveling Timetable

Standing on trains or buses can be put to excellent use. It's just the chance you've been waiting for. Spread your feet for balance and tighten seat, abdominal and leg muscles all the way down. You will soon find that the swaying can be handled beautifully. You'll find too, that your balance improves and with it your competence and willingness to try things you never dreamed of trying before.

Driving a car has its moments for exercise, too, quite apart from the unwelcome activity of changing a tire. Every time you come to a red light, let that light be your signal for tightening your seat muscles (pinching the buttocks together) and contracting the lower abdominals. Hold the contraction for the full length of the light, but don't forget to breathe. If you have a long trip before you, make a point of doing shoulder shrugs (index) every thirty miles. If you feel yourself getting drowsy, particularly at night or on turnpikes, stop the car and get out. Do the flexibility exercises (see index) with special attention to letting your head bounce way down so that a goodly supply of blood will rush to your head.

Whenever a car passes you, make that an occasion to tighten your hands on the wheel. Weak hands get tired, and before a month has passed, yours will be strong enough to tear a telephone book in half should the occasion arise.

When you wash and polish your car, use as many long stretches and reaches as you can. One of the very best car exercises involves character—leave it parked where it is and walk.

The habits that can be developed by travelers are many and highly necessary. The stay-at-home isn't plagued by timetables, lost baggage, business appointments he can't make or by the ruinous necessity to sit for hours and hours.

Most stations have endless flights of stairs. If you get there early, take a few. There is no law that says you have to use escalators forever. Most airports now have strong double rail fences behind which boarding passengers must wait. Men who are always dressed for action can put one foot up on the bottom rail, turn the other foot outward and using both hands on the top rail, pull their bodies close to the fence. It is as good a crotch stretch as the basin toe-drying act. Alternate legs, of course.

Carry your luggage whenever feasible and if you don't have anything to carry, look around. There's always somebody like me who has too much and would be grateful for a helping hand.

Get away from the idea that every delay must be laced with coffee and a Danish or a double Scotch on the rocks. If your plane is late, park your luggage in one of those lockers and take a walk, even if it's just around the parking lot. Then if the coffee urge is still with you, it won't be quite so damaging.

If you have to wait in line or in a telephone booth, utilize the wait. Tighten seat and abdominals and tilt the pelvis under (see index). Hold the contraction for ten seconds and then relax for ten. Never just stand.

There are several types of sleepers. There is the one who goes to bed and gets up by habit. Let the first ray of sunlight enter a room, and my father was up. This type may not go to bed—but he sits and nods all evening long. He is the Rhythmical Sleeper.

Then there are those who sleep eight hours no matter when they start. They are the Timers. There are those who sleep whenever they are not active. Let them put their hands down, and they're asleep.

One type of sleeper annoys everyone else: he goes into bed at five and is out again at seven looking fresh as the proverbial daisy. Then there are those who announce at breakfast that they didn't sleep a wink. They actually did —they just had waking moments. Whenever I've had a TV show to do early in the morning, I used to worry. When I worry I can't sleep. So with a mounting feeling of terror because I knew I wasn't getting the rest I needed, I would toss, turn and roll. It was a long time before I finally realized it didn't matter whether I slept, as long as I was resting.

There are emotional sleepers, who use sleep as an escape from difficulties. I knew one man under the care of a psychiatrist and all he had to do was to see the doctor come into his room, and he would drift off into slumber, not to be awakened until the doctor left.

When my children were small and I found myself engulfed in that morass of motherhood which is so difficult to reconcile with the racing creative personality, I found that I was exhausted by lunchtime and took a nap with Suzy. I needed another by dinnertime and couldn't wait to crawl upstairs by nine-thirty. Today with many jobs, I find I can get along quite well on about six hours. And I don't believe the people who tell me that they only need three. I don't believe, either, those who claim they need nine or ten. It has always been my experience that when I was fortunate or unfortunate enough to be in possession of ten undisturbed consecutive hours, I woke groggy and confused as to just where the shower was that morning. And there are better things to do with those extra four hours.

Another thing about sleeping late, you become one of those people who have never seen a sunrise, know nothing of the glistening of dew on the front lawn, the frost feathers on country roads and the marvelous warmth of early sun as it soaks into bones chilled by night. There is something about the morning of the day that is quite different from anything that comes later on. It is like the morning of life, and it would be a pity to miss it.

No, you won't die if you don't sleep. But it can certainly be an unpleasant sensation when one lies listening to the creaks of the house and the happy, gentle snores of the rest of the world. There is no point when you are keyed up and tense, and your mind is racing in twenty directions, in lying down, putting out the light and saying, "Now I'll go to sleep." The human organism doesn't work this way. The more exciting the evening, the longer it will take your motor to calm down. The man who takes a briefcase full of office work home each night is not going to fall asleep five minutes after he hits the pillow. The doctor whose patient has symptoms he can't yet identify is not going to toss off these cares lightly. Even when we do fall asleep, the mind, over which we have so little control, will do as it pleases, and sleep may be both interrupted and troubled.

You can do something about this. The mind lives in your body, as you know. And a tired, relaxed body will rest. Tired you may be, but are you relaxed? I think the silliest phrase on the face of the earth comes from the dentist who, with lethal weapons in his hands and a gentle smile on his face, says "Relax." Or the doctor who says "Don't worry." Your hand will obey your mind when you say "Pick up that apple." But just try telling yourself to go to sleep.

There is, however, more than one way to skin a cat. You can begin by tiring the body physically, and then the reverse seems to occur. The weary, relaxed body has every right to turn on the mind and say, "Shut up and go to sleep." Oddly enough, it often does.

People who have dogs are really more fortunate than they know. Since Jasper must be walked in the evening, and master or mistress must go along, they are unwittingly doing exactly the right thing for a tired, tense body. The fresh air is good, of course. The muscular exertion is excellent. And one more thing—the night outside is quite different from night indoors. Bright lights, the blaring radio or TV, the excited chatter of other people, the unfinished list of things to be done, the stuffy air—are quite different from the cool softness or even the bitter, biting wind of the world outside of walls. Night was meant for rest, and somewhere in our deep unconscious we know it. But where do we come in contact with night as it is, rather than the way our civilization has made it? Like jumping into a cold pool, you feel stimulated and relaxed, and when you return, it is even possible that the rhythm indoors may have slowed down.

People who are in love are also more fortunate than they know. The mere exertion involved in making love will bring on relaxation and rest.

There are other, less dramatic, preparations for a good night's sleep. A good book, a movie on TV, a crossword puzzle—certainly nothing that would stimulate creative thought on your own. Because once you mount *that* horse, you will be off to the races and sleep will be a phantom to be pursued but not captured.

What you really have to do is slow down. What method you use will be your own. What I do suggest is that for ten minutes before you crawl into bed you use the following exercise for relaxation.

HOW TO RELAX THROUGH EXERCISE

88 Tailor Rest

Sit crosslegged and allow the upper body to droop forward. Relax each segment of your body consciously starting with your head and working down neck, shoulders, arms, wrists, hands, back, legs and feet. Sit this way for about thirty seconds (that's longer than you think).

89 Supine Rest

Lie back with arms outstretched. If your back is very tired or stiff, bend one knee. Go through the same conscious relaxation of each part of your body. Take thirty or forty seconds for the run down.

90 Side Rest

Roll over onto your side and again go through the complete relaxation run down.

91 Prone Rest

Roll over onto your stomach and draw up one leg. This is a wonderful back rester. Go through the relaxation run down in this position.

A single record of a popular piece of music runs about two and one-half to three minutes—so put on some slow, relaxing music and let the music slow you. Those three minutes could not be put to better use.

CHAPTER SEVEN

Sexercise

This chapter is not for puritans. If you think that sex is a naughty word, and that any frank discussion of it is shocking, I can only advise you to skip to the next chapter right now.

My own feelings are quite the opposite. What shocks me is that it is necessary for me to be a pioneer in writing this chapter. As far as I know, this section of the book sets forth in print for the first time the simple, fundamental exercises every normal man and woman should practice in order to enjoy a full, happy and vital sex life. I will never be able to understand why there have not been scores of books published on this subject long ago.

I realize that there are numerous volumes in print on the art of love, many of them excellent within their limitations. But I am talking about something quite different. Handing one of these books to a newly-married couple is like taking a neophyte to the top of a steep ski slope, equipping him with boots, ski poles, skis and the rest, giving him some hasty instructions and then shoving him down the hill.

Nobody objects to the exercises taught a beginning skier in order to strengthen his muscles, improve his flexibility and equip him for the sport with some reasonable chance of success. Nobody objects to his continuing to utilize those exercises in order to keep in shape and improve his skiing technique. But apply the same simple, practical logic to something infinitely more important than skiing, and the air is rent with shrieks of protest. This merely demonstrates the extent to which we are willing to impair our happiness and take the bloom off the rose of life in the name of prudery and on the basis of a completely artificial code of morals.

Please do not misunderstand me. In making an analogy between athletic skill and sexual skill I don't mean to imply that sex is just another form of athletic contest. On the contrary, sex should be, can be, and must be, the physical expression of genuine love, and when it is anything less than that—well, you know the name for it as well as I. Wise men see love as a three-sided unit, with its mental, its spiritual, and its physical sides. In making whatever contribution I can to the third aspect of love, I do not mean to underrate the other two. I am merely concentrating on the phase that I feel has been most neglected and which fits into the concept of this book.

Despite Kinsey and sex education in the schools, people are still pretty confused about sex. Several generations of puritan thought, far from curbing our natural sexual appetites as was intended, have merely led to needless guilt complexes, indigestion and heartburn. In too many cases, this puritanism prevents us from ever enjoying one of the more universal of life's prerogatives and pleasures—lovemaking.

The postures of making love may seem bizarre to some, but if we had been meant to procreate by spitting over our left shoulder in the dark of the moon or by gazing soulfully into our partner's eyes, then that's what we'd be doing. We're lucky it's no more bizarre than it is.

Procreation is, of course, in the view of many, the basic reason for practicing the art of love. But we are fortunate that nature, in order to insure the future of the race, has made procreation so pleasant and has equipped us with a built-in sexual drive. This drive begins in our teens and can and should continue until the day we die, whether we're interested in bearing offspring or not.

In our multitudinous discussions about sex, for sex and even against sex, we have covered just about every aspect except one of the most important: to enjoy sex fully and to bring the most to our partners, we need good-looking, strong, flexible and well-trained bodies. It is a pity that now, when the work of psychiatrists is about to bear fruit, freeing people of inhibitions about sex and permitting them to enjoy this perfectly natural function, our soft civilization is producing more and more individuals who are becoming physically incapable of the sex act in any real sense of the phrase. And this is *not* because they have reached a certain age.

Most persons are unaware of the part that their body (and its ability to function) plays in enjoying sex, although it seems this would be obvious to all of us. I am reminded of the innumerable men I meet who tell me they wouldn't exercise for anything in this world. "Too dangerous," they say smugly, and quote that old saw about acting as pallbearers at their athletic friends' funerals. Most of these men are simply looking for a good excuse not to exercise, and I try to enlighten them as tactfully as I can, for I know that men who do almost nothing that requires physical effort usually do not do very well in the bedroom, no matter how good a game they talk.

Needless to say, the woman can just as easily be the one at fault. And only too often, *both* partners leave much to be desired.

In fact, one title I thought of using for this chapter was "First Aid for Ailing Marriages." Perhaps that isn't the most literary chapter heading in the world but it does describe the purpose and the potential of these "sexercises."

A famous divorce lawyer is quoted as saying: "People give me all kinds of reasons for seeking a divorce, but at least seven times out of ten, after I sift out all the 'good' reasons and get to the real reason, the problem turns out to be that well-known three-letter word, 's-e-x.' " Big Mama put it even more succinctly in the Tennessee Williams play, "Cat on a Hot Tin Roof." She points at the bed and says, "When a marriage goes on the rocks, the rocks are *there*, right *there!*"

If the divorce lawyer and Big Mama are right, and if I'm correct in my conviction that these "sexercises" can contribute new meaning, vitality and joy to tired marital relationships, then it is high time indeed that we take off our moral blinders and look at ourselves (and our bodies) as nature made us (and them). But I am interested in something even more important than rendering first aid to ailing marriages. And that is to contribute still greater happiness and significance to an already happy and significant marriage.

In lovemaking, if one has an unattractive body, simply turning out the lights isn't the solution (and besides, you'll miss a lot if you do). Loving gives tactile as well as visual pleasure, and there is hardly anything that robs desire more quickly than a gross or slack body, whether it's yours or your partner's, whether it's seen or felt.

The fact is, one essential to a satisfactory sex life is self-confidence: People who know that they are pleasing to look at are apt to take far more interest in sex than those who view themselves with shame and embarrassment. For that matter, the surest way to "break" a sex partner is to criticize the body before you. It pays excellent dividends to comment favorably on the width of shoulders—even if that's all that's worth commenting on— or the slenderness of hips. Never mind about the boyish bustline. If parts of you don't measure up to expectations —check with the index in the back—and change things.

An attractive body, however, is only one of the requisites for more pleasurable and meaningful lovemaking. Another is your ability to make that body function as it can and should. If you were setting out to be a skier, as I mentioned before, and if you were thorough, you would not settle just for skis, poles, boots and stretch pants. You would wonder about the muscles you were going to use and just what system you could employ to ski competently and avoid breaking your neck. The same goes for making love. The difference is that if the untrained skier breaks a leg, in time it will heal. The person unfit for love sometimes breaks a heart—and it is not always his own.

Almost all muscles, especially those concerned with keeping the body erect, have many uses. The muscles one needs for sex are also essential for many sports. If you set out to develop your sex muscles with exercise, you can for the most part keep them in shape with daily sports. If, however, you don't care for sports but do like to make love, then for you it's the exercises at the end of this

150

chapter, ten minutes a day every day for the rest of your life. Barring a few special exercises, the athlete need not run through the entire list except on the days he or she cannot get out and ski, ride, climb, play tennis, box or run.

Skiers need and use the pelvic tilt constantly. Tennis players, boxers, runners and gymnasts cannot perfect their form without it. Children, taught the pelvic tilt on a gym floor, can canter a horse bareback with only fifteen minutes of instruction.

Golfers use the hip swing, as do football and basketball players. Feminine grace in walking and masculine grace in sports come as a result of proficiency in this technique, along with flexibility.

Anyone with a sway-back or a backache desperately needs the gluteal and abdominal exercise sets. They are also marvelous for the new mother. There is no limit to their uses, but in this chapter we will consider them primarily in their application as exercises for sex.

There is no question but that the best lover is the one with whom we are in love. But how much better it is if this partner has a highly trained body. A Beethoven sonata will always sound better on a concert piano than on a kazoo.

But even the most beautiful, powerful, efficient body is limited as far as sex is concerned unless its owner takes time to enjoy the art of making love. We are a nation of hurriers. Too much of our lovemaking is done after long, grueling work days. Too many of us rush home in crowded trains, pushing and being pushed. We drink cocktails to relax and eat too much dinner, inducing a comatose condition that gives us all the *joie de vivre* of a pair of hibernating turtles. The wife is full of small chatter and the husband is just too tired to respond. One gloomy glance and she knows it's going to be a night like most nights, so she gives up any thought of love.

Lovemaking isn't just getting into bed and getting together. Good lovemaking must have as many facets as a diamond to make it sparkle, and each facet is important to the total effect. You cannot develop a feeling of intimacy with another human if you are busy reading the paper or going your separate ways. Tranquilizers don't enhance love, nor does alcohol. It's a rare man who can drink all evening and then can. It's a rare woman who wants to. A little alcohol is a wondrous thing, but not too soon or too much, because then all you'll be is tired.

Relax. Leave the work at the office. You can't plan a merger with Consolidated and with a woman at the same time. The mood of love is something that other nations appreciate better than we do. Fortunate is the American woman whose husband comes home to *her*. But there are two sides to this. Maybe more men would, if there were someone really waiting for them at home.

What you don't use, you lose. And that includes your desire to make love. Once a month isn't making love. If you've gone off the beam, you can certainly get back on again. But it will take time and patience. And effort. If it's hopeless, and you know it's all over, then don't make the same mistake twice. A woman needs to be loved a lot. A man needs to be loved a lot. It need not be violent, but it must be there. People who love can draw strength and emotional release from each other just by being close, just by sitting still and knowing that the other person is near. But the closeness has to be alive, and it has to be emotional as well as physical.

The "sexercises" that follow can afford you and your partner more enjoyment when you make love. But remember that emotional needs are more important than physical ones. Just knowing how is of no use in itself if you don't put time aside to look at each other and reach out to each other.

92 Gluteal Exercise

This first exercise trains you to pull your back in against your front, a motion basic to lovemaking. If you move in only one direction, it's like living in a two-dimensional

world when everyone else enjoys a three-dimensional world. In the beginning, practice this exercise lying on your stomach on the floor. Later it can be done standing or sitting. Then you can and should practice it anywhere: on trains, waiting for a light to change, in elevators. Often this surreptitious effort in a good cause will prevent board meetings and testimonial dinners from being a total waste of time.

Lie on your stomach, your head resting on bent elbows. Tighten your seat by pinching the buttocks together. Hold for a slow count of five, and then relax. When I say relax, I mean *relax*. To be efficient, a muscle must be capable not only of tension, *but also of giving up tension completely*. After a few practice runs, add the abdominal muscles. First tighten the buttocks, and then pull in the abdominal muscles. As you pull in one against the other, your pelvis will tuck under, as it does in the act of making love. Start with three and work up to a minimum of ten repetitions. Try to find time for two sets daily.

After the gluteal and abdominal sets have become routine (and these two exercises should be considered one, since they should always be done simultaneously after the initial practice periods), add a second step: the tightening of the inner muscles. This is primarily for women. A levator is a muscle that raises a limb or other part of the body, and the one we are concerned with might be described as lying along the floor of the pelvis. This is a crude way of putting it but the only clear way to indicate its position, and the only way to teach you to make it function at your conscious command, is to say that if you had to go and didn't have a dime, tighten whatever muscles would be involved in preventing leakage.

Other civilizations know more about the refinements of lovemaking than we do. They have learned that to be exciting to her partner, the woman need not at all times move her body visibly. It is the alternate tightening and relaxing of her interior muscles that heightens enjoyment for both partners.

Now hold all three: gluteals, abdominals and levator— and then relax. You will find that it is much easier to tighten than to relax at first, and therefore doing a set of twenty will take some time. As you gradually step up the rhythm, however, it needn't take more than twenty seconds to do twenty. You should try for at least one hundred a day.

93 Pelvic Tilt Supine

The next step toward achieving a good pelvic action is the pelvic tilt supine. The pelvic tilt is the natural forward and backward motion used instinctively in the act of making love. The longer you can maintain it, and the more you can control it, the better the quality of your lovemaking.

Lie on your back, bend your knees, and place your feet about eighteen inches apart. Keeping your seat and shoulders tight to the floor, arch your back slightly. Then force your spine down flat to the floor. While in this position, use the techniques you learned in the foregoing exercises, and tighten the gluteals, abdominals and levator. Hold for a count of three, and then relax. Do ten times.

94 Seat Lift

This is an exercise for people who have backs that behave. If you have one of those so-called "sacroiliacs," wait until the limbering series and general exercises have done away with it. The value of this exercise for the male is to endow him with the back strength he needs for making love in the traditional position. If the female can become

proficient at this exercise, she can reverse positions with her partner, adding variety and sparing his strength for later. She will also benefit from the increased strength of her back and will tire less easily.

In addition to lovers, people with "flat backs" need this exercise. Ex-dancers, divers, horseback riders and gymnasts will find it easy. Practice had better be done behind closed doors, because it does look pretty silly at the start.

We teach this exercise to youngsters by telling them to paint the floor in front of their chests with glue, place chest in the glue and stay stuck. Then raise the seat in the air. Hold for three counts, and then collapse. Alternate with *abdominal and gluteal set* for six repetitions.

95 Hip Swing

Not only is it necessary to tilt a pelvis forward and backward during lovemaking, but ideally also from side to side. Hip swings are useful for this purpose as well as for improving your walk, waistline, hip line, golf stroke or bowling. Even the football or basketball player, whose feet must act before his brain can, needs hip swings. The skier just can't get along without them.

Stand with feet apart and knees stiff. Shift the hips as far to the right as possible. Then swing to the left. Do not twist the body. Keep it flat. Tighten both the abdominals and seat as well as the thigh muscles and knees. Try to hold the shoulders straight and level. This has the effect of making the pelvic area into a tight, compact unit that moves by itself without apparent help from the rest of the body.

96 Pelvic Tilt Sitting

After the hip swings, we return to pelvic tilts, but this time they are more difficult. It should be noted that very little goes on in life without benefit of the pelvis. In addition to increasing the skill and pleasure of lovemaking, every exercise for the pelvis improves posture, guards against backache, reconditions after childbirth and affords a better figure for men as well as for women.

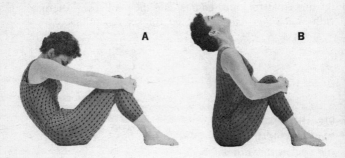

Sit on the floor and clasp your hands in front of your knees. If you have one of those tail bones that aches at a double feature, the floor will be too hard for comfort. Then take a bath towel, fold it in half. Take the two edges and fold them into the middle. Fold the outside edges once more to the middle, and you will have a cushion with a space running down the center. Sit on it so that the tail bone rests in that space. Now, no more of *that* excuse.

(A) Lean back as far as you can without tipping over. Drop your head down and round your back. Tighten the abdominals, gluteals and the levator. Hold for a count of five, and then sit up as straight as you can as in B. Get that back absolutely straight—even arch it, if you can.

As long as you are in this position, you might as well improve the chin line. Tip your head 'way back and look at the ceiling. Count five seconds for the "sit up" position and the same for the "sit back" position. Do five sets. Do eight of these each day.

After a few weeks you should be mighty proficient at "tilting," "tightening" and "relaxing." Now you are about to strengthen your thighs as well. With the next exercise you will find out just how far you have allowed your feet and ankles to deteriorate. And don't let me hear anyone say, "Oh, my ankles were *always* like that." If they were, you started to deteriorate very early, that's all. And it's no excuse. You'll have to repair it by working harder.

97 Pelvic Tilt on Knees

Get down on your knees and sit right down on your heels. Press the ankles flat on the floor. You can't? There are a couple of steel tendons in your ankles that won't let you, and your feet hurt? After you have finished the sexercises, turn to page 228 and do the limbering series for feet. In the meantime, roll up a small towel and put it under your ankles for support.

A   B

(A) When you sit on your heels, push your seat way out, even arch your back. (B) Now, without raising the level of your head more than a couple of inches, bring your seat under and the pelvis forward. Return to the first position and relax for two counts. Repeat this tilt four times for the first few weeks, and then gradually work up to eight.

At this moment, you will want to rest your feet. The pelvis and midsection get no rest. All we do for them is to go in another direction and so use them differently.

98 Stretch-outs

(A) Lie on your right side and draw your knees up to your chest. (B) Then extend the legs and arms and with the same swinging motion, roll over onto the left side. (C) Draw the knees up to the chest. Four to each side will serve both to strengthen and to relax.

A

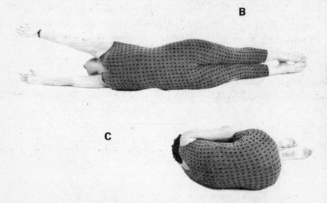

B

C

99 Standing Pelvic Tilt

No, you haven't learned all there is to know about a pelvis. The next step is the standing pelvic tilt.

(A) Stand with feet about eighteen inches apart—a little further if you are tall. Place your hands on bent knees, and thrust your seat out, even arching your back, as in the preceding exercise. You will look like a small boy watching a caterpillar.

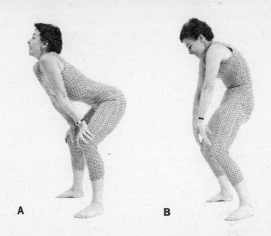

A   **B**

If someone were to walk up behind you and swat your seat with a canoe paddle, and it was against the rules to run, jump, let go of your knees or straighten your legs, what would you do? You would tuck your pelvis under and tighten your unprotected posterior into a hard knot. Do that, and one other thing: use all the knowledge you have acquired and *pull in everything*. (B) Hold for a count of five and repeat five times.

When you are contracting all of those muscles—and work especially on those interior ones—look down at your abdomen. You will find that it is completely flat. If you can't see that for the fat, poke yourself and you will feel the muscles lying there hard and smooth. That ought to be inspiration enough to justify an extra ten minutes of workout a day plus considerable attention to the chapter on diet.

100 Pelvic Tilt Walk

If you can't see why you should be doing this sort of thing while walking around, I can understand your puzzlement. But you'll have to do it anyway. Pelvic action has to be so much a part of you that you no more need to think about it while you are making love than you do about breathing or keeping your heart going. Also, the better you are at any skill, the easier it becomes.

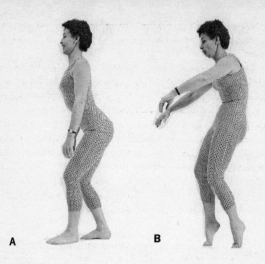

A   B

Start the pelvic walk in the corner of the room. As with all other exercises, it is much better if you use music. Keep your knees together, get your seat out, as you tilt the pelvis backward (A).

People look and feel so silly doing this exercise that, in class, I make everybody work at the same time. This keeps them too busy either to watch others or to worry about themselves. Also—I *never* tell them what they are learning.

Go all the way across the floor to rhythm with your seat so far out back that you could hang a hat on it. Any rhythm is good, but a rhumba is better. When you get to the opposite corner, turn around. For the return trip, tilt the pelvis under (B). (The word picture I think of is the wolf in a Mickey Mouse film as he tiptoes from tree to tree.) Keep the pelvis under all the way across.

Follow these trips with a four-and-four series: pelvis under for four steps and out back for four. You should practice this series for at least a week, doing about two minutes (one popular record's worth) each day. Then try doing two-and-two.

After a week of this, you'll be getting close to the big-time. Get off your toes and down onto the flat foot. Cross the room tilting forward as you step on the right foot, and back as you step on the left.

It looks like some African native dance. You know why? It is. Africans and many other people prepare their bodies for war and lovemaking with dances they do from earliest childhood. It certainly beats TV.

Incidentally, when you have "tilted" across the floor using the right foot for the forward tilt, come back using the left. And while you are paying so much attention to the feet, don't forget the original purpose of the pelvic tilt: tighten with each forward thrust and relax on each backward thrust. One record, or two minutes, ought to be enough.

101   Square Pelvic Tilt

This next step is primarily for women, since what you are learning here is to relax and contract the interior muscles. As we have said, older civilizations have developed refine-

ments in the art of making love. But we can profit by these only if we have bodies trained for the purpose.

This exercise won't hurt men, and will do their insides a lot of good. The more activity, the more chance all the parts of you have to get worked over and repaired.

Start by standing with feet about six inches apart and your knees slightly bent. Tilt the pelvis forward on a count of one. Thrust the hips to the right—really shift out to the side—and put most of the weight on the right foot. Tighten inside for the first count, relax when you shift to the right for the two count. On the count of three, tilt the pelvis back and tighten for all you are worth.

This is new for you. Up to now you have been tightening as you thrust forward. This time it's back, and most of the tightening will have to be done by the levator and anal sphincter, because the abdominals and gluteals are both in a somewhat stretched position.

On the count of four, shift the hips to the left and weight on the left foot. *Relax.* Now do this to a rhythm. Count very slowly so that you *never* become confused as to which way you are going and just what and when you are to tighten. After four sets starting to the right, do four starting to the left. (No use being one-sided.) If you can move every two seconds at first, you'll be doing better than well. Stay with this slow rhythm at least a week, even if you are sure you can do better.

When you have mastered the square tilt, then, and then only, should you go on to the circle. This one is so much easier than the square tilt that, being human, you are apt to say: "Why bother with the hard one, when I'm so good at the easy one, and besides it's more fun."

The circle tilt starts with the feet about a foot apart and the knees slightly bent. Tilt the pelvis forward, then right, back, left and forward in one continuous motion.

If you have practiced well, your interior muscles will tighten and relax at the proper times without any conscious direction from you. And when you make love, they will function automatically. That's why you practiced.

Do eight circles right and eight left for one set. Do eight sets.

102   Circle Tilt Prone

When you are standing, the main burden of supporting the pelvis is borne by the legs. When you lie on your stomach, the job goes to the lower back muscles. Nobody can enjoy making love to the fullest if he or she has to worry about a "trick" back. And the man who "puts his back out" in bed is as badly off as the guy who got a black eye running into a door. Besides, it's painful. If you have any sort of back problem at all, read the exercises for the back in Chapter 7 carefully; avoid the circle tilt prone until you are more than just adequate in the lower back area.

Lie on your stomach. Take the pillow from under your head and place it under your hips. Then perform the exercise exactly as if you were standing, as in the above exercise (the circle tilt).

103   Circle Tilt Supine

This exercise when done on your back is not less strenuous than when performed on your stomach, but there is much less strain on the back when you are lying on it (which is one reason women hardly ever get a backache from making love). Also, in the supine position, both the gluteals and abdominals (which by now you should have thoroughly trained) can take over.

Lie on your back with legs straight and feet about three feet apart. Do the pelvic circle exactly as if you were standing.

FOR WOMEN ONLY

The pelvic tilt has a use for women that is not widely known, and it is a pity that more attention has not been given to what may seem to be a small and unimportant fact. The most sensitive point of stimulation in the woman's genitals is the clitoris, rather than inside the vagina proper. When the man and woman are making love, this point may not be stimulated, and the woman may take overlong to reach orgasm, or worse, enjoy none at all. By learning to tilt the pelvis backward and holding this position, the woman can be assured of far more contact to her point of greatest sensitivity, and a great deal of frustration, not to say unhappiness, can be avoided.

Women who have developed their muscles to a high level will find that, instead of being merely the passive recipient, they can contribute far more to the act of love than they ever dreamed was possible. And they will discover that *the more they make love, the better their figures will be*.

Here is another exercise to help women learn to tense and relax the inner muscles:

Sit astride a straight-backed chair facing backwards, with arms resting on the back of the chair. For this exercise the abdominals won't help you very much, nor will the gluteals.

Tighten the levator inside and the anal sphincter, and hold for three slow counts. Relax completely, and it may take five counts to do it. You will have to *think* those interior muscles relaxed. Do it often enough, and it works. Patience is the key to this one.

As soon as you can, spend only three counts on relaxing and two on tensing. Eventually you will be able to work these ever-strengthening muscles down to one-half second for each action. Incidentally, as a post-natal reconditioner, this is wonderful.

104 Prone Leg Lift

In order to assure the male of that abundance of low back strength he needs for lovemaking, we have to start easy and work up.

Lie on your stomach on the floor and raise first the right leg, and then the left. Be sure to keep the legs straight. Start with eight to each side. Then roll over on your back and rest, with bent knees on your chest, for five seconds. This stretches the back muscles and relieves tension.

Return to the prone position, and repeat the set of leg lifts. Do this three times.

105 Prone Leg Lift Spread

By simply spreading the legs as you lie prone on the floor, you can make the prone leg lift (above) far more difficult. Don't start this one until you feel quite certain that the preceding one is very easy for you. Use the same system of lifts.

106 Weighted Leg Lifts

As you gain in strength, you will have to do more exercises to improve. This takes time, which you probably don't have. The answer to that is resistance exercise, which is described on page 201. Here it applies to leg lifts. Just hang the weight bags suggested earlier over each ankle and proceed as before. *Do not use more than five pounds on each leg* for a start. You can maintain the same number of lifts, and by adding weight gradually over the months, constantly increase your strength. It will also give the male that margin of reserve power which will enable him to make more prolonged and vigorous love.

107 Table Lifts

One further refinement for this important area of the back:

Lie across the length of a piano bench or a kitchen table. Hang the weight bags over the ankles, which we described earlier. Gripping the bench or table for support, straighten the legs until they are level with the body.

In some ways this exercise is easier than the prone leg lift because there is no hyperextension. Since there is none, you may do both legs together.

108 Head to Instep Exercise

Here is an important exercise based on the theory that strength without flexibility is only half the story in lovemaking. The greater and more varied the pelvic movement, for example, the greater the pleasure. Sit on the floor and bring your feet close to your body, facing sole to sole. Grasp the ankles and try to bring the top of the head down to touch the insteps in short, easy bounces. Start with ten and work up to fifty.

109 Crotch Stretch

Place feet sole to sole as in the *Head to Instep* exercise and grasp ankles firmly. Place your elbows on your knees and press the knees down toward the floor as far as possible. Hold that position five seconds and relax. Repeat eight times, always trying to get nearer to the floor.

It would have been very simple for me to have disguised the sexercises as something quite different. Since they are good for everything else anyway, it would have been no trick at all to call them "Good for What Ails You" or "Health through Strength and Flexibility," but I didn't, and for a good reason.

There are too many people who don't think they need "Health," whether it is obtainable through Strength, Flexibility or the eye of a needle. Far too many people think that "what ails them" is just old age creeping on. Sex, however, interests almost everyone.

Let's say once again, *there is nothing the matter with sex*, it is a wonderful part of our lives, something to be enjoyed and cherished. Mind, spirit and body are not separate units. They are all part of one miraculous whole, the human entity. And life is not lived in separate compartments. Anything that improves our ability in one area improves it in all areas. I have tried to do more than write a chapter on happier, healthier lovemaking. I have also attempted to contribute what I can to happier and healthier *living*.

CHAPTER EIGHT

Tension breaks for office workers

Tension is one of the disastrous by-products of modern living which man has unwittingly brought on himself, like fallout. Tension is rarely lethal in its pure form, although sometimes you wish you could die when you are in its grip. It is the by-products of tension that do the damage. Fortunately, with advance warning and knowledge of preventive measures, it can be controlled. Man's or woman's daily work is usually the major culprit—or rather his or her reaction to its sometimes crushing pressures and frustrations.

Once upon a time, men fought each other with fists, teeth and clubs. They fought for the same reasons they do now: for a better cave, an extra wing on the chicken, because he looked at your woman or your woman looked at him, or because he stepped on you. If you had lived then, and found yourself all stirred up and ready for a fight, you would have actually fought. Then, despite a bruise or even a busted rib, you would have felt great. If he'd won, you'd have slunk off, slept, and then gone looking for another cave, woman, chicken, or somebody *you* could step on. You would not, however, have suffered a headache, stomach ache, neck or back pain, or a deep, dark feeling. You would have worked off the whole deal with no emotional damage. (I suppose cave*women* released their tensions by burning the supper meat or beating the kids.)

Today, things are quite different. You still get ready to fight, or leave at a very fast pace if the odds are against you—but do you? You do not. With heart beating strong enough to lead a march on the double, blood pressure rising, muscles tensing, face and hands sweating and the adrenals pouring enough emergency power into your system to take on two wild cats—you swallow the whole thing, smile if it chokes you and walk slowly away.

Well, you say, it's poor economics to sock the boss or throw a phone at the secretary—poor family relations to wallop the wife or knock the kids' heads together.

So it is, and besides, there's another powerful deterrent—thousands of years of civilizing influences which you can't ignore. So what happens? Instead of hitting the other guy, you hit yourself, all your churned-up feelings go to work on your own body and the ultimate result is pain.

It all starts because you tighten various areas in your body whenever you are under pressure. The areas differ with different people, but each person tends toward a self destructive consistency and *constantly tenses the same areas in his own body*. Thus the stomach tightener gets a cramp just below his breast bone. The gluteal and back muscle tightener puts in for low back trouble. The shoulder type ends with a pain in the neck and the arm and thigh tighteners grow enormous in these areas that should be trim and smooth.

During tests to prove man's penchant for hammering away at special portions of his own anatomy, a man who suffered from tension headaches gave an excellent example. Electrodes were fastened to his left forearm and to his forehead. The latter spot was the usual center of his pain. He was then subjected to a very unpleasant interview and the impulses recorded on charts. The chart of the arm muscle tension mapped a gentle curve, slow to start and unimpressive in altitude. Within a few minutes however, the forehead recording was almost off the paper and our man had his headache.

After muscles have been tense over a period of time, the time intervals seem to vary according to the intensity of the tension and the sensitivity of the individual, they knot into spasms. It is then that you get news of what's been going on. It could be a feeling of uneasiness in the stomach area or a tightness in jaw or facial muscles. A typical sign of trouble is a needling pain that starts in the shoulder about two inches from the spine and one or two inches down the back. The technician peering into a microscope, the concert pianist with three hours of practice still to go, the proofreader, the architect, the fifth grade teacher, the harassed housewife—all know this tiny sliver of pain heralds misery that may last hours and often days.

When one muscle goes into spasm, it telegraphs the news to neighboring muscles through pain. Pain not only influences other muscle groups to join the party, but ties the knots harder in the original trouble spot, causing still more pain. Thus, spasm leads to pain and pain to further spasm. A truly vicious cycle. It slowly spreads down the arm, up the neck, behind the ears, up the scalp, over the forehead to pound home a lesson behind both eyes— *Tension.*

Once you feel the pain born of tension, it is too late to do anything about it until the cycle of spasm-pain-spasm is interrupted. This your doctor usually controls with medication. The only real and permanent answer lies in *prevention*—and yes, it can be prevented.

Muscles respond to physical activity by relaxing. If you work them intermittently throughout the day, especially if the day promises to be a rough one—you keep the muscles sufficiently relaxed to prevent the S-P-S cycle from getting under way in the first place.

The best exercises for neck, shoulder and head areas are called "the Shrug Series." Tie this series into habits that will be repeated often enough to assure you of continuing, well-spaced treatment. After each phone call, each new letter into the typewriter, each trip to another part of the office or after each household chore. Other members on the staff or family may think you have St. Vitus dance, but that's a chance you'll have to take. At least you won't have (or be) a pain in the neck.

The executive's office is usually pretty safe from observation, but sometimes the reverse is true. Those who find themselves in full view of their partners and employees will have to take a stand. The new and interesting things they will be doing are for the express purpose of keeping "the brains of the business" alive, vital, virile, attractive and in the office. So here you go on an office "routine" that will set the business world back on its heels and you on the path to a wonderful new life.

110 The Shrug Series

(A) As you sit in your office, at desk, drawing board or work table, draw your shoulders up to cover your ears. Really pull up hard.

(B) The second movement in the series is highly important. Press the shoulders down hard, stretching to make a long neck. Since most people start tension in their shoulders by imperceptibly drawing up, the *down* action gives release.

(C) In the third movement you round the back by pressing arms and shoulders forward and dropping the head. This stretches any upper back muscles that might be contemplating complaints. If you get into the habit of tightening the abdominals whenever you do this exercise—you improve your waist line as well.

(D) The fourth in the series presses both shoulders back as far as possible. Tip the head *slightly* upward and lift the chest. Hold each of the four positions about two seconds and repeat the entire series twice. The trick lies in spaced repetition. Since tension does its painful damage by constant minute repetitions, only repeated, extreme measures will serve to combat it. *Don't wait until discomfort tells you trouble is on the way.*

D

111   The Reach

Another useful exercise for tension is the "Reach." The higher and harder—the better. Reaching overhead pulls you up tall and releases tension throughout the body. This is also good for the figure—any figure.

112   File and Slim

Don't neglect the files. They are both a good reminder and a piece of apparatus. When you file it in the bottom drawer, place your feet apart and lean over from the hips being sure to keep knees straight (A). This stretches

A

B

both back and hamstring muscles, keeping your back young and limber. When you file it in the top drawer, do five deep knee bends on the toes and with knees together (B). This improves both the strength and appearance of your thighs. Then you won't be caught short for either the ski or swim suit season—since you'll be preparing all year.

113 Looking up the Number

When you look up a number don't waste the opportunity. Plant your feet about eighteen inches apart and twist both left and right three times each. There will be office gossip when you first take this one up. However, when you explain that you are slimming your waist and improving your golf score everyone will copy you, including the boss whose golf and waist need improving just as much as yours do.

114 On—Not Under—the Desk

Put your feet up on the desk. Your mother would probably have a fit, but those are not your mother's feet and she's not in nearly the danger you are. When your feet are up, your blood runs back into your body very easily. Cross one leg over the other and every once in a while raise both legs into the air and hold them aloft for a slow count of five. This works the quadriceps in the thighs and the lower abdominals. As the lower leg does most of the work, be sure to alternate.

115 The Chair Lift

The telephone is a convenience in any office, but it isn't a friend. More sweat collects on telephones, more rage and frustration pour through them and more agony is attached to them than to any business gadget in use today. Too often, after replacing the receiver, your impulse is to heave the whole thing at the wall. Far too often as you pick up the receiver, you are aware of weak knees and a curdling

stomach. All new telephones should come with a year's supply of aspirin, Pepto Bismol and hemlock.

Tension results from most business phone calls, so let's put phone calls to work cancelling tension. Every time you hang up the phone, place both feet on the floor and your hands on the arms of your chair. Do a slow push-up while keeping your body in the sitting position. Then lower yourself *slowly* and relax your arms. This will get rid of some of the shoulder tension you just built up. If the call was a five-alarm, do two armchair lifts. After your strength improves, you will be able to lift with legs held straight out at right angles to the body.

Just one chair lift isn't impressive, but let's say you weigh 180 pounds and that you lift that weight one foot off your chair. That would be 180 foot pounds lifted. Multiply 180 by the number of calls you will make or answer in a day—thirty is probably within the realm of possibility. That would add up to 5,400 foot pounds lifted by shoulders and arms plus some work for the abdominals. Not a bad workout. As it will take only five seconds a lift, the cost in exercise time is two and a half minutes. Should the day be a rough one and require two lifts per call, you will pile up 10,800 foot pounds, dissipate considerable tension, work off at least one large dollop of fat and really give your muscles a going-over. Time cost—five minutes.

If your chair is a tipper, place your hands on the chair arms at the farthest point forward. This should stabilize the chair, but check carefully before lifting in order to avoid surprises.

If your chair has no arms at all, you will find that the lift works your back and abdominals more than your arms. Place hands at the forward corners of the chair, keep arms straight and lean the upper body forward. Your seat lift will be made primarily by the contraction of your upper and lower abdominals with the help of the upper back. For a paunch flattener, there are few better exercises to be found anywhere.

116 The Chinning Bar

The Chinning Bar, already recommended for the home, should have its mate in the office. Business is business to be sure, but if the business requires a man to run it, opportunity should be afforded to keep that man in a full state of masculinity. Put the bar in the doorway to your office and if your secretary is a smart woman she will encourage you to use it and keep track of your improvement. If she is wise as well, she'll use it herself, thus guaranteeing a trim bust line and smooth, slender arms.

You will soon discover that others, both in and out of the office, have remnants of the competitive locker-room spirit. I know of one office that gives prizes each Fourth of July to the highest scoring man and woman. As the prizes are not insignificant (a weekend for two at a famous resort)

a lot of extracurricular practice goes on all year. I understand that each member of the office staff has a chinning bar at home (which must influence families as well). The firm's president tells me that absenteeism has dropped noticeably.

Almost anyone can do one chin-up—so as you go through that door, reach up and chin *just once*. (If you can't do even one, check index.) Let's say you leave the office ten times a day. Say also that you weigh 175 pounds. Your arms, hands and shoulders will have to lift 175 foot pounds twenty times or 3,500 foot pounds. Can you imagine the impressive shoulders that will appear in about a month's time!

To get the most benefit from combining office work and chinning bar, alternate the direction of your hands on the bar according to your own direction in—or out. Palms toward you on entering will work biceps. Palms away on leaving, the triceps.

117 The Tension Break

A leg slimmer and strengthener comes with the water cooler or coffee break. Skiers, golfers, walkers, tennis players and swimmers take note: lean against the wall and slide down to a sitting position. Hold both the position and the look of nonchalance as long as possible. To create a sensation, start practicing about two months before you exhibit your prowess at the office. Incidentally, competition is great for leg muscles. In fact any muscles.

118 Modified Push-ups

Modified push-ups are important, but remembering to do them is difficult. When you walk into your office, *don't sit down to the mail.* Place your feet as far away from your desk as you can manage easily—and do five modified push-ups with hands on the edge of the desk. As your performance improves, stand farther away from the desk and still later use the chair seat. When you move into the big-time, do one-handed push-ups at desk or chair. They are just as good as two-handed push-ups from the floor.

119 The 9 O'Clock Bounce

Flexibility suffers every time you work yourself into a tizzy. The madder the pace the tighter the back. Keep this in mind when your back feels stiff and remind yourself pointedly that eighty per cent of all backaches are caused by muscle deficiency.

Every time you get out of your chair, whether it be to leave the office, fix a blind or pick up some material, do a few "Back and Hamstring Bounces." Place your feet wide apart, hands behind your back and keep your head up. Bend forward from the hips and bounce the upper body downward five times straight ahead, five right and five left. Let gravity do the work. *Don't push.* Then drop the upper body toward the floor letting arms and head dangle downward. Do the same five bounces to the center, right and left.

120 "In Conference"

There is often more to be gained from rest than from food. We eat too much most of the time anyway. Even the President gets a lunch hour, though too often he doesn't take it. If you are in a business turmoil you'll be safer (and thinner) if you'll have a glass of *skimmed* milk or a bowl of soup alone—than a

three-course meal under pressure. No animal eats when it's nervous—why should you? Then hang up the "In Conference" sign—and take a nap.

So damaging have been the losses in the top echelons of big business from what appears to be a preventable condition known as cardiac failure—that business is now taking an interest in its prevention.

I was asked by the Executive Furniture Guild to help design a small space to be incorporated into the offices of the modern, elegant but very functional new buildings. It was to be called the "Tension Easer Space" and perform precisely that office.

The Tension Easer Space has one side entirely of mirrors. Mirrors are apt to be more truthful than tactful —which is exactly what many royal heads need. It holds a chinning bar, and two resistance poles where the angry man can do what he'd like to do to old J.P. and nobody the wiser. There is an angled wall for push-ups and an exercise bench that teams up with a notch in the wall for specific exercises outlined on built-in exercise charts. There's a stationary bike with all the latest bells, timers, speedometers and over-loaders—but far more important, directions for how the thing is to be used—besides just ridden. There are glittering weights that look like something else and a small scale that looks like a small scale. A threatening tape measure hangs in full view next to a chart that reports loss or gain of inches. In the corner is the simple Picas: two slender poles sprouting from a support that leans against any convenient baseboard. It bears the seal of approval from the Institute for Physical Fitness—and its recommended exercises.

What is the purpose of this space? To keep a man a man—and alive.

Golf is fun but it can't do *that* job. Anger won't wait till the weekend and he can't take time out from an impossible day to go to the club. There's no guarantee that the club can provide more than a steam bath and a rubdown anyway. Anger, like fat, mounts up—and like fat, is dangerous. Anyone has ten minutes here and there throughout the day—if not, fire the secretary! Take ten minutes (coffee-break time) in the morning and the same in the afternoon and you've put aside one hour and forty minutes a week for exercise that can do nothing but good.

You should understand that it is not the last twenty repetitions—after you feel you can't do a single one more—that do the job. Exercise is cumulative like the food you eat. Not everyone could take an hour and forty minutes at a stretch, but anyone can take that amount in bits and pieces. The best part is you can take it in a Tension Easer when you need it—not five hours later when tension has already worked into muscle spasm, and pain.

A program such as the one provided by the Tension Easer has another notable advantage. It's been a terrible day at the office—it is also Mary's birthday and you have reservations for dinner, theatre tickets, and exactly the present she's been hankering after. You wish it had been any other evening. Well, get off coat, tie, shoes and shirt and go at it for fifteen or twenty minutes. You probably can't see what good that would do, but oddly enough, exercise does not tire you out further. It speeds heart action and circulation. It sets the adrenals to work and forces the lungs to provide the body with more oxygen. Fatigue and tension drain away, leaving you relaxed, stimulated and ready for a wonderful evening.

121 The Picas

The Picas is a simple piece of equipment that can be stored anywhere. There are hundreds of exercises that utilize the Picas. For example, Figure A shows one exercise where you start standing back on your heels and then lunge forward to hang on the poles. The weight of your body is enough alone to stretch the chest and shoulder muscles. The arched back assures both back and abdominal strength. In B, the body is turned to the side, and supported by the strength of the right arm.

Vacations

One final word—about vacations. The habit of taking a vacation should be encouraged just as emphatically as the habit of considering oneself indispensable should be opposed. Start tomorrow to find different ways of taking vacations. Vacations don't have time limits. Once in a while, I tell my secretary I'll be out of the office for the afternoon. I'll be busy, I tell her, but I'll call in. I leave and physically it's exactly as though I were headed out on a job. Psychologically it's quite different. I'm on my way to play hookey. When a heavy snowfall makes returning from a ski weekend impossible, I notice that all my skiing friends manage to survive the enforced vacation. Why not simply take an extra day? Naturally time clocks and employers are deterrents, but they are never as strict as a conscience even at their orneriest. If you can, get away illegally occasionally.

Americans' habit of taking two weeks' vacation in the summer is murder. In the first place, everyone else is trying to get one at that time, too, and overcrowding is only one of the perils. There are so many others clamoring for space, who needs you? Service can be pretty miserable. Then if the innkeeper is delightful and you always go there because you enjoy him, he's usually too busy to spend much time with you. It would be quite different after the season. I always make a point of going on small surprise-vacations just before or after the season anywhere. Acapulco is hell over Easter and a half-priced heaven one week later. The Florida Keys are wonderfully empty just before Christmas, and you know what it's like right afterward. Our East Coast beaches swarm with humanity all summer long but the Labor Day broom sweeps them all back into the cities, leaving incredibly beautiful shores and sparkling still-warm water to gulls and sandpipers.

Winter vacations are becoming more popular as more people take to skiing and scuba, but where do they all go? Right to the nearest mobbed resort. This is probably profitable for the mate seekers, but for the others it might be novel, restful and delightful to go to a place everybody else isn't.

One should be in shape for a vacation. All too often, you work right up to the very last minute—packing suitcase or car in a dripping frenzy. The first day of vacation finds you beginning to unwind and without the strength to get out of bed before noon. Now there's absolutely nothing wrong with staying in bed till noon if that's what you want to do, *but* vacations are supposed to recharge batteries and very little of that happens when you are flat on your back.

You find yourself in Sun Valley. The weather's great, snow conditions never better, but after two runs you have such cramps in your feet that you've got to go in. The water's fine in Nassau, but unfortunately you never took the time to learn how to swim. You'd love to take up the invitation to play tennis with those new people who arrived yesterday, but you haven't touched a racket in years and would just be a drag. The same mountains you scrambled all over when you were eighteen are glittering above you, and you're too tired to put on your climbing shoes.

Vacations are every bit as important as making a living, and they can bore you to death or keep you young. If it's swimming you want to do, go down to the "Y" and learn how now. Every "Y" is putting in courses in scuba diving. Why not investigate a new world under the sea? If it's hiking you want, practice daily and check the section on walking. Want to ski? Start on October 1 to train. Check the section on sports for your program. The important thing to remember about vacations is, it isn't the place you go, or the clothes you wear, or even the people who go there. What's going to make or break your vacation is the way you feel and the things you will be able to do.

CHAPTER NINE

The art of walking

The art of walking has many facets and the least of these is getting where you want to go. I've heard it said that we won't *have* to walk ever again. That's almost the same as saying, "radio communication will soon be so good and so universal that we will be able to close our eyes and never have to look at the world around us again." What a priceless gift is the not-so-simple ability to get up and walk somewhere—anywhere! Once, when a skiing accident put me into traction for three months, I had a lot of time to notice how people managed that great giver of independence. Some of them walked lightly, with a pleasant sense of energy. Some shuffled. There was one person whose irritating, brusque personality was preceded by the sound of her feet pounding up the stairs. My nurse had a very slight and completely disarming limp. As she whisked around the room, competent and tireless, the limp was noticeable more as an accent than a handicap. There was one woman who toed in, and, as a rather comical balance, her husband toed out. A walk is a dead giveaway, and habits of thinking and moving make it what it is. Often a person's walk can change five times in as many minutes, as that person's mood changes. For the next few days, watch your friends (and enemies) walk.

Pigeon toes make wide-eyed little girls of three look delightfully vulnerable. Their tiny turned-in feet make them appear to be helpless and in need of cuddling. The same stance on a five-foot nine, 145-pound college senior is something else again. Pigeon toes shriek immaturity and weakness. Try and find them on the self-assured woman. You will have to search a long time. There is something about self-assurance that almost outlaws a weak walk or poor posture. The problem of pigeon toes seems to be mostly confined to girls, and barring some extreme congenital abnormality, is very correctable with exercise.

122 Correcting Pigeon Toes

Start by walking across the floor (preferably to a record) with the feet in an exaggerated turn outward. Pretend you are on a tight rope and find a crack in the floor or a pattern on the carpet to follow, being very sure that the knees are stiff and the pelvis tilted under (index). (A) Step forward, turning the foot outward *before you touch the floor*. Touch first with the toe and then set the heel down *slowly*. Stand tall and relaxed except for the

A

B

tipped-under pelvis and tightened seat muscles and the ever-working abdominals. The steps should be average length when you go forward, but double or more as you backtrack.

(B) Walking backward will be harder at first, but is great training for more than just pigeon toes. The stand foot is turned out and the stepping foot stretched backward in the extreme turned-out position. Place the toe on the floor and then press the heel down. At once you will feel pull in the heel cords and since you took a long step and had to bend the stand knee, you will feel strain in the stand thigh. Keep your upper body straight and the pelvis tucked under. This will force the thighs to open, which is what you are after. The steps are similar to the position taken for fencing.

This comes under your special program, but it will not be enough to change a habit that should have been corrected before you were ten. You'll have to incorporate it into daily habits. Concentrate on a moderately turned-out walk wherever you go. Very often, only one foot will turn in. That's the one you *always* turn out to the point of limping, even if you are only going across the hall.

Flat feet used to keep boys out of armies. Now if they accepted that excuse we'd have no army. Babies, kept standing during the first critical months on soft padded playpen floors, on crib mattresses, generally overfed and under-exercised, have developed some of the worst looking and most inefficient feet in the world. While there seem to be more turned-in feet on girls, boys take most of the prizes for the turned-out condition that often accompanies flat feet. Feet can be as flat as pancakes and still do an excellent job if the anterior tibialis is well developed. Put your foot on the floor, pull the toes up toward the body and rotate them inward a little. Now slide your hand down the outside of the front of your lower leg—that swelling is the muscle you are looking for. The exercise that would have given you good feet if you'd done enough of it as a child is walking, especially under the weight of a pack and on uneven terrain. Now you will need that and a bit more. Use all the foot exercises (index) and try to walk with toes well turned in when in private and at least straight ahead when on the street. To get that tibialis working for you, work it. Sit when you can, with legs outstretched and heels on the floor. Pull the toes up and inward. Hold for a slow five count, relax and repeat. This can be done under desks and tables, too, and can utilize time that would otherwise be lost in utter boredom.

Interval training has been used with success by many coaches. For example, you run at top speed for a given length of time and then trot along easily for another given period of time, then you are off in a flash again. This alternating of effort with rest seems to both build and relax muscles. I use a similar system on the streets of New York and nobody knows I'm doing a thing except walking. For a person of my size there are 105 steps in a north-south block and fifteen steps to a street. I keep my seat tight and abdominals contracted for the block and leave them on their own as I cross the streets. Push them hard and then relax. Try as you go along to pull your trunk in so far that you can't feel your belt. Never waste a minute. If you are wearing a coat that covers your seat, you can overwork that area very easily. Bottoms have two sides and they *can* move independently. Stand with feet slightly apart, weight on the left foot and right just resting at the side for balance. Now, tighten the gluteals (seat muscles) on the left side. (You would find it more difficult to tighten both together in this position.) Now relax and shift the weight to the right side. Tighten that side. Now take a step forward on the left foot, tighten and *relax*. Take a step forward with the right foot, tighten and relax. If you feel awkward, imagine how a baby must feel his first week on feet. Practice this at home until it goes well, then add it to your bag of tricks designed to improve each shining hour.

The duck waddle or wet diaper walk appears on women more often than men—although they are not all immune. If you watch carefully, you will notice that their steps are taken along parallel lines and never overlap. The greater the distance between the parallel, the more grotesque the walk. This walk often goes hand in hand with turned-out feet and swaybacks, but it can appear by itself. It looks awkward and is tiring. This, too, should have been corrected at an early age. Very few girls who had good dancing lessons in childhood are so afflicted later on. Correction will take time and awareness of the problem is the first step.

123 Correcting the "Duck Walk"

Do exactly the same exercise as the pigeon-toed, but exaggerate the crossover, putting each foot down about six inches to the outside of its mate. You can't very well do this on Main Street, but you can keep a check on each step by making your knees rub as they pass each other.

Worn down heels on your shoes are a sign that you are putting weight where it shouldn't go. Notice what happens to the tread on cars when wheels are out of alignment, and imagine what's happening to your joints. You will need all the foot exercises (index) and you should walk, walk, walk. Any muscle that is worked will improve and if it is worked correctly, as it will be in the foot exercises, it will improve faster.

Awareness is the habit to cultivate. You probably are not aware of your walk, do not really know how you sit down or arise from a chair, climb stairs or get into and out of your car. The really adept notice less than the painful or clumsy because they are not reminded by a twinge or spilled milk. Partly because so much of nature has been taken out of our environment and partly because we were never educated to notice, we lose the ability to hear, smell, feel, see and taste on the high level of healthy children and animals. This is really a terrible loss and it is a crime that those who should be educating us to increase these sensitivities are themselves unaware of their beauty and importance.

Running can be beautiful to watch—or funny as all get out. If I had to pick a team in a hurry out of a thousand applicants, I'd put them all to the test of running once around a gym keeping pace with a good, fast record. You can pick out the women who were tomboys, the ones who were dancers, swimmers, and the powerhouse athletes. The awkward, the weak and the inhibited, reveal themselves before they've gone twenty feet. Now we are back again to awareness. How do you run? If you ever could, you can again. If you never did, you still can learn. It will take time but is certainly worth the time invested. Your heart, lungs and endurance will improve, which knocks out fatigue, and your legs will strengthen and *stay* strong.

I found out something about running on city streets one day when I was giving a demonstration at Radio City and had a TV show scheduled at the Waldorf Astoria Hotel four minutes later. No cabs were handy so off I ran, wearing tights, white lab coat and ballet slippers. My manager was with me and we were planning the program as we ran along. On the other side was a reporter assigned to me for the day. Pretty soon who else was running? Two cops. I left manager and reporter to explain and made the opening with thirty seconds to spare. Like the walker on country roads who is offered a lift every half mile by incredulous motorists who know nothing of walking for pleasure, the runner is equally unbelievable. Then, too, there's the problem of women's shoes. You probably don't know this, but the shoes we gullible gals wear are the remnants of an earlier day when the male hobbled his mate to keep her close to home. That sort of control doesn't work anymore, but the fashion persists. Ladies will have to choose their running locale with more care and limit it to times when they are dressed for the sport. But men, RUN.

Let's say you are thirty, in good shape and the doctor says he wishes he were you. Start your build-up by running fifty steps. This can be done out in the country on the way to the train, at the beach or right in the center of town. Walk the next fifty and if you are still breathless, push that fifty walking steps up to one hundred. Then run another fifty. That's one hundred running steps that day. When you can cut down the walking to a fifty-fifty ratio, take on one hundred fifty running steps—that's three sets of runs and three sets of walks. If time is at a premium, you can improve by cutting down on the walking steps in between runs, or by adding more sets. Either one works. The main thing is to do it. I have three friends who asked me to take a walk around a five-mile circuit last summer. The youngest was fifty-six. It was a beautiful day and I asked them if they would like to try an experiment. Would they run five steps with me? They would. One hundred steps later we ran five more. I wanted to see what effect it would have, and I found that they didn't get breathless and the rest period was more than enough to quiet pulses. Further, the fact that they were used to walking five miles at a clip and that they were walking at the time, prevented any stiffness. We all had fun and I forgot all about it. Last week I was invited again. Imagine my surprise to find that they kept up the routine and increased it gradually. They now run one hundred steps and walk fifty for the whole five miles. They say there is only one trouble. They get back too fast.

CHAPTER TEN

You're never too old to be a winner

Sport began at the same moment man learned to throw the first stone. The first game probably went something like this: "I can throw farther than you can."

That was also the beginning of competition, and I doubt very much that as long as man exists, we will lose either one of them. In the thirties there was an odd trend among educators toward the outlawing of competition in athletics. Unfortunately, they succeeded not only in getting rid of competition in many instances but in getting rid of athletics as well. The intramural programs that were supposed to fill the gap too often lacked the excitement and importance of interscholastic competition.

Another trend, and one that is far more deadly, was ushered in by the same group—the trend toward excessive attention to safety. Note that I said excessive, not sensible. The basis for this trend is fear—which results in overprotection. Girls are the prime target for this neurosis. Participation is often cut to "rest" them, and fields of action narrowed so that they will not "over-do." This succeeds in boring them, and they avoid the narrowed fields altogether. So dull do most high school girls find their physical education programs that they use any excuse to get out of them. To judge by the numbers of excuses pleading menstrual periods presented to the instructors, one can only conclude that the young American female is in this condition the entire nine months that school is in session.

While I understand the idea of balance between an intramural program and interschool competition, I believe that the methods still being used to achieve this balance can result in nothing but tragic failure. Many people in physical education (those actually on the gym floor—not the people working in research far from the madding crowd) feel the same way.

As a varsity athlete and one who played on winning teams most of the time, I loved competition. Indeed, I had to be grown up and far away from school days before I realized that everybody didn't love it and that being on a team, even the third team, wasn't everybody's idea of living. Having lived through a very difficult early childhood fraught with anger and frustration, I needed the polished battlefield of the gym floor. There I could legitimately war—within a framework of rules and sportsmanship. It was a far better outlet for excess energy and pent-up fury than the rock-and-roll dive of today—and every bit of effort had to come from my own sinews, not the gas line of a hot rod. When the game was over, both body and emotions had played it out fair and square. Further, there was an all-important training field for *winning*. It is important that we learn early to fight each battle—no matter how small—to win. If more of us had had that practice, there would have been less uncertainty in Korea. Indeed there would be less give-up-itis in the constant daily battles of life. While each battle may seem small and insignificant, the sum total of those wins or losses is the life story of the man or the woman.

Youngsters with drive, passion, enthusiasm and often unseen pain, need tremendous doses of competitive sport. Take these qualities and channel them, train and discipline these young people and you get a leader. Frustrate or dissipate them and you get what we've got too many of—jd's.

True, there are children with entirely different personalities. The child whose life is a gentle stream—even though it is often a lonely one—can go his quiet way with neither interest nor need for competition. Fighting and winning are as remote as the stars. When forced to action he often performs very well, but left to himself, he would rather not. Such a child finds his way into sports such as sailing, skiing, hunting, fishing—or any other in which nature plays an important role. It is to be hoped that there is a sailing, skiing, hunting or fishing parent in the background—who can introduce him early to these pleasurable and healthy outlets.

Another group, and by far the largest, is made up of a great potpourri of ages, sizes, body types, and levels of intellect. Many would love to compete. Some would just like to get out on the gym floor to find out what it's like and still others want nothing in this world so much as to do a flip on a trampoline. They all have one thing in common—*they need physical activity for the building of strong efficient bodies and as an outlet for emotional stress*. None of this group, however, is physically endowed for competition. The doors to this phase of school life are closed to them before they register in kindergarten, for they lack the strength, flexibility and coordination to qualify for anything more active than team manager or water boy. These are doomed to watch—whatever the game may be. Since they perform poorly, they are not even welcome in the intramural program which is designed to bring games to the masses. Even the masses don't want to be hampered by a dud.

The failure in our sports programs, whatever the type, lies in the phrase "too little much too late." Any strong, healthy, coordinated body cries out for action. Sick bodies do not. To correct this deficiency in school will take time. While other, more progressive nations are spending billions on gyms, apparatus and well-trained instructors, we are expanding our school bus programs. When you travel abroad, give attention to the differences in body condition and builds between foreign children and ours. A good place to observe this is at the beaches.

There should be opportunity in our country for the varsity athlete—we have every good reason to cultivate him *or her*. There should be a chance, too, for the boy or girl who prefers hiking, skiing or swimming just for the kinetic pleasure they afford. There should be a chance for anyone who wants to enjoy physical outlets that will build them into better, stronger, more stable, valuable people. If that chance comes early enough, every child will seize it.

Start yours in babyhood and build strong, sturdy youngsters. Then insist that the schools be given an opportunity to provide good daily programs of calisthenics, apparatus and tumbling. They can play games after school if they want to. We did. Those programs should start in kindergarten, not Junior High where it is already too late to offset the ravages of sedentary living.

Every American who is denied a good body is a potential burden for every one who has one. The weak, the sick and the deranged must be cared for by the healthy and strong. It is within our power to increase the numbers in either group, and our present trend toward building more of the weak, less capable people and less of the strong emotionally stable—seems to me to be sheer folly, bordering on suicide.

There are almost as many sports as there are people, but one rule applies to every one of them: the better the physical condition, the better the performance—even in so easy a game as shuffleboard. If you begin early in life with a good body, train and work it well, there is no reason why you should not continue all the days of your years in fine health—ready to take on and enjoy anything and everything.

There is an important thing to remember in connection with all sports. You get in shape for sports—you don't use *them* to get into shape. This is dramatically apparent in the sport of skiing. If you reverse the maxim, you could very well end up with a broken leg. Football and basketball are rarely well played without lead-up exercises. The gymnast cannot begin serious training before he develops the muscles for his chosen sport. Even the simple Virginia Reel needs lungs, a strong heart and good legs. Whatever sport you select for your own, be in condition to profit from it and enjoy it. Let's first consider the various types of sports.

Some sports come under the heading of *Spike Activities*. These involve short quick stops and starts which build strength but work against flexibility. Since both are important to coordination, special effort should be made to do flexibility exercises as well as engage in the sport itself. Another argument for this extra effort is the prevention of injury. Spike sports are made up of unpredictable action peaks calling for all-out effort without warning—injury is therefore always a possibility. Tennis, squash, badminton, paddle tennis, volleyball, hand ball, soccer, football and even baseball are spike sports. There are many others, but these are good examples.

The driving personality will derive a great deal of satisfaction from spike sports as well as a quick outlet for suppressed steam.

Rhythm activities are quite different from spikes. The swimmer, the gymnast and golfer know exactly where their bodies will be at the peak of action, and they can prepare in advance for the danger zones. While the swimmer who is constantly reaching and stretching as he glides through the water is always improving his flexibility, he will need to work overtime for strength if top performance is to be achieved. Bob Kiphuth, coach of the great Yale swimming teams, had his young team members on the gym floor daily for nine weeks before they got their feet wet. Swimming is great as a relaxer and the person who enjoys kinetic pleasure and his own thoughts can find enjoyment merely in swimming laps. The adventurous spirit need only add scuba diving to find himself in another world.

Age has very little to do with the selection of a sport, but the condition of the individual is all important. Some of my best rock-climbing partners have been well over fifty and even sixty. I have seen veteran tennis players who could put Junior National players to shame. The questions to ask yourself are:

What do you like to do?
Where do you like to do it?
Are you a team type or an individualist?
What sort of body do you have?
What condition is it in today?
What was it like when you were 12?

Do you like a lot of people around, a few, or none at all?
What sort of people are available to you?
What part of the country are you in?
What sports are to be found in your area?

If you are an individualist (we find that the scientist, doctor and musician, as well as a lot of other people, seem to fall into this category), you will probably prefer skiing, hiking, and fencing to football, hockey or baseball. There is also the problem of getting up a team. While there are always enough players for one- or two-a-cat, it is almost impossible to find eighteen players with two free hours on a Saturday morning. Football is pretty much out of the question as you'll never find twenty-two plus the armor to go with them although there's nothing that says you can't get up a darned good game of "touch" with almost any number, anywhere.

Soccer is a wonderful example of this kind of flexibility, and it is one of the all-time great games for developing strong bodies with quick reactions. The beaches of Europe are one long soccer game in which one group runs into the next.

Hiking is something that can be done almost anywhere, and even if it takes two hours by car to get to country nice enough to hike in, it's worth it. There are groups all over the land which have formed themselves into clubs for the express purpose of walking in the fields or hills or woods. Last year when my fall program came from the Appalachian Mountain Club, I was amazed to note the number and variety of programs available. Trail walking, trail repair trips, canoeing, rock climbing, Sunday walks, bird watching, nature lectures (that may sound dull to an ex-football player, but to a professor aware of the intricacies of life on our planet it could be a fascinating day).

Scuba diving, one of the latest fads in our country of many fads, is a wonderful sport and is booming in every YMCA pool in the country. Don't stop there, however; Nassau, Hawaii and the Mediterranean await the practiced (and solvent) diver, and you *can* have a lot of fun at Jones Beach.

For some time, *rope jumping* has been out of favor. This came about when theorists (certainly nobody who had ever jumped rope) turned things about. They felt that the delicate bodies of little girls would be endangered by any bouncing motion that might dislodge highly important organs of reproduction. The reverse is true. By strenuous physical activity little bodies are made strong enough to safeguard reproductive organs, and develop the muscles and coordination necessary not only to reproduce but also for the lovemaking which precedes it.

Dancing may not qualify as a sport, but like sex it is certainly a physical activity that can be both extremely physical and extremely active. Primitive people prepared for war and lovemaking through dance and as a consequence, were neither inhibited nor dismayed when faced by either in adulthood. Ballet and modern dance can be very active indeed and a course in ethnic dance supplements sexercise. For the person with creative ability, dance is a wonderful outlet that will also keep the body young and attractive. Again, however, one must keep in mind that there are areas that are totally disregarded, namely arms. (Ask your dancing daughter to do ten push-ups and see what happens.)

Swimming is good for almost everything—but *swim*. Florence Chadwick set a style in one Midwestern YMCA pool by tying herself to the base of the lifeguard's stand and swimming for two hours in one place. The number of youngsters who emulated this novel workout made the pool look like a spider web. The fact that they were held stationary while swimming through water doubled the workout for the time invested.

Gardening, while it may not be labeled SPORT, certainly bears all the earmarks, from competition ("My tomatoes are bigger than your tomatoes") to spike activity. (Ever move a tree?) Preparation for gardening should be started in midwinter, however, if "gardener's back" is to be avoided. If it's too late for this gem of information, and you are already in a knot while the weeds multiply, do the limbering series on page 228.

The *gymnast* needs preparation in both the fields of strength and flexibility. While the sport is rhythmic and therefore predictable, it has this quality only when the performer maintains a high degree of fitness. Let him make an error in timing and his sport becomes a spike sport of a very dangerous kind. It is one thing to be off balance on a tennis court and quite another on the flying rings. Gymnastics are graceful, precise and beautiful. The sport has a very high rating in kinetic pleasure, discipline and personal courage. Constant exercise, both during its performance and in extra calisthenics, is the price of excellence.

Golf is a sport that improves or deteriorates according to physical condition, mental attitude and practice. Like many sports, it suffers from the law of diminishing returns. The better you become, the less effort it requires and therefore the less physical benefit it provides. It is a sport that can be enjoyed by even the very old and has one great advantage—it must be played out of doors. If the golfer wants to improve his stroke he must use specific exercise and keep in mind that while it stretches the shoulder girdle, it does little for the flexibility of the back and legs. These must be worked on the side. One look at the average golfer's midsection tells you it isn't the answer to *that* problem either. If he (or she) is healthy and uses a golf cart, a pail of balls at a driving range would be more beneficial. The golf cart's major purpose, aside from tangible evidence of status, is to get you to the nineteenth hole without the necessity of moving your action-hungry body. Golf *can* be relaxing. If you use it for business only, it *can* get you an ulcer.

Horseback riding combines rhythm with spike, and the more mettlesome the horse, the greater the opportunity for unpredictable action. The rider gets a good workout for pelvis, inner thighs, upper back, arms and hands. He must also govern his emotions before he can govern his animal. What happens to legs, abdominals and feet? The Cossacks on the steppes developed an answer to that. Fierce warriors all but grown to their small, shaggy mounts, they once lacked the leg strength to be effective when unhorsed in battle. Wise commanders instituted special cavalry calisthenics which we see today in Russian folk dancing. The tremendous leaps and leg action done to wild, stirring music started early in childhood and gave them striking and staying power. We would be wise to emulate these exercises to offset the debilitating effects of school buses and family cars.

Skiing, one of America's fastest growing sports, has the same drawbacks (though to a lesser degree) that golf has. The more proficient the skier becomes, the less physical effort he will need to put forth and therefore, the less physical benefit he will derive. The novice, dragging his snow-covered carcass out of every other drift, works up a lather in fifteen minutes. Two years later, as he floats down the trail swinging his hips gently and shoulders not at all, he has cut effort to a minimum while increasing pleasure to a maximum. To be sure of enough strenuous activity for good performance and accident prevention, the skier should start a strong calisthenics program two months *before* the ski season and keep it going between weekends on the slopes.

One good way to assure a sufficiently strenuous workout would be to forego one or two trips on the lift each skiing day and climb up on foot. For safety's sake, however, stick to the edge of the trail. The wearing of climbing skis would multiply the benefits. The weight of the skis acts as resistance and thereby conditions the legs. Further, no footprints will be left in which to catch a ski tip when you descend.

Tennis, squash, badminton and paddle tennis are in the spike category. It should be noted that any game played in cold weather is a great calorie burner, but at the same time presents the danger of injury if special attention is not given to warm up *before the play begins.*

Basketball, dodgeball and volleyball, like the above, are spike sports. Attention should be given to flexibility and warm-up. Volleyball can be made into quite a game if a medicine ball is substituted for the regulation light ball.

Football stands in a class by itself and is mentioned here only in the hope that fearful parents will permit enthusiastic offspring to play it *when it is properly taught.* Life is no bowl of cherries anyway, and the sooner a boy learns to take his lumps the better. However, you must be sure that the coach knows his business and is not bucking to win the Conference no matter who pays the bill. Football needs more pre-season training than any other sport and if your boy does not engage in rough, tough sport all summer as well as football in autumn, I'd rather see him playing soccer, which is a better conditioner and a faster game anyway. While our sons are certainly bigger than they were a generation ago, they are generally much weaker. Size plus padding looks impressive, but breaks like a matchstick unless there has been intensive training before the game.

Baseball is fun but is not a builder of men (or women). If the player has a good body to begin with and top flight coordination, he *may* play a good game of baseball. The game, however, will not give him these qualities as it is played. Do not count on baseball to do very much for your children other than entertain them. If it is the extent of the school sports program, be sure that they get gymnastics and swimming somewhere else.

Hunting and *mountaineering* (as well as hiking) do a good job on legs. The addition of a pack will aid abdominals and backs, but you still need something for arms, hands and shoulders. Woodchopping is an excellent supplement, but not everybody has a tree. Check the section on "Resistance" for exercises that will round out these sports. Incidentally, if the hunter is an archer, he will get plenty of work for those areas.

Running works the legs, but not the arms. Riding and apparatus work the upper body, but not the legs. Try to provide the ingredient missing from your favorite sport by alternating with a sport that stresses exactly that.

Fencing, a wonderful sport combining speed, grace, skill, and power, has one obvious failing. It is unilateral. And since one should not be one-sided, it would be well to alternate with a sport that is aggressively bilateral, such as rowing for the arms and running for legs.

Biking, roller skating, sportscar racing and *sailing* can be tough—or as lazy as a summer afternoon. They are exciting activities and each develops some part of the body, but cannot be used as overall programs. Another sport will have to be added, or a good calisthenics program. If you think driving those little cars is nothing, you may be interested in a report by a doctor friend of mine. In the last six months he has had five cases where worried young men came into his office complaining of terrible chest pain ("could it be my heart, doctor?"). It turned out to be muscle strain due to non-power steering!

Incidentally, roller skating and ice skating are great at any age. But if bones are brittle, it would be the better part of valor to choose a sport with more predictable action. If you have skated all your life, however, there is not a reason in the world why you should not continue.

Judo, boxing and *wrestling* not only develop strong bodies, but the ability to "take it" and the ability to make quick decisions. Naturally there should be a lot of conditioning taken before and along with such activity. It's too bad that girls never get a chance to do any of these things. They have to "take it" so often.

Bowling, deep sea fishing, rowing and *canoeing* all do fine work on arms, hands and shoulders. Whenever possible, running or hiking should be added.

Don't forget that every sport can be made more difficult. The golfer *could* carry his own clubs, but if status precludes this, then make status pay off. Step into a sport store and buy a set of scuba divers' diving weights. Sling them bandolier fashion over each shoulder. "Why th' hell are you wearing those?" can always be given the enviable answer—"need a tougher workout." The hiker need only add a couple of cans of fruit to his pack. Incidentally —and I suppose this doesn't belong here except that I think nice things belong where you find them—if it's a cold brisk October day, the hiker will find that a bottle of good red wine tucked into his pack can make a festivity out of a lowly picnic.

So what you did at ten, you can do at twenty—only better. There is no reason to slow down for thirty. I'm better after forty than I was at thirty and there's no reason why you shouldn't be, too. That's ten years more practice. The difference between forty and fifty is negligible and anything you did then, you should be able to carry right on through life *so long as you stay in condition.*

If you are to enjoy a sport—any sport—you have to have two qualities in your pocket *before you begin.* They are *strength* and *flexibility,* two parts of the world's true wealth. You need them in varying amounts depending on what you want to play and how hard you want to play. If you don't have them, you won't do well and you will probably quit before you get the hang of things. Exercise will give you both of them and rhythm will help with timing. Repetition should increase your control over intensity, just be sure that the pathways you follow are correct.

When a child is learning to play the piano he plays scales. They are simple enough to learn. If they are played slowly, correctly and often, pathways of motion are beaten and fingers rarely step on a wrong note. Later, when the moment comes for these tools to be used for the pleasure of playing a piece of music, the same system should be followed. The piece should be learned and played at about one-quarter speed, well under control. Much later, if impatience has been conquered, the piece will be ready in a flawless state. The trick then is to put it away and not look at it for about three months *never having played it up to tempo.* We absorb what we have learned only while at rest. At the end of the absorbing period, the piece can be played up to tempo as flawlessly as at one-quarter the speed.

The novice skier who takes the trails at full tilt does so at his (and others') peril. Only constant practice of correct movements at slow speeds completely under control will insure the form for a racing descent. The absorption period applies in the case of the sportsman, too. The skiing we learn this winter only becomes a part of us next winter. The golf swing we worked over all summer will only begin to win stakes next summer.

The natural athlete moves correctly from birth. He is the one who is really born with the golden spoon in his mouth. He is always in balance and control and seldom under- or over-reaches in any play. But he is the rarity, not the rule, and a great deal can be done to train muscles to behave correctly in even the most average body. Stress, poor diet and disease can ruin the natural just as it can the average. Work, good diet and training can build the average beyond his wildest dreams.

Correct basic movement is the key to all successful engagement in sport. The tennis player who puts too much top spin on every ball within reach, will end up with a painful "tennis elbow" and a mediocre game. The basketball player who hasn't learned to jump correctly, will injure knee joints. The inflexible track star loses six inches of distance on every stride which makes the difference between running, winning, and even making a record. The tense, inadequately trained football player runs grave risk in every scrimmage. The secret is simple. Develop the basic quality of pure movement first and put in additional effort preparing the particular quality needed for your favorite sport.

Building Your Resistance

Weight lifting or weight training, or resistance called by any other name, is still a great body builder and absolutely essential to excellence in *any* sport. Until a very short time ago the word "weights" or "barbells" elicited a gasp from the average female and a raised eyebrow from the male, and it came by its questionable reputation quite simply. There was a man who said "Once I was a ninety-pound weakling, and look at me now." A lot of people did. They went to work, emulated him and improved. But there were the weight-lifters who lifted incorrectly and ignored flexibility (which is true also of many football players). Their muscles bulged and bulged some more. They had to have special clothes made and then found they were too muscle-bound to get into them. "Obviously, the sport was harmful." To these were added the ones who lifted too much too soon. Their torn muscles were waved like so many tattered flags of warning.

There is just as much science to lifting weights as to any other sport. Do it one way and you improve strength while building smooth, neat muscles. Do it another and you produce a monstrosity. You are to do it the first way.

In the following pictures, I use two telephone books as weights. While you may not have barbells or even weight bags on hand, you surely have a couple of books. They work fine for a start. Later, when you have become accustomed to the idea and the program, get a set of barbells. Seventy-five pounds is plenty for the average family. Below you will find directions for using them and also your progressive scoring sheet.

WEIGHT TRAINING

124 Clean to Chest and Press

Lean down keeping the knees relaxed as in A. Grasp the weight with palms facing toward the feet. Keep the pelvis tucked under and stand erect, bringing the weight to chest level as in B. Press the weight overhead as in C and then return it to the chest level position B. Finish by lowering the arms to full stretch and bringing the weight to rest at the top of your thighs. This exercise gets the whole body stretched to a good start. It strengthens the back, leg and arm muscles.

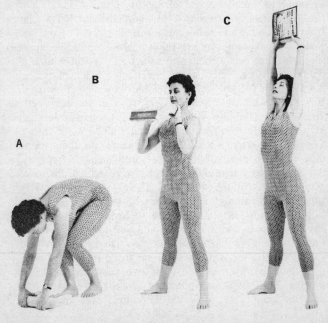

125 Reverse Curl
Bring the weight again to the chest level as in exercise 124 (B) and then lower to the floor.

126 Curl
Reverse your hands so that the palms face away from the feet. Stand erect and curl the weight against the chest (C). Replace the weight on the floor.

C – D

The *Curl* and *Reverse Curl* work the upper and lower arms, wrists and hands. These three exercises make up the opening set. When you have completed it, stretch the arms long and lean over for a hamstring stretch (see index). Do ten "opening sets" with time out to stretch between sets.

127 Bent Over Row
Stand with feet apart and knees straight. Lean forward from the hips and grasp the weight (A). Keeping the body still in the forward bent position, bend the arms bringing the weight even with the chest (B). Lower to full arm stretch without touching the floor and repeat ten times. The ROWING exercise strengthens the arms and, more important in this instance, the upper back.

A

B

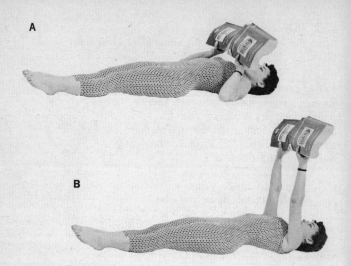

A

B

128   Supine Press

Lie supine holding the weight above the chest as in A.
Extend arms straight overhead as in B. Do ten. This
exercise strengthens the muscles of the chest, back,
shoulders and arms.

129   Knee Bends

Place the weight behind the neck
and, keeping the knees together,
rise to the toes and then drop
slowly into a deep knee bend.
Rise and return to the flat foot
starting position. Try to keep the
back straight. Do ten. This exercise
works feet, ankles, knees and legs.

130   Pull Over

Lie supine with weight extended overhead (A). *Keeping
arms straight,* carry the weight in an arc until it almost
touches the thighs (B). Do ten. This exercise works the
muscles of the chest, back, shoulders and arms. As it
stretches the rib cage it is also excellent for the lungs.

131 Lateral Stretch

Lie supine with weights extended to the sides (A). Keeping the arms straight, bring the hands together overhead (B). Return to side extension and repeat ten times. Works arms and chest muscles; improves bust line.

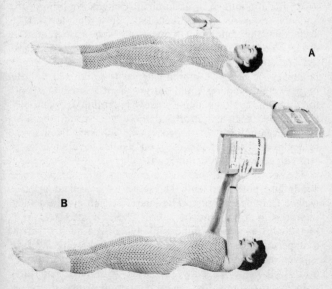

Breathing is important and most people rarely really fill their lungs. As you stretch with weights you will find that your body needs more oxygen and the stretches almost compel you to open your lungs fully. Try to fill *and empty* the lungs completely during each exercise.

Weight bags can be used in the foregoing exercises in place of books or barbells. By holding them in hands or draped over ankles almost any exercise in this book can be made more difficult—and more beneficial. As your strength improves, add pounds rather than repetitions. This saves time.

Weight training is not a hit-or-miss affair. It is very methodical and carefully designed. Many people think you walk up to the biggest weight you can find, seize it, grunt, grunt again, turn purple and heave it overhead. They also think it's crazy. If they were right about the method, they'd certainly be right in assuming it insane, but they are wrong on both counts.

Success lies in the gradual increase of resistance. For instance, if you were to do ten bent-knee sit-ups (index) a day for a month, your abdominal strength would improve and the exercise would feel easy. In order to further strengthen the abdominals you would have to increase the dosage. You could double the number of sit-ups, or increase the resistance by carrying a weight in your hands behind your neck. A month later you could add a little more weight and it would never be necessary to spend long boring minutes doing many repetitions. Eventually you would reach capacity and there you would stay. At no time would you have been in any danger from over-exertion and strain, because you would have built your strength slowly and methodically.

The opening set, bent over row, supine press, knee bends and pull over lend themselves very well to a basic weight training program. The lateral stretch can be added if you wish to be sure of a firm chest or attractive bust line. If this exercise is done while lying on a narrow bench that permits the arms to hang down below body level, it is even better. First you must understand the principle. Start well below capacity, work up to a peak and then reduce the weights for a cool-off period. Since the peak is well above your starting weight, you limit it to fewer lifts. This permits overloading, but prevents fatigue. The chart shows you the warm-up-peak-cool-off principle.

The next record shows you how to chart three days' lifts. I think you will do a better job if you limit your weight training to every second or even third day, using the intervening days for a sport or running. Don't neglect a short calisthenics period daily. The addition of such a program will work considerable change for the better on your appearance.

Chart 14. EVERY-OTHER-DAY WEIGHT TRAINING CHART FOR EVERY-DAY PEOPLE

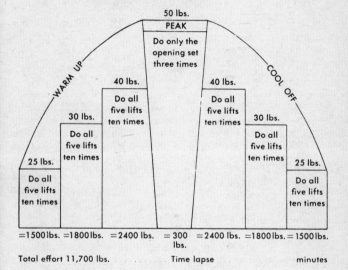

=1500lbs. =1800lbs. =2400 lbs.   = 300 =2400 lbs. =1800lbs. =1500lbs.
                                   lbs.

Total effort 11,700 lbs. . . . .   Time lapse   minutes

(If you are a beginner, you may want to lower the starting weight. As you improve you will want to raise it little by little.)

Chart 15. PROGRESSIVE WEIGHT TRAINING RECORD

No.	Exercise	Weight	Total	Total	Total
10	Opening set	25 lbs.	500		
10	Supine press	25 lbs.	250		
10	Bent over row	25 lbs.	250		
10	Knee bends	25 lbs.	250		
10	Pull over	25 lbs.	250		
			1500		

10	Opening set	30 lbs.	600
10	Supine press	30 lbs.	300
10	Bent over row	30 lbs.	500
10	Knee bends	30 lbs.	300
10	Pull over	30 lbs.	300
			1800
10	Opening set	40 lbs.	800
10	Supine press	40 lbs.	400
10	Bent over row	40 lbs.	400
10	Knee bends	40 lbs.	400
10	Pull over	40 lbs.	400
			2400
Peak— 3	Opening sets	50 lbs.	300
10	Opening sets	40 lbs.	800
10	Supine press	40 lbs.	400
10	Bent over row	40 lbs.	400
10	Knee bends	40 lbs.	400
10	Pull over	40 lbs.	400
			2400
10	Opening sets	30 lbs.	600
10	Supine press	30 lbs.	300
10	Bent over row	30 lbs.	300
10	Knee bends	30 lbs.	300
10	Pull over	30 lbs.	300
			1800
10	Opening sets	25 lbs.	500
10	Supine press	25 lbs.	250
10	Bent over row	25 lbs.	250
10	Knee bends	25 lbs.	250
10	Pull over	25 lbs.	250
			1500
Day Score			11,700

Enter pounds lifted at the conclusion of each group. Enter elapsed time.

132 Advanced Weight-Lifting Exercises

A

Place weight bags on each ankle and do a slow bicycle action (A). This works both the leg and the abdominal muscles. (B) Then, hold weights in your hands for a crawl stroke to work the shoulders, arms, upper back and hands. If the legs are kept straight, the added weight also stretches the hamstrings. Make a circle around the head with a weight in the hand (C). This will stretch —and give strength to—the shoulder girdle, chest, arms and hands.

B   **C**

THE INCLINE BOARD

Your resistance exercises will be much harder—and much more effective—if you work *against* gravity. One way to do this is to use an incline board. All the sit-ups can be done head down with feet held secure by a strap.

133 Leg-Chest Stretch

Leg-chest stretch. Start on hands and knees with the knees at the high end of the board and the hands almost at the bottom. Raise the right leg in the air and at the same time bring the chest as close to the board as possible. This exercise strengthens the back, gluteals and arms and gives considerable stretch to the chest and shoulders. After each leg raise, return to the hands and knees position. Alternate sides, starting with two and working up to eight.

134   The Flag Pole

The flag pole, which you have done on the level floor earlier can be made much harder on the board and still harder by bending the held down leg. Start supine with head down and the left foot thrust under the strap. Swing the arms back to touch the bottom of the board and raise the right leg straight overhead. Swing the arms up to grasp the raised foot and then sink *slowly* backward

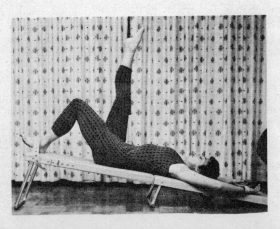

taking five seconds to complete the descent. Start with three on each side and work up to six. To increase the difficulty, carry a weight bag in each hand throughout the exercise.

Get in shape for the sport, don't use the sport to get in shape. Start before the season to condition your muscles, heart and lungs for top effort. Since different sports develop different parts of the body and also do little about other parts of the body, you will need supplementary exercises to make sure that no part of you becomes rusty. Note the exercises needed to supplement your current activity.

Chart 16. TRAINING FOR YOUR FAVORITE SPORT

The Sport	Start Training with These Exercises One Month Before the Season	Supplement the Sport of the Season with These Exercises
	(Numbers refer to exercises.)	
Baseball	71, 14k, 14L	71, 14k, 14L
Basketball	71, 14k, 14L	14k, 14L, 15, 37, 67, 68
Volleyball	71, 14k, 14L	14k, 14L, 15, 37, 67, 68
Handball	71, 14k, 14L	14k, 14L, 15, 37, 67, 68
Football	71, 14k, 14L	14k, 14L, 15, 37, 67, 68

Tennis	71, 14k, 14L, 10, 2, 37, 68, 77, 27, 28	14k, 14L
Paddle tennis	Same	Same
Badminton	Same	Same
Squash	Same	Same
Ice hockey	71, 14k, 14L	14k, 14L
Field hockey	Same	Same
Soccer	Same	Same
Lacrosse	Same	Same
Swimming	71, 14k, 14L	14k, 14L, 132
Scuba diving	Same	Same
Downhill skiing	71, 14k, 14L, 50, 31, 32, 35, 37, 15, 16, 27, 46	14k, 14L
Slalom	Same and add 36	Same
Cross country	71, 14k, 14L, 31, 32, 35, 37, 15, 16, 18, 46	Same
Water skiing	Same	Same
Ski joring	Same	Same
Boxing	71, 14k, 14L, 6, 10, 31, 32, 35, 37	14k, 14L, 6, 10
Wrestling	71, 14k, 14L, 59, 60, 61, 64, 6, 10	Same
Judo	71, 14k, 14L, 6, 10, 2, 15, 16, 27, 37	Same
Dancing	71, 5, 6, 15, 14, 12, 27, 28, 29, 30, 37, 46, 47, 51	71, 5, 6, 14, 12, 27, 28, 29, 30, 37, 46, 47, 51
Fencing	Same plus wgts	Same plus wgts
Diving	Same plus wgts	Same plus wgts
Acrobatics	Same plus wgts	Same plus wgts
Gymnastics	Same plus wgts	Same plus wgts
Apparatus	Same plus wgts	Same plus wgts
Figure skating	Same as dancing	Same as dancing
Tumbling	Same plus wgts	Same plus wgts

Rowing	71, 14k, 14L, 6, 10, 18, 37, 59, 73, 74, 84, 83, 107	6, 10, 14k 14L
Canoeing	Same	Same
White water	Same	Same
Aquaplaning	71, 14k, 14L	71, 14k, 14L
Archery	71, 14k, 14L, 6, 10, 18, 37, 59, 73, 74, 84, 83, 107	71, 14k, 14L
Hiking	71, 14k, 14L, 18, 15, 22, 25, 27, 28, 51	71, 14k, 14L
Climbing (rock)	Same plus 136	Same
Mountaineering	Same	Same
Hunting	Same without 136	Same
Fishing	Same with 136	Same
Camping	Same	Same
Bird watching	Same without 136	Same
Riding	136, 71, 14k, 14L, 20, 62	71, 14k, 14L, 20, 62
Bike riding	14k, 14L, 71, 10, 15, 16, 70	14k, 14L, 71, 10, 15, 16, 12
Roller skating	Same as ice skating	Same as ice skating
Sailing	71, 14k, 14L, 136	71, 14k, 14L
Sports cars	Same	Same
Running	71, 14k, 14L, 12, 15, 16, 18, 22, 27, 28, 29, 31, 32, 59, 60, 61	71, 14k, 14L, 73, 35, 36, 37
Track	Combine rowing and running series.	Same as rowing, running.
Golf	71, 14k, 14L, 136, 3, 5, 9, 11, 15, 37, 116, 95	71, 14k, 14L, 136, 3, 5, 9, 11, 15, 37, 116, 95
Bowling	136, 71, 14k, 14L, 1, 5, 8, 10, 9, 15, 16, 73	71, 14k, 14L
Gardening	14, 1, 2, 3, 6, 9, 11, 12, 15, 59, 60, 69, 71, 73	Continue all flexibility exercises for season.

CHAPTER ELEVEN

(Almost) Strictly female

Different doctors have different ways of breaking this particular bit of news. But the sum and substance of it is: "Mrs. Jones, you are pregnant."

As with everything else, reactions will differ to an announcement of that kind, depending on the circumstances. If you're under thirty-five, chances are that this is the happy plan for the last of the line. If you're thirty-five or older, the news probably comes as quite a surprise and may take a little time to adjust to, particularly if you went back to work after the child you thought was your last was in nursery school and your eldest firmly ensconced at Groton. How is this little surprise going to fit into that job routine of nine-to-five-with-cocktails-afterward? Then there's the problem of schedules. Your eldest will be graduating in June, and his commencement is going to rather conflict with yours.

Just what your reaction to this will be is hard to say. But there is one thing you'd better do, right away—get in shape for the event and, even more important, for coping after the baby arrives. It could be wonderful, you know, if you can stand it. But to stand it and also enjoy it, you'll have to be strong, flexible, enduring and attractive. Remember, there will be a child of yours now at every level of need. Those who can talk will be saying, "And *this* is my mother." The tone of voice carrying that pronouncement will depend on you.

There is still another reaction to the news of pregnancy —if it is happening to your daughter and not to you.

You went with her to the doctor, because for weeks she had felt wrung out and miserable. It was probably a virus. Almost everything was, wasn't it? Well, if it's a virus, in about eight months you will have to give it a name. You are going to be a grandmother. And if the doctor is clever, he'll put *you* on a diet, too. Say it, try it on for size: "I am going to be a grandmother."

As it slowly sinks in, you are going to have a good many reactions which will vary with the time of day. It's more startling just before dawn and somehow rather sweet around evening and bathtime. But as you sip a martini in a bar, you may feel little rustles of fear. "Oh God, me a *grandmother*." Visions of Whistler's mother and Grandma Moses will hover in the smoke of your cigarette as it curls about your very sleek and not at all white hairdo.

You wonder if your daughter will bring her new baby to visit you. Well, she will. You are going to be the kind of granny that any kid will want. You'll be in on the ground floor, and the second and third floors, too. Soon there will be a sleepy child with soft, feathery hair saying, "And God bless Granny." You'll wonder why you never took the time to enjoy your own children quite like this.

You plan to give the child not only a horse, but the boots, pants, saddle and bridle, too. You wonder fleetingly if you ought to take up riding again yourself. You play a good game of tennis right now, and you can ski up a storm. You wonder if you can keep it up till you have small company on court and slope. Well, you can and you better. This business of sitting in chimney corners is for the birds, not grandmothers.

Now put away your dreams of glory for a few minutes, and let's get down to cases. The baby will get here soon enough. In the meantime, you have some very important work to do to begin your own fitness program.

And if your pregnant daughter was one of those carefully mechanized youngsters who had little of the physical in her youth, you will have to do some tall planning to help her through these next months, and see to it that she keeps her figure, her disposition—and her husband.

Whether it is you or your daughter who will have the

baby, you both should know the reasons for the expectant mother to get and keep herself in good physical shape. There is still no better way to deliver a baby than the normal, natural way and for that, the mother needs strong abdominal muscles, a relaxed body and good breath control. Bearing a child is called "labor" because it's hard work. If the mother is so weak that her contractions are not sufficient to expel the baby from her body, complications ensue.

One of the ways to keep in shape is to keep from gaining too much weight. Your doctor will advise you on diet so that you do not gain more than twenty or twenty-five pounds during your pregnancy. Being too heavy puts an additional strain on everything, especially the back. You'll be more comfortable if you keep your weight down. Recovery of your normal figure after the baby is born depends on the tone of your muscles and on how much weight you have gained. Many women who gain more than the twenty-five pound limit never regain their trim figures after pregnancy, because it is so difficult to lose the extra pounds after the baby arrives. As in most things, prevention is easier than correction. The stretched skin will shrink back to normal, if it hasn't been filled with fat.

The day is long gone when the pregnant woman could gain with good conscience because she was "eating for two." About two thousand calories a day is usually the limit set by the doctor for his pregnant patient.

Far too often I receive a tragic letter like this: "Dear Miss Prudden, I have four children, the oldest is eight. I weigh 195 pounds, and my husband is off looking in other pastures. I can't even blame him. You should see me. I weighed 134 when we were married. I don't know how it happened, but with each baby I got fatter. Every day I feel more and more trapped. My friends say it's the situation, but I know it's the fat. Please help me. I know it's my fault, but I've got to get started, and if I looked like a human being, it would be enough for a start."

Naturally this could not happen to you or your daughter. Whatever else, you are going to see that it doesn't.

One young doctor I know never mentions the health of the coming baby to his patients. When they gain too much, he talks figure, carriage, posture and attractiveness to them. He has been heard shouting to some poor "stuffer" about his unwillingness to treat unattractive females. "Look at her—hair a mess, nails a mess, dress a mess. Does she think having a baby is any different for her than the Queen of England? She is to be back in one week two pounds lighter, hair done properly and her dress in order. Anyone with a face as pretty as hers has an obligation to be beautiful, pregnant or not." This young doctor was taking care of that baby's future as well as its prenatal life. Whether he knew it or not, and I always thought he did, he was taking a strong interest in the happiness of the baby's father, as well as its mother.

In addition to diet, there is the problem of keeping the legs and back in shape to carry the weight of the child as it grows heavier in the womb. Most doctors recommend a daily walk in the fresh air and housework during a normal pregnancy. Others feel it is wise to engage in any sport you wish, as long as you do not become over-tired. Some doctors advise only mild forms of exercise during the early months when the danger of miscarriage is greatest. If your doctor gives permission for you to engage in normal physical activity, the exercises listed as pre- and post-natal in the index are designed to help you become strong and flexible for carrying and delivering your baby and help you gain good muscle tone for regaining your normal figure after birth.

Preservation of the bustline is very important. Under that beautiful lifted line are the same pectoral muscles which every healthy human being has. If these muscles are functioning well because they are being worked, they will kept the breasts shapely. By wearing a good firm brassière (even to sleep) you can help prevent breakdown of tissue. After nursing a baby, the breasts usually become soft and lose some of their lift (exercises to overcome listed in index). What is lost in gland size can be made up in muscle size. If you look at those muscle-man magazines, you can see how a breast can be increased, even on a man, by the simple method of doing resistance exercise.

After the baby is born, the mother should do post-natal exercises, if the doctor has no reason to object. Usually he won't, because he is almost as anxious for the new mother to be steady on her feet and attractive when she takes over as she is. As soon after birth as she is rested enough to wink an eye, she should start to tighten here and there. At first nothing responds to that order, but soon there is a flicker and then a full response. (Check Limbering Series on page 228 and the Armchair Ballet.)

Nobody wants those platinum lines under the skin that seem to accompany childbearing. Any stretch to excess will cause them so KEEP YOUR WEIGHT DOWN. Also you can help your skin by keeping it lubricated. Don't overlook the value of sun and air.

The minute you know you are pregnant and have checked with your doctor, start getting in shape. Every minute counts, and nine months is hardly long enough for all the wonderful things you two have to do.

MENOPAUSE AND
THE PROMISING YOUNG MAN

On a particularly beautiful, somewhat nostalgic Indian summer afternoon, they were sitting together at the card table. The breeze that came in through the open windows carried a trace of burning leaves and warm earth. Perhaps it was the sense of summer ending, or the inescapable crowding presence of autumn and harvest, who knows? (We know as little about the effects the seasons have on us as the effects of color, smells and architecture.) However, Evelyn was moved to drop her bomb.

"Well girls, I'm menopausal." For years the word *menopausal* had been used by the four to describe any older woman who didn't meet their standards of grooming, mental alertness, physical attraction, in fact almost any shortcoming at all. It had always been their most unflattering adjective. Naturally, stares followed Evelyn's announcement.

"Yes, I've had my first *hot flash*. No question about

it kids, I'm menopausal." A shiver of apprehension went around the table. The breeze suddenly felt chill and unpleasant. The already dealt cards lay where they had fallen. While it was Evelyn who had sustained the first blast of winter, it couldn't be long before it touched each one of them. Four perfectly sound hearts were squeezed with anxiety. Four beautifully coiffed heads were filled with unfounded "facts of life." The fearsome stage had arrived.

Had Evelyn seen a doctor? No she hadn't. Well, didn't she think she ought to? After all, menopause had been known to cause all sorts of problems. Some women even went, well, they weren't quite themselves for a while. Then it began. Every old wives' tale and half-truth came pouring out.

Evelyn's symptoms got a thorough airing every Tuesday and by early spring, Marge, too, was reporting "hot flashes." Her periods became irregular and she had "splitting headaches." Then something very unusual and alarming took place. Marge the gay, the delightful, the lighthearted, so full of warm Irish humor, began to have "fits of depression." Her doctor gave her a check-up but could find nothing. She had a small fibroid tumor, but she'd had it for eight years, and if anything, it was smaller. He said she was in fine shape for fifty.

After the visit, Marge had gone home and looked for a long while at the face that stared back at her from the mirror. She'd never been one to think much about age. She had no fetishes about wrinkles or a double chin, but lately she'd begun to wonder if Harry was aware of the changes taking place in her. She'd always been so sure of him. Harry was such a good sort, stayed close to home, loved his family, home and golf. They'd always spent three weeks at the lake each summer and weekends were pleasant enough. Business was good and they had a fine life. Their sex life had slowed down some over the years, but when they felt the need for each other—up to now—it had always been warm and satisfying. Nothing was really different. Why, then, was she so depressed? Everybody grew older and fifty hadn't seemed so far along, not until she started "losing her capabilities."

Marge's emotional state is better understood if one knows that to the woman whose role is "mother" the reaffirmation of potential is a form of fulfillment. Each new neighborhood baby reminds her that she, too, could add another life to humanity if she just had the time or the space for another in her small house or if current expenses weren't so high. While she can think this way she is forever young, forever fertile, forever attractive, needed and fulfilled. What, then, is menopause to her? It is the end of spring, but not the beginning of summer. Menopause is the sudden break in the rhythm, the ominous silence between heart beat and beat—the promise that is no more.

Analogous to her is the fellow who for years has been considered a "young man of promise." One day he reaches the age of forty. He is so accustomed to his "promising" role that he cannot face being merely a man and retreats into a nervous breakdown. A man is not less because he arrives—a woman because she is no longer pregnant with the possibility of children.

Certainly there are some physical changes that come with the ending of the fertility cycle, but most of them can be controlled with medication. The unpredictable factor is the woman's attitude. If that is healthy, problems are rare. One of the really foolish fears at this time is the fear that sex will be lost to her. No matter how often doctors say that this doesn't happen, most women are convinced that it does. What they are confusing is the cause for the loss of the sex urge. Not menopause but laziness causes that to fade away. How many women over fifty (or men over forty) have kept the trim lines of youth? How many still look on life as an exciting adventure? One of the most embarrassing thoughts, if not impossible thoughts for adolescents to entertain, is the possibility of "oldsters" over forty making and enjoying love together. This is not because of the chronological connection, but *because of what they have permitted their bodies to become*. Women could save themselves a lot of grief if they would place blame in the right place and let menopause go its very normal way without tears or fanfare.

One day Marge's husband was sent overseas for UNESCO and Marge went along. She was hired as an interpreter and spent three exciting years being overworked, overstimulated and underfed. She lost fifteen pounds and her letters never mentioned another menopause symptom. Following her lead, Dot, too, got a job. That dissolved the bridge club. Evelyn's two sons seem to be trying to populate the world all by themselves and "Granny" is almost offering a bounty for each downy head. I never saw such a delighted lady in my life nor such a busy one. The importance of fertility is apparent still, but the proper shift has been made to the next generation and the whole family will probably live happily ever after.

Not so with Jean. Menopause for Jean is a disaster. She drifts as so many do, without reason or direction. But then she never had any before, either. The change in the only status she ever possessed found her unprepared either to slip into the excitement of interesting work or the substitution of another generation. She overeats and each disinterested glance in the mirror sends her scurrying to the icebox for more. Her husband's sidelong glances at attractive neighbors and perfect strangers send her into furies of jealousy, and quite naturally menopause gets the blame. It is certainly easier than accepting her own shortcomings.

Many of the discouraged and discontented—one might better call them the "discontinued"—envy the smooth cheeks and slim vital bodies of youngsters, thinking, "I'd change all of this if I were only young." They don't realize that they wouldn't change a thing. Youth is not the answer. Stronger perhaps, and fresher, it is also lacking in both first-hand experience and the ability to interpret correctly the experiences of others. Each of us has been given a problem to solve. It is unique in that it is ours and we are unique. Marge was fortunate in having a man who loved her and who took the trouble to show it. She also had good luck. A new experience was dropped in her lap just when she needed it. She would have deserved more credit for her successful negotiation of the menopausal shoals if she had foreseen the dangers and prepared for them. Marge was lucky.

The correct interpretation of another's experience helped Dot—plus her ability to go after what she felt was right. Evelyn, submerged in the altogether normal cycle of home, family and babies, accepted her continuation once removed gracefully and with enthusiasm. That's what she wanted to do anyway. There is no way of telling how it would have gone with her had she been denied any of the steps that led to her maternal satisfactions.

Is the proper handling then mostly a matter of luck or can we do something about it? We certainly can and tomorrow is not a day too soon. Children are born and spend a little time in our houses, but forever in our hearts. They grow up and go away taking their laughter with them. What then? Prepare now for the day when one of them comes with the "wonderful news" that she is marrying Bob, and they'll be stationed in Tokyo. Perhaps a son will inform you with all the fierce pride of the chosen, that he got the job in Brazil and leaves two weeks from Wednesday. A third wants an apartment so she can be "on her own." If you have looked at the future squarely and accepted these possibilities, you must also have wondered what you would do with your spare time. If not, do it now. Your life will have to be so full of interests that you can let them go emotionally as well as physically, and their going must not leave you empty.

If menopause is D Day, where do *you* stand? D Day minus twenty years gives you quite a bit of time to play with—just don't forget that you'll need to be starting a new life about then, and make plans. D Day minus a year or two means *start now*.

Before you can launch into a new phase you have to look and feel the part. Check the fitness tests and eight weeks from now check again to determine your progress. It will be considerable, but that's not the time to sit back. Keep at it from now on.

CHAPTER TWELVE

Special exercises for special problems

At one time or another during a lifetime, each one of us hits a snag. Some can be pretty difficult and stay with us a long time. We'll call these snags "specials" and treat them individually. Since no one knows what life has in store for him, it behooves us all to stay in the best possible condition all the time. That way we are set for surprises. If, on the other hand, something has already occurred that shakes us up, we should take comfort in the fact that there is *always* something to be done to improve our lot.

"Specials" include such misfortunes as the bad back and the coronary, the lady who is afraid to move because of her varicose veins or her hysterectomy, or the man whose brush with death has left him partially paralyzed. The person who can't hear and the one who can't see have special problems. Here are the questions for the little black book:

1. *Exactly what is my special problem?*
(If you have a back like a board when you get out of bed each morning, you will have no trouble answering that one.)

2. *What exactly do I want?*
I once asked that of a bitter young man who had lost his left leg in Korea, and he almost screamed: "I want my leg back, damn it." Well, there are limitations. If he had said, "I want to ski the Nose Dive next January," I would

have said "Fine." Try to make your wanting within the realm of possibility. The higher you aim, the farther you can go, but let your aim be possible.

3. *How much can I get?*
That depends on the material you will be working with —yourself—and the difficulty that will attend your effort, and just how much you are willing to put into it. We'll describe a few people who were willing to work—sometimes inhumanly hard—and you will be able to see how far *they* went. This may be encouraging to you. It was to me.

4. *What is my major weakness?*
This is not the simple question it appears to be at first glance. A blind person can't see, but that is *not* his major weakness. Since he cannot see, he is not quite the same in one respect as the person who can. His weakness may be an inability to orient himself in space. It might be lack of balance, or a fear of people. It might be the feeling of being excluded, helpless or forgotten. These weaknesses are just as real and serious as the recurrent muscle spasms of the angina heart patient. They can be just as difficult to manage as the unpredictable contractions of the person with cerebral palsy. List the areas in which you think you should be stronger.

5. *Where is my major strength?*
The amputee or polio patient may find that the limb left to him is inordinately strong or that his shoulders and arms are able to help out. The deaf person finds he has the knack of reading lips, the back sufferer, that he has developed all sorts of ways to save himself effort. Sometimes, if things are really bad, the only strength you seem to have is the will to hang on. This is the greatest strength of all. I once saw a great hulking man who had neither a scratch or a pain, reduced to tears, gasping and vomiting, because he lacked this ingredient in the face of an emergency. I also saw a little boy whose mangled body had been very nearly torn in half under a speeding car. They had wrapped him gently in a sheet in the hope of

holding him together, and as they laid him on the stretcher he looked up with a grin at the young intern, and whispered, "Hi, Doc." Something in the man was dead. Something in the boy burned with a bright flame. It was the will to hang on, to fight back.

6. *How do I begin?*

At the very beginning, do as little or as much as you can for as long as five minutes. You start by understanding the problem. After that, you will, like everyone else, set up a program in your little black book. And you will stick to that program as if your life depended on it—because it does.

Let's begin with the back sufferer. He is numbered in the millions, and back pain can ruin a life faster than the loss of an arm. The first thing you should know about backache is that its chief cause is muscle deficiency. Eighty per cent of all the backaches in the United States can be traced to muscles that are either too weak or too inflexible. Sometimes they fail in both areas. The Minimum Muscle Test was given to over five thousand back patients, who were also tested by a whole group of doctors ranging from orthopedists and neurosurgeons to gynecologists, psychiatrists and internists. They were X-rayed and given blood and urine tests. Everything was done to make the examinations thorough. Twenty per cent had something organically wrong, but eighty per cent merely flunked the muscle test. When the eighty per cent were given a program of therapeutic exercises, they passed the test and lost their pain. Then, being human, they went home and sat down. In no time at all, back they came with the same pain and the same muscle failures. Brought to safe levels again, they recovered. You must understand right at the outset that *there is a level of muscular fitness below which you may never go,* and this is no different for you than for anyone else.

If your doctor has told you that your X-rays show nothing is wrong he is not hinting that your backache is really in your head, although it is a rare backache that isn't accompanied by tension. The damaging muscle injury may have occurred years before during a modern dance class or soccer game, been sore for a while and then disappeared only to reappear now when you are under pressure.

A typical back sufferer is the man who played sports all through school, played tennis and swam for two or three years after school and then had to "buckle down to business." With success came the need to "make it while the going was good." There was no time for exercise, and too much time for selling—under highly caloric conditions. Our man put on fifteen or twenty pounds. One day he leaned over to pick up his brief case and couldn't straighten up. He felt as though a knife were in his back. A muscle had gone into spasm. (See earlier discussion of muscle spasm.)

Once a perfectly delightful friend of mine listed to port. His back looked like a sidewise hump. Three days before, he'd started on a backache when he got out of bed and it was getting worse. What could he do? He had a TV show to do tonight. I asked him if he could straighten at all. Oh yes, he could straighten. The only trouble was, if he straightened, his left foot came six inches off the floor.

The first spasm had hurt him, and pain leads to more spasm. The muscle had responded by tightening further and hurting him more. That brought in the neighboring muscles one by one or in bunches. Pretty soon he couldn't tell where it had all begun. He was under terrific pressure (most TV people are) and tonight was the night. The mere fact of a deadline is often enough to make a back even worse.

I have another young friend who is a writer. She wrote for a national magazine for a long time—with all the attendant frustrations of such a position. She had a very responsible job, and she had to be right. Over-tense and caught in the three-hour three-martini lunch trap, she put on weight, lost tone and met deadline after deadline. She used to get up from the typewriter, put both hands in the small of her back, straighten out slowly with many painful grimaces and some choice epithets, walk around the office two or three times and sag back into her chair. Life sometimes wasn't worth a roll of typewriter ribbon. Needless to say, her private life wasn't easy. It almost never is for people with backaches.

Then there was my friend who was pregnant. She had no physical outlets at all. A maid took over any muscle work in the house. As pregnancy progressed, my friend sat more and more. When she'd sit for a while, the "jelling" pain on rising was so unbearable, she'd go lie down. She began to worry.

Well, what do we do about it? None of the people I described had anything the doctors could pin down as pathological. On the other hand one can't spend years on a heating pad eating aspirin. What caused the trouble? Weakness, inflexibility and tension. My TV friend had tension to burn and hadn't played so much as a game of golf in ten years. My pregnant friend wasn't fit for much activity in the first place and the weight of her growing child had pulled her so far out of line that she didn't have the strength to hold the adjusting position.

Next time you see your doctor, ask him if he objects to your giving yourself the Minimum Fitness Test on page 30. If you flunk, you know where the trouble lies, but before you can do any tough exercises, you will need the "limbering series." Ask him if you may try them.

A

135 The Limbering Series

A. Lie supine with knees bent and arms resting at your sides. Bring the left knee as close to the nose as possible. Lie back and stretch the left leg straight about ten inches above the bed or floor. Return to beginning position and relax for *three seconds*. Alternate legs and do four repetitions on each side.

B

B. Roll over onto your right side and take a comfortable relaxed position. Draw the left knee up as close to the

chest as possible. Stretch the leg down parallel with the resting leg, but about ten inches above it. Lower the leg and rest for *three seconds*. Do four repetitions.

C

C. Continue the roll over action until you are prone with head resting on bent arms. Tighten seat and abdominals. Hold for five seconds. Relax for three seconds. Repeat four times.

D

D. Roll still further until you are resting on your left side and do the same exercise as you did in B.

E

E. Finish the roll over on your back with knees bent as in A. Arch your back *slightly*, keeping both seat and shoulders touching the floor. Press the spine down hard, keeping it flat to the floor, tilt the pelvis as far as you can and hold for five seconds. Relax for three seconds. Do four repetitions.

Exercises to keep back muscles relaxed and limber will only work if done often throughout the day *before* tension has a chance to build up. Start the Limbering Series before you even get out of bed and keep at it throughout the day. Eight times is not too often, but less than five times is too little.

At the first sign of a twinge, down you go. Don't be satisfied with one complete revolution. Whenever you have time for two, take it. Don't hurry the exercises. Half the trouble is tension, anyway, and you will have to teach your body to relax. Here's your chance.

After you are without pain, you can start to add some of the general exercises. Use the ones you need first (they are indicated with the tests). If you have a posture problem, correct it. You will always be under strain as long as you are out of line. The correcting exercises are listed with the posture faults in the index.

BE SURE TO SLEEP ON A HARD BED. There are special mattresses and bed boards, but a slab of quarter inch plywood slid under your present mattress may do as well. If you share a double bed and your partner complains, tell him or her that the sexercises work far better on a hard mattress than on a soft one, and also, that everyone gets used to the change in surface in less than a week. Not only that, but neither of you will be as tired in the morning—backache or no backache. The word "soft" should always frighten you.

Time and again, women came to my exercise classes not to exercise, but to be assured that they can go back home and sit down. They'd love to exercise, they tell me, but they just had a hysterectomy or they have had two children by Caesarean section and *naturally* that leaves them out. No such thing. Whatever happens to you, if you want to live, *what's left has to move*. I merely sympathize with them for the work they are going to have to do to get their figures back. Then I put them in attractive tights and into class. Operations are usually done so that you can get back to enjoying life—not so that you can have an excuse to avoid it. You will go back in easy stages. If the operation was abdominal and recent—and by that I mean the last few weeks—take it easy for a while. Start with the "Armchair Ballet" (see index) when the doctor says you can. (By the way, tell him what you intend to do. Don't just say "exercise." Doctors have hundreds of professional publications to read each year just to stay abreast of their specialties and the word "exercise" can mean anything from barbells to knee bends. Then, with his permission, get going.)

After you have some of your strength back (which should be in a week) start with the Limbering Series. After two weeks with those exercises, you will be ready for real action. Then test yourself and get at it.

If the operation took place some time ago, what are you waiting for? If you are fit to get around, you are fit to build yourself up. The only admonition is—start *slowly* and stick with it. Just by way of reminder, eat a high protein diet.

I know an unfortunate lady whose even more unfortunate family is being made to suffer day in and day out. The lady, once slender and attractive with a most disarming smile, spends every waking hour eating bitterness and pastry. She calls herself "the little half chick." A year ago she underwent breast surgery which today has replaced what used to be certain death from breast cancer. A woman's breasts bespeak her womanliness. They are connected with children, love and beauty—and to lose one or both breasts can be both painful and shocking. BUT IT ISN'T THE END.

I have had the good fortune to work with many women who have had this type of operation. One spring at my crash course at Springfield College, there were two ladies who waited to tell me until the course was almost over that they had recently undergone the operation and had come to get their figures and confidence back. That means they weren't quite sure it was the right thing to do, but didn't want to be stopped. Far from stopping them, I would have introduced them to each other and given them extra exercises. As it was, everything turned out just fine. After three days in class, they, like all the other women, were in tights and leotards and far too busy to be self-conscious. Through those ten murderous days of fitness classes they never peeped, but at the end they proudly exhibited full range of motion of the arms—and also that one arm did just as well as the other. Their carriage had improved dramatically. Anyone who has observed my classes comes away with the indelible impression that I spend nine-tenths of the time shouting "Get your bust UP" or "Tighten your abdominals." I probably do, but it's necessary. These two ladies had learned the lesson.

Again comes the admonition to start easy. The stiff shoulder series (see index) should be used along with the Armchair Ballet and Limbering. Ask your doctor if there are any exercises in these groups you should not do. If he gives you the go ahead, go ahead. Start with five-minute stints ten times each day. That mounts up to less than an hour and you won't be more than a little tired. If you are, you certainly needed it.

While we're in the area, let's talk about painful shoulders that show nothing in X-rays—and your doctor says that fortunately there's nothing wrong with the darn thing except it hurts. Well, if there isn't anything to pin it on, look for a habit. I had one. Years ago, when rope tows were in fashion and every lazy skier was pulled up the mountainside by a continuous rope, I had both shoulders injured when the skier ahead of me snapped the rope as he got off. About five years later, I started having trouble brushing my hair. The pain in my right shoulder was so excruciating that I seriously considered having my hair cut so short that I could shake it into place. X-rays were negative and there wasn't any reason for me to have a pain. That sure makes you feel like a fool. You can't very well say, "But doctor . . ." Then I remembered reading somewhere that wrong movements could cause trouble. I started watching myself. My tennis shots were hard but flat. No top spin was to blame. I carried heavy loads, but not overhead and it never hurt to carry. I rode horseback, but reining in was a clean bilateral pull-back motion. Fortunately I was so intent on finding that "wrong action" that I even worked at it in my sleep. One night I woke up with the pain burning in my shoulder. I lay perfectly still wondering what was causing it. Both arms were overhead, almost touching the top of the bed. I had to move slowly and with considerable pain to get them down. *That* may be the criminal I thought. The next day I bought a pair of heavy cotton pajamas and a big safety pin. That night I pinned my right pajama sleeve to the pants and went to bed. Ten times each day I did the shoulder series and three days later the pain was gone. It comes back every so often, and when it does I go for my pajamas, safety pin and shoulder series.

Years later I met a doctor who worked on the same theory. A man with a bad shoulder, irritable disposition and no time at all, came into his office. What sports did he play? None. Did he use his arm at work? He was an executive and worked with his head! Well, describe your day. After the description it was clear that the only habitual thing this man did all day was telephone. Then came the crucial question—"Where do you have your telephone?" The man made a twisting motion reaching behind him for an imaginary phone. The motion immediately caused a grimace of pain. *There* it was and the sleuthing was over for the day. Prescription? Move the phone.

Old injuries plus bad habits of motion are good for a pain almost any year.

Doctors tell me that varicose veins are hereditary, but nobody needs to look like a road map of Long Island. Standing still too long at a job, or having babies seems to hurry their appearance, but keeping in good shape will retard them. The walls of the veins and arteries are muscular too, and if the muscular parts of you are in good tone they have a better chance than if they are soggy and flabby. Then, too, the simple action of squeezing the blood along as muscles contract is an assist. There is one thing to remember. If your doctor recommends "stripping" or removing the broken down veins, the recovery time is cut way down and the results far superior if you are in top condition. That goes for any operation, incidentally. If the legs are very bad, ask your doctor if you may do the lying-down exercises which will put no strain on legs, but will improve strength and flexibility as well as circulation. Take the book right to him so that he knows what you are talking about.

One day Harold walked into my Institute. It was a great and new day for me because it was then that I started to learn about a whole new world. Harold was blind. He was also weak, had a terrible walk and did disconcerting things with his hands to his eyes. When his mother was talking to me, his non-seeing eyes would rove all over the office or he'd be pushing his knuckles against them as though they itched. I asked him why he did it, and he said he didn't realize he was doing anything at all. This was a good clue for later when all sorts of jigsaw pieces fell into place.

Harold wanted to be an athlete. He was a good chess player, pianist, writer, cook. But he wanted at the quite natural age of eleven to be an athlete. Chances were pretty dim because he did very poorly at baseball, basketball and volleyball (our national sports), and you can't swim all year round. We started Harold in exercise class, and from him I learned that you don't have to see to do gymnastics, tumbling, judo, wrestling, track or lifting weights. In fact, all you need for those things is determination and guts. At the end of the second year, Harold was doing fine in all of those fields and had won the gold cup we give each year for courage.

Harold prepared me for the many blind people I have met since. Alice was a blind gentlewoman farmer whose sheep insisted on heading for distant thickets when their lambs were due. The well-insulated sheep were unaware of the danger to newborns often born in sleet storms, and Alice had no way of knowing where the delivery room was. If you can't find wandering sheep, how do you keep them home? Alice shaved the heads of all expectant ewes and the first icy blast drove them back into warm shelter where lambs could be born in safety.

Then there was the pretty little twenty-year-old who attended a clinic I held for a state organization in New York. After the lecture I set up all sorts of equipment from sawhorses and ramps to rocking platforms. The sighted helped with the blind, but after a turn or two this one very lithe and graceful girl was bouncing on and off everything like a trained gymnast. I said she must have been awfully good in school. "Oh no, I never did this sort of thing in school. The teachers were all afraid I'd hurt myself." What a waste of childhood!

Today I often have blind students in my classes. They have learned the exercises from my records and plan to teach other blind and even sighted people. After all, movement and rhythm are for everyone.

The first thing a blind person must know and accept is that he (or she) must start at once to widen his horizons. The more protected and pampered, the more impossible will his life become. The first thing to be considered is physical fitness. Blind or sighted, a good body is a must, but blind, it is the key to freedom. The exercises in this book can be done by anyone whether or not he or she can see. Start first with the Armchair Ballet, then the Limbering Series. Use music all the time to improve your rhythm and ultimately your balance. *Omit no exercise* and pay tremendous attention to the walk exercises. Instead of using a crack in the floor, lay a strip of adhesive down and walk on it barefoot so you know where you are. Do the stair exercises until the neighbors think that's where you live. Find a place where you can safely walk *fast* without anyone's help. When you have gotten your directions, start slow running. Harold used to run our track following another boy. The Boy Scouts are very helpful when it comes to providing running "pacers." *Stop depending on other people.* I know of one school for blind kids that permits them to travel from room to room *only when led.* I saw a camp that "protects" its inmates by stringing wires all over the place. One mother who visited me with her blind twelve-year-old was wiser. She took her out in the fields and let her run through the high grass at will—*just to feel freedom.*

Do hand and arm exercises and pay attention to what they are doing all the time. Stop looking into space and looking past people when they talk to you. You may need someone to show you exactly where to look when people talk. Later the sound will help, and the habit more than anything. Develop habits that may seem ridiculous at first, such as using a mirror for make-up, looking at the finger-nail you are clipping. And *clip* them. You can, you know. At first you may clip too short, but you'll learn. Make a science of the whole business. All of a sudden, life will be very exciting. If you plan to get a guide dog—and you should—keep in mind that you *and the dog* must be fit. There should be time set aside for both of you to walk and run free. There is nothing so beaten looking as a dragging moth-eaten dog accompanying a dragging moth-eaten mistress or master. Feed both of you properly. Groom both of you carefully. Do your exercise daily and then, with your head held up, you will be the equal of *anybody* as well as equal to *anything*.

The blind tell me that it would be worse to be deaf. I can't understand this, but maybe they are right. However, for the deaf, who can see danger ahead, it should be physically easier to avoid some problems, but they, too, must have strong bodies and quick reactions just as any-one else. And if there is partial hearing, they must be on guard against constant turning of the head and tensing of neck muscles which can lead to the condition called fibrositis. Be sure, if total or partial deafness is your dif-ficulty, to use all the exercises for tension many times throughout the day. Try not to withdraw from people simply because you cannot hear what they are saying. Sometimes it isn't worth very much anyway, but their companionship is. Sports can be enjoyed without talk and so can the art of love. I remember being very much in love (for two delightful summer days when I was sixteen) with a German boy in Heidelberg. We had a marvelous time, and I know we didn't understand one single word of each other's language. We were good mountaineers, however, and we danced well together. We were attractive with the beauty of youth which doesn't need much help. You can be good looking, strong and flexible if you set your mind to it and there are all sorts of things to be done in this world. Get into top physical shape, then learn something entirely new, then go enjoy it.

Some amputees are stay-at-homes but I've never known one. I met Burt at Pico Peak the year I joined the ski patrol. I was a good first-aider, but was still having lots of trouble getting over the fear born of my ski-fractured pelvis. I was so embarrassed to be wearing the brassard of the Patrol while I fell over myself that I took to standing still. When no one was around, I'd grit my teeth and bomb a few feet, black out with terror—and fall again. One day a tall boy was standing still on a hummock with me. We were both covered with the kind of snow that doesn't come out of the sky, but out of a sitz mark. He grinned at me and said, "Nobody'll believe how hard it was snowing up here." I grinned back and he took off. His right turns were stupendous, but on the second turn left, he was down. I skied down to where he was standing, brushing snow off his pants and he said, "That was better, you weren't so tense—that's because you weren't thinking of the turn, but my fall." I laughed and said I'd go ahead and fall too. Maybe it would help him. We spent a wonderful afternoon and only later that evening did I learn that he had been a very promising racer and lost his leg in a race only a year before. He had been trying a new invention on his prosthesis, trying to improve those left turns. I've met lots of one-legged skiers, since—some who lost legs after they'd learned to ski and others who took it up simply as a challenge. Real skiers are a funny bunch. The first question they ask in the emergency room after they've had an accident is "When can I ski again?" If this be insanity, it's a very healthy and enviable form. All amputees should be so crazy.

Amputees are missing all or parts of one or more limbs. The rest has to take over—just how much or how well depends far less on the extent of the maiming than on the drive and desire of the individual. If there is an abundance of those two ingredients, the rest may not be easy but it will be interesting and successful.

Mark was seventeen, good looking and too bright. He did more thinking than seventeens can usually handle and not enough moving. He liked cars that went fast and boats that went faster. One night in a fog his fast boat met up with a very slow rock and he lost a leg. He spent six months waiting for the soreness to leave his stump and the ache to go out of his heart. Then he came to us.

Mark's frame was good, but he'd never done much with it. He hadn't been team-type material in school so he was undeveloped physically. Our job was to give him a body and a reason for living. He wasn't exactly for it. He *was* game, however, and we put him through some pretty grim days. Parris Island has nothing on us when we get going. He wrestled, learned Judo, did apparatus and tumbling. He lifted weights and did knee bends until he could do as many as the other boys with two legs. Then one day he fell in love. According to my way of thinking, that's always great inspiration. I learned to get along in two foreign languages simply by falling in love with boys who spoke them. We sent Mark up to ballroom dancing. A year or two earlier, with two legs, he would have balked like a steer. Now, wanting very much to be noticed, he practiced rhumbas and mambos by the hour. Anyone who is missing one leg will limp unless he is fully trained in rhythm and has power to burn. It turned the trick. The exercise gave him the power—especially in the abdominals. The dancing gave him the rhythm and the girl gave him the reason. Mark is much too busy to be bitter about that long-ago accident. He went back to school, then college, graduated, married (sorry, different girl), has two children and a good job. He knows that for the rest of his life he will have to exercise hard to stay ahead, but then so should anyone living in our too comfortable society.

If this is your difficulty, get going first on abdominal and back exercises, even before you work on the limbs remaining. The trunk is by far the most important part of your body—and usually the first and most neglected. After all the exercises have become familiar, start adding resistance.

The loss of any limb brings the danger of imbalance. That is one good reason for trying to replace the missing member with a prosthesis. A history teacher I know who has been without his left arm since he was sixteen, does absolutely everything anyone else can do—from flipping open a can of beer to chopping wood. He wears no prosthesis, and as far as practicality goes, really needs none. However, his left side weighs less, it takes less muscle to twist that side of his body, and he has a tendency to lift his left shoulder, rather than hold his shoulders even. If these are difficulties for you or someone you know, call attention to the shoulder exercises, especially the tension reliever and also the upper back and abdominal exercises.

Mrs. Case was no youngster. She had married a second time, had the responsibility of bringing up two healthy and obstreperous grandchildren and thought living was the greatest thing anybody could spend his life on. I hadn't seen her in a long time and I was upset to find her leaning on a cane and limping along in obvious pain. She thought she had "a touch of arthritis" and "no, she hadn't bothered the doctor; he had enough to do without old biddies pestering about their lumbago." I didn't like the looks of things so I badgered her into seeing her doctor. He packed her off to a specialist and the next I saw Mrs. Case she had come in "to be reconditioned." The ball and socket joint in the hip had begun to disintegrate, and the surgeons had performed an operation in which they fashion a new socket which is then set into the pelvis and made fast. The ball part of the joint is made fast to the top of the femur, the long bone running from hip to knee. Too often, operations are a complete success, but the patient gets no benefit from them. The doctor informed me that this patient was to get full benefit from his hard work, and I was to see to it that she exercised correctly and built up the muscles she would need. I will always remember Mrs. Case, legs waving, perspiration, gasps and groans. Three days a week like clock-work with never a complaint, and cascades of laughter. First we went after the trunk muscles. Then lateral leg stretches because she hadn't done anything like that since the operation. I was quite sure she expected to come unstuck somewhere along the line, but she kept at it. We did all the flexibility exercises, not just those for the operated area. Mrs. Case didn't have a muscle we didn't find and work. It took six months, but she walked tall and proud when it was over—and has ever since.

Unless there's an absolutely valid reason why you should not move, exercise helps. Sometimes it's the difference between dying and living, and it is always the difference between excellent and indifferent performance.

There is more discussion today about heart attacks than any other disease. It happens to our men more often than to our women—at least until the onset of menopause. There are many theories about the causes of heart disease and they change with the seasons, but there are observations that remain constant. Fat is a contributing factor and so is a poor level of physical fitness. How many fat eighty-year-olds do you know? Not many. Octogenarians are usually thin, spry and have years of considerable activity behind them. A study done in England revealed that twice as many inactive people have heart attacks as do active ones, and in the first attack, twice as many die. If for no other statistics than these, it behooves us to MOVE. But now let's suppose that the worst has befallen and you have your attack. The orders will be "exercise as soon as possible." If you had to cop one, be glad it's now and not twenty years ago when you weren't permitted even to bat an eye at a pretty nurse. In fact I think it was my father who told me all pretty nurses were forbidden to enter the heart wards lest somebody die of sheer imagination.

How do you begin to exercise after a heart attack? First you ask the doctor if there's any reason why you shouldn't have a small rubber ball. He'll probably say it's too soon for a game of "catch." At that point you explain that you wish to squeeze that little rubber ball and get back your hand strength. That will probably be all right with him. You take that ball and you squeeze it every time you think of it—but with a system.

136　The Squeeze
Lying supine, hold ball in right hand as it rests at side. Squeeze—relax. Then shift ball to other hand and squeeze —relax. Do this simple exercise for a few days then add the "clock."

137　The Clock
Start with the ball in your left hand at "twelve o'clock," which is overhead. Squeeze once and relax. Move the

hand clockwise to "one o'clock." Your arm will be a few inches away from your head. Go on to "two o'clock" and at "three o'clock" it will be at right angles to your body with the hand over the edge of the bed. Keep squeezing once to the move. After the left hand has finished at "six o'clock," the right takes over. Repeat "six o'clock" and go on up to "twelve." If you tire along the way, *stop*. Rest, look at TV, close your eyes—anything you wish, but one hour later, start over.

138 Time Clock

That was pretty easy you feel. Well there's no trick at all to making it difficult. Start holding the squeeze for two seconds and then relaxing. Keep track of your efforts. If you get round the clock once every hour at two seconds per squeeze, and you start at 9 A.M. (what else can you do?) and quit at 9 P.M. you will have contracted one or another group of muscles one hundred eighty-two times. ("Twelve" and "six" o'clock got two squeezes.) As they were held for two seconds each, you worked those muscles hard for six minutes and four seconds. By the simple expedient of working every half hour (like I said—what else can you do, they certainly won't give you a phone), and holding each contraction five seconds, you will net twenty-nine minutes and ten seconds workout in twelve hours.

139 I Must, I Must, Develop My Bust

This is a wonderful exercise for doing what it says, but men need not worry, nothing unusual will happen! Clasp your hands together over the ball with fingers laced. The ball should be held a little outside of the palms, more on the heels of the hands. Squeeze—relax. Now insert this maneuver between each hour position. This will carry your arms in and out as well as utilize the hand contractions.

140 The Check List

Fortunately and importantly, you are not just hands and arms. Keep the ball in your two hands. You will squeeze and relax your hands in between each of the next contractions. This will help you to relax in other parts of your body. The idea in this exercise is to get a clean, complete contraction and relaxation of each area. The longer it takes, the better. Speed only causes the two opposing actions to run together.

With legs and feet parallel, curl your toes. Relax. Squeeze the ball, relax.
Point toes—relax—squeeze ball—relax.
Rotate feet outward—curl toes—relax—squeeze ball—relax.
In rotated position, point toes, relax—squeeze ball—relax.
Rotate feet inward—curl toes—relax—squeeze ball—relax.
Return to parallel position—tighten knees—relax—squeeze ball —relax.
Tighten thighs—relax. From now on, it is understood that you will squeeze the ball and relax it after each new contraction.
Rotate feet outward—tighten knees—relax.
In outward rotation—tighten thighs—relax.
Rotate feet inward—tighten knees—relax.
Same position—tighten thighs—relax.
Feet parallel—tighten seat and levator ani (check sexercise Chapter 7)—relax.
Tighten abdominals—relax.
Rotate feet outward—tighten seat and levator—relax.
Tighten abdominals—relax.
Raise head and look down at toes—lie back and relax.
Turn head to right and raise—relax.
Turn head to left and raise—relax.

All the above "Check List" exercises done with one second contractions add up to seven minutes and two seconds in the contracted state and probably close to fifteen minutes' worth of workout time. If you do that every hour, with your doctor's permission, you'll be spending one quarter of every day building yourself up. If you had given a fraction of the days that went before your attack to this most profitable pastime, you'd look like a million, feel like a million and you wouldn't be in the hospital. Never mind. Get to work and get into shape. A mild heart attack is the best thing in the world for bringing home true values. While you are busy contracting, start planning what you are going to do with the life you have suddenly found so invaluable.

Needless to say, you can make this workout tougher by holding the contractions longer or adding contractions. If you happen to be in a room with someone else who has your problem and has a doctor who believes in mobilization, work together—it's more fun. *However do not set up any competition.*

After you have improved considerably and the doctor comes in one morning with that smug satisfied look that means "Thank God this one's okay," ask him if you may hustle along into the Limbering Series on page 228. This you do along with, not instead of, the foregoing.

When you graduate to a chair, ask the poor long-suffering doctor to look over the Armchair Ballet. Don't forget to use music whenever you can. I think one of the funniest sights I ever saw was a friend of mine who had had a coronary lying in his bed wearing the ear plug to one of those tiny transistor radios, tightening and relaxing, with a beatific smile on his face and in perfect silence. On his night table was a complete list of his exercises and the number of minutes he was devoting to it. He was so charmed with his records that he had just enough time to say hello and get back to work.

Almost anyone stuck in bed will find these exercises helpful. There are very few conditions under which strict immobilization is ordered. The man in traction with the compound fracture had better tighten and relax the rest of him or he'll get the shock of his life when they let him up. The rules to observe are:

1. Get the doctor's permission.
2. Don't ever over-do. If you are tired, you did. Do a little less until you have worked back your strength.
3. Start with next to nothing and work up.
4. Keep a record of what you did each day, and if you feel fine, try to do a little more the next day.

CHAPTER THIRTEEN

Retirement: An end or a beginning?

I used to think that forty was old. Now I'm not even sure about eighty. I've come to believe that there's no reason in the world why people can't go along being active, good looking and vigorous until they are ninety. Then it's permissible if they slow down a little. The day of the chimney corner, however, is long gone, and anyone who sits in one does so at his peril.

Aging brings changes to be sure, but most of these changes are brought on by habits that are far more telling than the accumulation of years. Habits assumed by both our bodies *and our minds* determine in large measure not only how long we shall live, but how well we shall live and even by what means we shall take our departure.

Every fall I spend a day with two elderly friends in the country. We have been friends since I was seventeen, and I know a little about the way they think and a great deal about the way they have lived their lives. One fall, we sat up late on Saturday, and there was so much to talk about that we went on till after midnight. The old gentleman and I had canceled out each other's Presidential votes, and the arguments were hot and heavy. I envied his concise thinking and his wealth of historical knowledge.

Sunday morning I heard him go downstairs at six-thirty, and I rolled over for another snooze. He woke me at nine because I had promised to go walking with him and he had waited patiently long enough! After breakfast we started out. He had found some seedling oaks we had to see. They were on top of a high hill. The rocks in the lower glen were covered with some new kind of ivy and I shouldn't miss it. Would I like some azaleas for my garden? He had some beautiful species, and they were only a quarter of a mile away. We'd hardly gotten there and marked the selections when he had a wonderful idea. We had ridden horseback together every Saturday and Sunday for many years, and the bridlepath had been unused for some time because a parkway had cut off the access. Why not take a stroll over there and look around?

After lunch we had to part, unfortunately, because I was headed back to town and he had a date with his sister-in-law for their usual daily three-mile walk.

My young friend is over eighty. He has white hair and stands as straight as the cavalry officer he once was. His skin is smooth and a fresh pink color. His collars are too big for him because his wife took me seriously when I said, "If you love him, reduce him—he's getting a spare tire." I would rather spend a day with this wise, educated, interested and interesting gentleman, than with any other man I know.

His wife used to beat me at tennis. She won every game we ever played until she was over sixty. Then *I* gave up tennis for serious rock climbing. I have the uncomfortable suspicion that if she put her mind to it, she could beat me today. She, too, is bright, interested and interesting. Artistic and a painter, she is a grandmother with much to offer. Two years ago, she fell as she was getting into a boat and stirred up an old knee injury. Way overweight, she hobbled about all out of balance and pretty soon her hip began to show the typical arthritic symptoms caused by "old age." "You are overweight," I told her. "You are overweight," her husband told her. Finally she looked in the mirror and said to herself, "I am overweight." That, of course, was the turning point. She took off thirty pounds, her aging hip grew young again, she tossed her cane in a corner, got a new permanent and went on a trip with her oldest granddaughter, who is my oldest daughter, Petie.

These two people have always been active, but they are not two of a kind. She was a natural athlete with tennis as a hobby all her life. He was an awkward little boy and everything had to be painstakingly learned. Born in Europe, he walked (even as we did once upon a time). He hiked, climbed mountains and rode horseback. One thing they had in common, however—everything they had done as children they carried into adulthood. What they were doing as young adults they were still doing in their middle and late-middle age. Now, by chronological standards, they are old. Physically and mentally, however, they are still very young, active and enjoying the adventure of life. They've had physical troubles. The big problem just now is his eyesight. He will have an operation soon, but in his condition, it should be a complete success. They've had tragedy too. I don't know anyone who lives very long who doesn't come up against it some time, but they survived, and found that time is really the healer they say it is—if you help a little.

The two biggest problems that older folks face are dependence, due to physical deterioration, and loneliness, due to mental attitudes. BOTH OF THESE ARE IN YOUR OWN HANDS. The second problem is more closely related to the first than most people suspect. The body, mind and heart have the same needs and desires as young bodies, minds and hearts, yet most people act as though old people live on a different planet. If Aunt Martha gets a twinge in her shoulder, she is urged to rest it—preferably in a sling. If she does, it gets rusty. Then it hurts more. If it hurts, she will move it less, and pretty soon she can't turn over in bed. I met Aunt Martha four years ago, and she was quite an old lady. She called up to find out exactly what type of wheel chair she should use. I told her my job was to get people out of wheel chairs—not put them into wheel chairs—and what was her trouble? "Old age," she snapped. I guess I snapped, too, when I told her that that was no excuse for quitting. We had quite a chat! It ended when I told her I couldn't say anything more on the phone, and she would save both of us time if she'd come in to the office. I never expected to see her, but in

246

she came about a week later. To be truthful, she didn't look so good. I asked her if she had been sick in bed recently. In bed? Yes, she always spent Monday, Tuesday and Wednesday in bed. Sick? Not unless you called rheumatism, arthritis, and a miserable backache sick. The trouble was, she couldn't get about any more and would I *now* tell her which chair.

A lot of questions elicited the information that her doctor had told her she was suffering from old age, and that with her years she'd just have to bear it. She liked bridge, but two of her friends were also housebound, fortunately in the same house. When she and their "fourth" couldn't get around any more, there would go the game. She definitely needed that chair. I asked her if she wouldn't rather go on foot without a backache.

What did I mean by that? I explained that her bed rest routine was the worst thing she could do for herself unless there was a medical reason. No, she said, no doctor had ordered her off to bed, it was her own idea for "conserving energy." We put her on an exercise routine, to be done ten minutes out of every two hour period every day in the week—no time out for Sundays. You know the type of old lady Aunt Martha was, indomitable. Furthermore, she really *wanted* to play bridge.

In six months, Aunt Martha was walking three miles a day. She had badgered her housebound friends into joining her on the floor. The fourth wasn't allowed to escape into "old age" either. Those four little dears kited off to Athens last summer (in a jet naturally) and they haven't returned yet.

The end of life comes to everyone soon enough, but Aunt Martha learned that it was quite unnecessary to hurry it. For all I know she prolonged her stay on this planet long enough for a quick trip to the moon. In any case, she has certainly spiked the present with excitement and independence. I know a lot of young folks who have neither.

I learned a great deal about old people when I did a pilot study on "Exercise and Age" in a home for retired ladies over seventy. I had been asked to lecture on my first book, *Is Your Child Really Fit?* One look at my audience convinced me that they couldn't care less, but probably had nothing better to do with the morning. Without a backward look at the youth of America, I altered my lecture to "Over Seventy, The Last Fit Americans." I talked about *their* childhoods and how much they had done in comparison with today's children. We talked about the bodies they had once built and about the aches and pains they had developed through dis- and misuse. We argued the merits of various brands of girdles and bras. (Do you really think that elderly ladies and gentlemen are less vain than young ones?) I showed them the exercises needed for their stiff backs and creaky knees. They tapped their feet and bounced their hands to wild Russian music. We had quite a ball! After it was over they asked if I could possibly give them a class, and we started two weeks later.

THE ARMCHAIR BALLET

(The armchair ballet is good for anyone who must get off to a slow start.) All of these exercises should be done to music—first slow and later a stepped-up tempo.

141   The Knee Lift
Place both hands under the upper leg and lift as high as possible. This strengthens arms and stretches the back. After doing this a few times, lift the leg as before, but then remove the supporting hands and try to maintain the lifted position of the leg. Lower *slowly* and alternate four on each side. This exercises the abdominals and thighs, stretches the back unilaterally, and prepares for harder work. When the knee lift has become easy, replace with the following exercise.

142 Knee Kiss

Place hands on the arms of the chair and bring the left knee as close to the nose as possible. This stretches the back and strengthens thighs and abdominals.

143 Knee Cross

Slide your seat forward in the chair and lean back. Cross the left knee over the right and then alternate. Start with two or three and work up to sixteen. This exercise stretches and strengthens the legs, and strengthens abdominals. When the knee cross has become easy, replace with the following exercise.

144 Knee Cross and Kick

Keep the same body position, but each time you cross one leg over the other, kick as high as you can.

145 Knee Cross Pull-up and Open

Cross the left knee over the right, bringing the foot over the thigh. Grasp the left foot and pull it up toward the body to stretch the back, seat and thigh muscles. Then swing the leg to the left and drape it over the arm of the chair. Replace the foot on the floor and alternate legs. Do four each side.

146 Neck Rest

Sit relaxed in the chair and let your head fall forward. Let it hang for about five seconds while you try consciously to *let go* wherever muscles in the neck, shoulders and upper back resist. Then roll the head *slowly* to the right side. When it is over your shoulder, move it gently back and forth, trying to make the other side of the

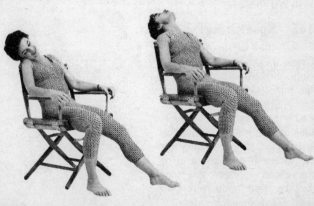

neck relax. After about ten seconds of this, roll the head back. Open your mouth to relieve tension and repeat the gentle rolling motion, again trying to make tight areas relax by feeling where they are and working them over. Roll to the left and then drop forward. Do this series twice, first to one side and then to the other—but do it often throughout the day. This exercise rests and relaxes tight neck muscles.

147   Feet In—Feet Out

Place the feet about ten inches apart and rotate them inward, bringing the toes together. Then rotate them outward as far as possible. Start with about ten rotations and alternate this exercise with the Heel Lift for three sets.

148   Heel Lift

Place feet parallel with heels flat on the floor. Keep the toes and ball of the left foot on the floor and raise the heel. Try to arch the foot and push the instep over the toes. Lower and alternate feet for ten lifts each.

149 Toes Up—Toes Down

Slide forward until the seat is at the very edge of the chair. Lean back to rest the shoulders and stretch legs forward. Keeping the feet apart and parallel, press the soles of the feet flat to the floor. Then, with heels still resting on the floor, pull the toes up toward the body as far as possible. This exercise stretches and strengthens the muscles in both front and back of the legs and improves both strength and flexibility of the ankles. Faithful work in this and the next exercise improves both appearance and function of feet, legs and ankles. Repeat up and down motion ten times and alternate with Toes In—Toes Out for three sets.

150 Toes In—Toes Out

Stay seated with legs outstretched. Rotate the toes inward as far as possible and then outward, trying to bring the outer edges of the feet to rest on the floor. This exercise stretches and strengthens the muscles of the ankles, legs and feet. Do ten rotations. To increase the value of these two exercises, add foot circles by combining them. Press the toes flat, rotate outward, then up, inward and down. Reverse the circle to start down, then in, up, out and down. Do three circles in each direction whenever possible throughout the day.

151 Seat Lift

Place hands on the front of the chair arms and straighten arms to lift the seat in the air. *Lower slowly* taking five seconds to accomplish the descent. This exercise strengthens the arms and shoulder girdle. Start with two and work up to six.

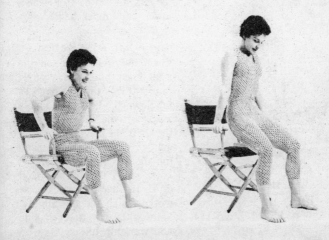

152 Back Stretch

Sit back in the chair and place feet apart, parallel and flat on the floor. Keep the hands on the arms of the chair and lean forward to drop the head between the knees, or as close to this position as possible. Bounce the upper body gently downward three times. This stretches the back, shoulder and chest muscles. Do four sets.

153 Waist Twist

Keeping feet well apart and flat on the floor, twist the upper body around to the right, bringing both hands as close to the back of the chair arm as possible. Swing to the left and repeat the same action. Alternate for four to eight times. This exercise loosens and slims the waist, lower and upper back.

154 Shoulder Reach

Place the right hand on the right knee, and with a single motion place the left hand as far down the back as possible and twist the upper body to the left. Change direction and swing to the right, placing the left hand on the left knee and the right hand down the back. This exercise works for shoulder flexibility. Start with two to each side and work up to six.

155 Arm Circles

Sit forward on the chair and place feet parallel and flat on the floor. Lean forward from the hips stretching arms out in front. Sit erect and raise hands straight overhead pressing shoulders back. Open the arms wide and press back and down in wide arcs. Grasp the backs of the chair arms, lift the head and chest and press the elbows toward each other. This exercise stretches back, arms, chest, shoulders, and neck. Repeat the action four times.

156 Upper Torso Twist

Lean down and reach around to grasp the outside of the
right ankle with the left hand. Return to the erect position.
Do this same movement to the other side. Then reach
down between the feet and around the back of the right leg
to grasp the outside of the right ankle with the left hand.
Repeat the same movement to the other side. This exercise increases the flexibility of upper torso, arms and
shoulders. Repeat the series three times.

157 Body Lift

Move the seat forward in the chair and grasp the forward ends of the chair arms. Stretch the legs straight out
in front pressing feet flat to the floor. Keeping legs straight,

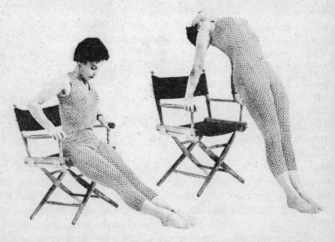

raise the entire body, arch the back and let the head fall backward. Hold the arched position for a slow count of three and then *slowly* lower to the original sitting position. This exercise stretches the abdominals and chest muscles and strengthens the arms, upper back and shoulders. Start with two and work up to six.

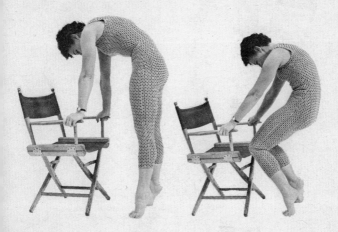

158   Pelvic Tilt Assisted

Stand with feet flat and apart and hands resting on chair arms. Rise *slowly* to the toes tightening abdominals, leg and seat muscles. Keeping head down, *and seat tucked under* do a half knee bend. Straighten and return heels to the floor. This exercise helps you develop the pelvic tilt, so necessary to posture and freedom from back fatigue. It also strengthens the feet and legs.

159   Knee In—Leg Out

Start by standing in front of the chair and grasping the chair arms for support. Bring the left leg up to rest on the chair seat. Swing the left leg backward and at the same time lift the head. Do four and alternate with four on the other leg. Do three sets. This exercise will stretch back and abdominals and strengthen the same areas. It is particularly useful for improving the seat line.

160 Push-ups

Be sure your chair is anchored so it cannot slip and
also that your feet are secure so that you cannot slip.
Stand back from the chair (the distance will be greater as
you improve). Grasp the front part of the chair arms.
Place the feet wide apart at first, this makes the exercise
a little easier. *Slowly* lower body into the let down position of the push-up. Push up to the straight arm po-

sition and return to the standing position. Then place hands in the small of the back, pressing elbows and head backward. Try to stretch the whole body tall. Start with two and work up to as many as you can manage.

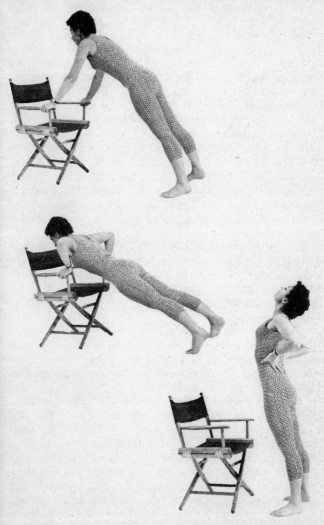

Our class was quite unorthodox. First of all, I put all of them into tights. Now *that* was quite a sight. For the first ten undressed minutes, they kept trying to pull their tights looser, lower and higher—anywhere but where they were. At the end of two lessons they were far too interested in progress to give any time to current appearance. Also they were "pulling in" already and looked younger and better. We used rhumba music, cha chas and African rhythms. Their mothers would have been horrified, but they thought the new look in music was just great. It was in this class that the Armchair Ballet (page 248) was born. My little old ladies were a sensation at the Golden Age convention. Four months later they made their very successful debut on TV.

I did have one bad moment, though. After we'd been going about three weeks my oldest student, age eighty-six, came to me before class and said, "Miss Prudden, I'm having a terrible time with my exercises." You can imagine my feelings. The study was an experiment and one in which I had great faith, and I earnestly wanted it to be a success. Here was the first snag and who could guess how serious that snag might be? I made a fine show of unconcern as I asked for her symptoms. "Well," she said, as she stepped back about three feet, "When I do this (she did three perfect apart-together jumps), the people downstairs complain."

Sometimes things have gone to pot already. If this is true in your case, you may feel there's really no way out. Well, there is. I was old at twenty-two and again at thirty-five, but I feel younger and happier today than at any time since I was twenty-one.

As you know, in December, 1936, on a steep, wonderful hill in Vermont, known appropriately as "Suicide Six," a surplus of enthusiasm and a deficiency of know-how left me upside down with twisted skis and a pelvis broken in four places. Today, patients with the same injury would be up on crutches in a matter of a few days, but in those days it was traction and a cast. I was told that to move would cause more damage, so for months I hung head down waiting for healing. Weekends I cried warm tears of self pity as I heard my husband and his friends packing ski gear into the car. There is no misery quite like the feeling that life has gone on without you.

When I was finally unveiled in April, the good legs I had taken to Vermont had wasted away to pipestems. There were pressure sores on both hip bones and all down the calf of one leg. As I was rolled onto one side, my abdomen sagged like an empty bag, and there was no pulling it in either. I was given crutches, but atrophied leg and arm muscles, not to mention the all-important back and abdominals, refused to support me. What a shock for an athlete used to instant obedience from all members of the organization.

For months, my circumference of movement had been within a cast, within a bed, within a room, within a house. The less I could do, the more tired I became, and of course, the more tired, the less I did. Does it sound familiar? It should, because it is the pattern of deterioration. I noticed something else—and this is a terrifying lesson that should be learned right now and never forgotten. The less stimulus I had from outside sources, the less I thought—beyond myself. I became interested primarily in *my* trouble, *my* chart and *my* pain. Since I couldn't use my body, it had deteriorated and with it, my thinking and my sense of humor. And all that in just three months.

Today when I spot the thin legs that spell disuse—the formless torso or stiff, bent shoulders that usually accompany them—or the loose, uncontrolled abdominals and the strained, unhappy faces that come with badly handled years, I think of myself at twenty-two.

I became old again at thirty-five. This time emotional distress came first and the body went dutifully along. I was miserably unhappy in my marriage and the world closed in, filled with tension and the ghosts of what might have been. Time was rushing by, life was rushing by and I was growing older. I couldn't believe that of the wonders it had promised this was all there was to it. The haunting words of my mother kept whispering through the house: "I'm still waiting for something to happen. . . ."

I took to overwork as an antidote for discontent— washing, painting, scrubbing, polishing. My sense of virtue was only exceeded by my sense of loss. I grew snappish and put on fifteen pounds. My back hurt and I thought I had an ulcer.

The doctor I finally consulted was wise and sparing of words. "What do you do with your days?" When my list came to an end, she asked the second question. "And what would you like to do?" I mentioned some of the things that had given me happiness: teaching, painting, writing. The last question was far too short for the weight of its meaning: "Why don't you?" Naturally I brought out every excuse in the book. Too much work, not enough time, no concentration. "Nonsense," said the wise lady. "Do at least one of them or you'll end up in a hospital."

So I did what I wanted to do and grew young again. Oh it didn't happen overnight. I had to begin slowly and keep at it but the ship was out of irons so-to-speak, and going somewhere. The moral of this story is: If you want to do something, then go and do it, whatever your age or circumstances. The major ingredient in happiness and progress is desire.

Sometimes growing old brings loneliness. Contemporaries fade from your life because they are restricted in theirs—or because they have gone on to whatever lies ahead. One cure for this (and it is also one way of keeping a young point of view), is to make friends with young people. To appreciate the wonders of your world, you should show it to someone else. To really understand what it is to be alive, you have to watch a healthy young animal who feels, smells, hears, tastes and enjoys on a more intense level than you remember, and you have to go with him.

Remember when you rolled down a hill of tall grass just because you felt so good? You broke the brittle ice on November puddles and walked home through spring freshets in the gutter. Remember the smell of fresh rain on cement walks, and burning autumn leaves? Can you still recall the taste of baked potatoes charred black in camp fires? Remember the pain of skinned knees and stubbed toes? And the way handkerchief bandages would never stay up? You probably snitched grapes or apples or sweet corn. Once or twice you broke windows and had to pay for them.

These are the things that today's children know all too little about. If you have children or grandchildren or even great-grandchildren, they need you. *You* grew up in a day when children *did* things rather than watched unreal sequences performed by unreal people on a TV screen. For their sake as well as your own, bring your world back for them.

Don't wait until the children "grow up and get sense." When that day comes, they will be far away and it will be too late. Go now while they can still give you back the days of your first youth because they live there. Take them on a hike even if you must drive to the start of the trail. Take a knapsack full of lunch, or better, let the youngsters carry it for you. That way they will grow in strength and pride. Don't walk too far the first time. Both his young and your not-so-young legs will have to walk back. Go prepared for rain and hope that it does. Controlled emergencies are exciting.

When you are lying, full of fresh bread and butter and maybe chocolate cake, in a warm sunlit field and you can't return until you both have rested, you are caught. You'll have to listen to frogs, crickets and the wind. You watch great, fat clouds sail by. An ant may crawl on your wrist and a blade of grass tickle your ear. Your legs will ache pleasantly and your walking shoes feel heavy and firm.

When you finally let your old bones down into a hot tub that night, you'll know you've been somewhere special—and so will your young companion.

As people get older, the question of retirement comes up. Some men can't see beyond that fateful day and it is almost like a wall. They dread and fear it because for them it spells the end. Our retirement policies are stupid and wasteful, God knows, and will only change when managements realize that experience can't be acquired except over a long period of time. While our life expectancy used to be somewhere in the forties, it is now in the seventies *and with more attention to maintenance,* could go to the hundreds.

Present shortsighted policies, however, can be put to good use. *You* can get out of the rat race at sixty or sixty-five. Fifty years from now, people will probably be seventy-five before they can escape. The big question—and one for which you should start preparing at thirty—is: What do I want to retire *to?* This has to be well thought out and lined up just like the choice of the college you wanted to attend. Enforced leisure can be a frightening void for a man or a woman used to girding each morning for war. Don't ignore retirement—you want to plan at least ten years before just what you will do with all those new and shining hours. Retirement makes sense only when it frees you for a more exciting and interesting life.

One couple retired to Acapulco and built a motel. After years of business travel, they felt they knew exactly what was wrong with motels from the guests' point of view—and they designed the place to provide the ultimate for the traveler. They look and feel younger than ever, and have stopped fussing about taxes taking away their life's blood.

It all boils down to attitude and physical fitness. If you are physically fit, you remain physiologically younger—which in turn keeps you young in heart (both ways). Exercise is important and so is diet. Stretch your mind as well as your body, and "old age" as we know and fear it simply won't happen. Never confine either your thinking or your activities. Stir yourself in almost any direction, and something is bound to happen. Take a course at college—something you never thought of studying and preferably something like geology that demands field trips. Go out for a new sport. If you ever skied, water skiing is great (and soft for impromptu landings), and scuba diving isn't just for kids. There's a world down under that needs experienced eyes—yours. A friend of mine who used to hunt a great deal told me yesterday he had a brand new hobby. Armed with a new Japanese camera, he goes back into the woods and just sits still. "I don't move, or smoke or make any noise at all. Last week I had a bear lying not twenty feet away. *He joined me.* I've got a million pictures to take, and I'm starting next month when my retirement comes through."

If you've never done anything in your whole life worth talking about, or if you haven't been active lately, the formula is just the same. Check back with the "how to" chapters and then start out. Do the Limbering Series on page 228 and the Armchair Ballet in this chapter. Keep at it until you feel ready for the general exercises. You will find that as you improve in strength and flexibility, you will have more energy. More energy always begets new ideas and new ideas lead to action. Nobody is ever going to have to tie your shoelaces for you. Now get at it and show the young folk what it can mean to *live*.

CHAPTER FOURTEEN

What's new, pussycat?

As far as exercise is concerned, everything in America is new. Ten years ago I had to call my work "conditioning" because people were so afraid of the word "exercise." At that time we couldn't even protect ourselves by asking for preclass medical checkups from people who were not really healthy, but who needed us desperately. Many who eventually lost smothering fat, lowered high blood pressure, came to need less insulin, strengthened their tired hearts, improved flagging circulation, breathed easier, and even found release from mounting tensions within themselves, would have been forbidden to come by their own doctors. A decade ago the medical profession was deeply involved with *curing* disease, and had little training in its *prevention*. Some of those people would have been told to "slow down," and that "straining in middle age could be harmful." Others might have been admonished to "accept limitations." A few might even have suffered the humiliation of hearing the words, "Act your age."

It was President Eisenhower's heart attack and Dr. Paul Dudley White's unorthodox treatment of it that ushered in the new era of exercise in medicine. Prior to that time, if your heart set up a holler you were immobilized, which either crippled you or at best made life a nervous bore. Today men are urged to *"run* for their lives" long before those lives are in any serious danger.

Ten years ago women thought exercise would make them and their daughters look masculine. They pointed out the hefty Russian women who threw the discus as examples of what exercise would do, rather than examples of what kind of activity already big, strong women were best fitted for when it came to Olympic competition. Now they know that, unless they and their daughters exercise, they won't have attractive curves—or at least they won't keep them long.

Fat people called their problem "glandular" and skinny ones called theirs "hereditary." The fat ones alternated between feasts and famines while the skinny ones tried beer and bananas.

Pregnant women were afraid to raise their arms above their heads, twist in any direction, lift, tote or hurry. They also ate for two.

People (male only) who lifted weights were called "weight lifters" or "Muscle Beach boys," and their sexual leanings were suspect. Opportunities for developing fine athletes, boys *or* girls, were so limited that often elementary and high school youngsters with gymnastic potential had to be sneaked into college gyms after hours. Most physical education colleges in the business of turning out female physical educators cut down their students' *physical* activity so far (no running or jumping, no accidental or otherwise collisions, no sweat or heavy breathing, no activity that produced endurance) that they developed several generations of nonphysical physical educators. Often overweight and lacking the ability to set an example, these educators convinced every student with eyes that physical education turned out big, heavy, masculine types. "If it makes *her* look like that, why should *I* go to class?"

Little children were "protected" from just about everything except permissive parents and teachers. Their physical activity was sharply curtailed at that precise moment in time when the automobile, TV, "designed starvation"* and the anxious mother (courtesy of the *interpreters* of Freud) all came together to form a lethal quartet. Millions of children became obese (you can be starved for real nutriment and still be fat). Other millions suffered from various forms of "hypokinetic disease." Arteriosclerosis, heart problems, even diabetes and tooth decay fit in that category, and so do emotional problems. The mean age

* Read on—you'll come to it.

for matriculation in mental institutions has dropped steadily over the years.

It should also be noted that the children born into this freak era where adults worship children on the one hand and irreparably damage them on the other are the ones who are "freaking out" with marijuana, LSD and other assorted escape mechanisms today. When the word "why?" comes up, I wonder if we should not consider the start they got. Those of you who still have young children may yet prevent the worst fate of any human being—that of being simply wasted.

Twenty years ago things had already come to such a pass that the elderly ladies at The Osborne Home in Rye, New York (nobody under seventy) had a better K-W rating in minimum muscular fitness than the Rye High School girls. When we finally publicized the fact that the United States had the worst rating of any country we had tested (and there were many), it produced the first real jolt to our national ego. A lady from the National Education Association of the United States told us we were "unpatriotic" to say such things about Americans, but President Eisenhower said it was "shocking" and that "something must be done about it."

In the last ten years a lot has been done about it. Volumes and volumes have been written (even one by the lady patriot), all telling us how to get into condition. The paper in these volumes is new, but most of the contents is just more of the same old stuff discarded years ago. Sometimes the recommended programs were just plain dull, but often they pushed exercises that would have been difficult for the very fit. For the typical American they were out-and-out dangerous. Take for example that old-time favorite (often of obstetricians), the double leg lift. You remember it. You lie on your back and lift both legs simultaneously and then lower . . . slowly. Those with weak abdominals (twenty-five percent of the American kids and one percent of the Europeans) can't do that exercise without substituting—in other words, arching their backs, which is bad for them. However, somebody wrote it in a book, and others who knew no more than they used it.

268

Next we come to the "GI backbreaker," the straight-leg sit-up. It is probably responsible for more backaches in World War II, Korea and Vietnam than all the lugged packs and ammo. When you lie on your back with legs outstretched and do sit-ups (fast *or* slow), you engage the hip flexors or psoas, and that brings in your back rather than just abdominals. Pull on that back enough, especially if you lack flexibility (forty-four percent of the American kids lack it and seven percent of the Europeans), and you'll work into a backache. It should be enough to fight a war without feeling as if your back is broken.

They even brought back running in place and "jumping jacks" as *warm-up exercises.* Then all you need for a muscle tear is a fight with the teacher, a stiff exam or a left-over problem from home. If the exercise is done outside and it's cold, you double your chance of injury.

Just about this time it became stylish to write papers on athletic injuries, and up popped one on the damaging effect of the "duckwalk." I was there when that one was first presented to a thoroughly gullible (because to that date they knew nothing about *exercise*) group of physical educators. The study had used football players and weight lifters who had incurred knee injuries presumably when in the deep knee-bend position. The writer had picked two of the three most knee-damaging sports for his study. I wondered why he had left out basketball. Those knees the writer talked about were not injured *just* on the day they gave way. They had been overworked (and often undertrained), strained and battered (especially in the case of the footballers, who sustain innumerable blows *from the side*) until they were ready for the final push and the final tear.

Furthermore, those injuries were sustained by *Americans.* We grow them big these days, but that does not mean that their strength has kept pace with their height. Big kids play football in high school, but for such safety as they get they must rely mostly on equipment. Training often starts when school does in fall, and three weeks later the team is in a game. The boys *look* impressive, but tendon tears, torn shoulders, sprains and strains plague coaches—even the ones who *know* where the trouble is. That doesn't help much, because there's a rule that says you can't work your team through the summer. Human beings cannot afford that luxury, particularly would-be athlete human beings. Nobody would dream of bringing an expensive racehorse up to the gate without *plenty* of training. What makes people think they can do it to boys?

The net result of that totally mistaken paper was that children in *elementary schools* were told knee bends were dangerous (so was everybody else, but imagine *elementary schools!* That's just one step past the time when most of what children do quietly is done from a squatting position). We've been years and years trying to undo the mischief, and I'll wager it has cost the life of many a soldier. Can you imagine getting into or out of a slit trench or foxhole without the strength to more than half bend a knee?

The next joker out of the box was the "isometrics" craze. Now there's nothing wrong with doing *some* isometric exercises, which are the ones where muscles are tightened (push one hand against the other hard— and hold for six seconds) but no movement ensues. The trouble with isometrics lay with the claims. *Amazing . . . Only a few minutes a day . . . Lose weight without dieting . . . Take inches off your waist . . . Grow strong the easy way . . .* and Americans, cheated out of exercises since 1930, bought it. A manufacturer brought an isometric gadget to me for endorsement as an exerciser for women. A famous athlete had his name attached to it already, but for men. I told him he was cheating people. There never was, and I doubt there ever will be, any single answer to exercise, and certainly not in any six minutes a day. He asked me what I'd suggest, and we worked out a kit in which his isometric gadget can also be used isotonically (movement with resistance), and we added free exercises and a jump rope for endurance. The women now get the program, but the men still get the athlete's six-minute isometric gadget—period. Who do you feel was the biggest fraud—the manufacturer who was uninformed and willing to change or the athlete whose name so many trusted?

We don't hear much about isometrics any more. A great many studies were done in research laboratories, and they came up with the news that isometrics don't net much unless you work up to sixty percent of capacity, and at that point the blood supply carrying oxygen to the working area is cut off. Certainly that form of exercise does nothing for our major need, the release of tension, and our next biggest problem, inflexibility. It does nothing *for* joints and may do something *against* them. Isotonics (work through full range with resistance such as weights) gets better results and lasts longer if you stop your program for a while. Isometrics won't do a thing for your endurance and may have helped to bring on the current craze, aerobics, which in its way is just as limited.

Aerobics hit the fan just this last year—and there is a hallelujah change. Instead of buying the idea hook, line and sinker, people asked questions. The one I heard most often was, "Is it right that exercise doesn't do any good?" Well, if the man who brought out aerobics said exercise doesn't do any good, of course he's wrong—but did he? I am inclined to believe that were he faced with a very beautiful woman of sixty who had arthritis of the hip and was either forced to live with it or perhaps get along on a prosthesis because running was out, rope skipping was out, long walks were out and no pool was available, he'd accept exercise as having value. Most of the confusion about exercise is caused by semantics.

What did that man really say? I *think* he meant (and don't you think I didn't read what he *said*) that of all the forms of exercise available to us, those that make the heart pump harder, lungs take on greater loads of oxygen and our circulation carry that oxygen to all parts of the body are the *exercises* our bodies need the most. Without a strong heart that gets a good workout, we cannot possibly take on the fuel we need through well-exercised lungs or carry it to all the places where it is needed. There is nothing wrong with that idea. But he lost many of the people who make up my audiences and clinics when he implied that *calisthenics* didn't do any good. He did add, however, that *he* did calisthenics, though he was not very clear why. Mean it or not, what came through to "people" was that although *aerobics* were essential, no other form of exercise was.

The studies on aerobic exercise were done by a military doctor on a military base with military personnel. In essence, he was directed by the needs of the people around him and limited in his observation by *their* age range, background and motivation. I have two friends who were on American international basketball teams; one had played in Brazil and the other in Russia. Both are young women, strong, attractive, beautifully put together and in the field of physical education out in Denver. *They* took to aerobics immediately. Strongly motivated by the will to compete and the possession of well-trained bodies, they couldn't *wait* to get out on the high school track. I wanted to see what *I* could do in my pool. A third athletic friend likes to combine biking with running and swimming. However, in the hundreds and thousands of letters I get because of my TV shows, *not one woman has mentioned aerobics as a possibility*. Without question most (if not all) would profit by some form of endurance exercise, but many could never come even close to the thirty points demanded by the exponent of aerobics. Even if they could, their *wants*, if not their needs, are elsewhere. The young mother of four with a floppy abdomen doesn't want to be told that what may be called calisthenics isn't going to help her. The 200-pound gal who has just joined a diet club *must* exercise, but she could do a lot of damage working for those thirty points. Ever tried to walk even a few blocks carrying 200 pounds?

The word *calisthenics* seems to be a problem. Just as there is exercise and exercise (from golf to skiing), there are differences in exercise forms or calisthenics. For instance, if you want exercises that are very good for building endurance, such as running, biking, swimming or rope skipping, give Exercises 32, 33, 34, 35, 36 and 37 a try. Don't try too hard at first—and not before warm-ups— but do try. Do a couple for a couple of seconds now, add seconds first and then more exercises as the weeks go on, and you will be doing aerobic exercises as well as exercise that will improve your flexibility (very important) and your strength, heart, lungs and endurance. It is perfectly true on the other hand that Exercise (or Calis-thenic) 9 won't do much for your heart, lungs, intake and distribution of oxygen or endurance, but it will help the person who has a swayback to correct it. It will pull in a protruding abdomen and clear up menstrual cramps (men don't seem awfully interested in this aspect, but I know people who are). The "sexercises" were not designed to increase heartbeat, lung action or circulation during re-hearsal; however they might induce all three in at least one person during phase two.

It comes back to the same thing—there is no one final answer to physical fitness needs. I've seen businessmen at the "Y"s who could run all day, yet they have paunches like teddy bears. There are people who could swim half way from Dover to Calais, yet they have a constant nag-ging backache (and don't you believe the ads). For eighty percent of the backaches, it's going to take specific exer-cise patterns. There just is no single *complete* answer that fits every need—just as there is no answer to "How long will it take?" "What should my measurements be?" "What exactly must I weigh?" "When should I exercise?" "How long at a time?"

There is only one thing about activity that fits everyone and that is that one must move. While you can make your program interesting and pleasurable, there is no such thing as instant fitness, and there is no "easy" way—and that brings me to jogging.

Jogging, like aerobics and isometrics, isn't new. Little children (if they are healthy) jog everywhere even if it's just to the kitchen. In the olden days, we used to jog to school (when we weren't running full tilt or skipping rope). Indians used to jog, and so did our first American settlers. Physical fitness "nuts" jog and so do plebes at West Point. Lately jogging has become very much "in," and it may very possibly be here to stay. But it doesn't do everything. On the other hand it does a lot, and it doesn't cost much. Comfortable old clothes will do unless you are a clothes nut like me. I have a beautiful blue jogging outfit that is as far from the old-fashioned sweat suit as a miniskirt from a flowered flannel nightgown. You *can* get along with sneakers, especially if you have good feet, but there are very snazzy running shoes available now, even for women. They are of leather and give a little extra support.

Jogging cannot (as many joggers would have you think) be done just anywhere and at just any time—especially if you happen to be a woman. Years ago in New York we used to jog around the Reservoir in Central Park, but only a fool would try it today—alone. In cities like New York you should join a "Y." Most of them have measured their gyms so you know how many times around them make a mile. May I remind you that there is also a half a mile and even a quarter of a mile. If you can get the teacher or physical director to put on a good brisk record you will find. it's more fun than listening to your breath whistle. If you are just starting, set yourself a goal (and keep track in a notebook). If you can only run ten steps, that's a start. Then walk fifty for a rest. But week after week add running steps to your program and when you are running fifty and walking fifty, start lessening the walks. Note the time it takes each week.

If you can get a friend to go with you—whether it's to the "Y," an exercise club, the school track or just down the road—it helps. You encourage each other and support each other on those days when it would be easier to stay home. If you don't like kids to kid you, run during school hours, and if it rains (and you don't like rain), run in the living room changing direction often. Sometimes you can interest your husband in running by telling him how badly *you* need .it, but you are afraid to run alone. While protecting you, he will also protect his heart.

If you are a man and you want company, ask her, whoever she is, to run along and keep you from being bored. If she says she has never run, believe her and take lots of time to break her in. You can always sprint to the corner and back to her for extra workout. One way to get a wife or a husband going is to get the neighbors interested after supper. In which case, keep a log and celebrate 100 milestones every time someone accomplishes one. You can check the distance of your course with the car.

I used to run the high school track early in the morning. We started before it was light and felt both Spartan

and noble. The only fly in our liniment was a large iras-
cible shepherd whose back door faced his track. It was *his*
track, and don't forget it. Every morning I said, "Good
morning," politely as I passed him standing in a most
threatening attitude behind a one-foot box hedge. From
experience we knew he was likely to stay there, but carrying a crop, light switch or thin, short curtain rod that
won't interfere with your stride will give you courage and
dogs something to think about.

The other peril when you are out of doors is, of course,
traffic. Women can run when the traffic is light and the
kids are in school, but men will be limited to before breakfast (once the train, bus and commuter traffic start, it's
just no fun and it's dangerous besides) or after dinner.
There is nothing against using your lunch hour a few
times a week at the "Y" or athletic club.

For best results, for protection against small muscle
tears that can be painful and ruin your resolution, do your
warm-ups *before* you start running. You only need do
enough to feel warm and loose. Incidentally, stitches in
the side are helped if you use "running sticks." Those are
¾-inch dowels cut to about five-inch lengths (bigger
hands, bigger sticks). Squeezing them as you run does
help.

Along with all the books, pamphlets, articles and news
releases that have inundated the public, there has come a
veritable avalanche of "new" equipment that is as new as
whalebone corsets. It ranges from fairly inexpensive jump
ropes that have value if *you* do the jumping to fancy
electric bikes that claim to do everything. There were
(and I'm afraid still are) rubber suits that in theory become your own private sauna, but in actuality are as
dangerous as some of the football gear that has caused
illness and death from heat stroke. (The body is designed
to sweat in circulating air.) At the other end of the price
list there are now very posh saunas that can be installed
right in your apartment, brick by insulated wooden brick.
In keeping with our understandable desire to invent a
means to attain fitness without lifting a finger (except for
that button), every conceivable machine and gadget is
now available. You can lie full length on a couch, sit in a

chair or stand up in such a variety of vibrators, rollers, squeezers, shakers and chafers (all guaranteeing weight loss if you eat less), it's hard to choose, not only the gimmick you want most, but just which promised benefit.

Weight lifting, accepted for men (if that was what you wanted to do) has now become not only acceptable for women, but even desirable. Men's magazines have added pages and pages of pictures showing girls with mammoth mammaries accomplishing this questionable condition with pink, blue and chrome dumbbells.

The old-time resistance assisters such as springs, rubber cables and barbells moved from men's weight-lifting rooms in the basements of YMCAs to new quarters. Chromium-plated and often wired, they stood expectantly in glamorous emporiums called "health clubs." These were mostly franchises run by people whose interest was in financial returns rather than a quality product. Some were out-and-out frauds. Wall-to-wall carpeting, soft music, "tropical" swimming pools (potted palms), Finnish saunas, sexy hostesses in leotards, they advertised as follows (parenthetical remarks mine):

- *Ultramodern Health Club for Men* (Machines, massage, no program)
- *Luxurious Figure-Contouring Salon for Women* (Mirrors)
- *Patented Electrical Reducing Machines* (Patented does not mean guaranteed to reduce)
- *Mechanical Body-Reproportioning Machines* (What do you suppose *those* machines do?)
- *Mild Progressive Resistance Machines* (Getting close to real effort. Thus the word "mild")
- *Roman Swirl-Pool Treatments* (Presumably with swirlers like the ancient Romans used to have!)
- *Finnish Sauna* (No "emporium" is "in" without a sauna)
- *Private Ultraviolet Beauty Ray Sunbaths* (Quick total tan . . . slow itchy peel)
- *Fabulous Indoor Swimming Pool* (Small, lukewarm and crowded)
- *Private Thermostatically Controlled Showers* (Hot and cold)

276

- *Personal Supervision* (Lest you get hung in a cable or come unplugged)
- *Individual Programs and Extraordinary Personal Service*

Now that can mean almost anything, depending on the manager and the personnel, but one thing for very sure, it won't mean a well-designed exercise program, which is what you really need. I was once shown the "work book" for one of the biggest "health" studio chains. The first half was concerned with the "sell" and the second half with "sue." In the middle was the program—one page.

All of the above "offerings" I copied from a clipping that came in today's mail, along with the admission that you can't fool everybody forever. Smack across the top of the ad in two-inch letters it says *60% OFF*.

Naturally there were the pictures of a man and a woman in the ad. They were "Before" and "After" pictures, and they were, if not faked, at least slanted. This is how you can tell. The "Before" picture of the man was in profile. His abdominals were so relaxed that had there not been a button on his navel, the intestines would have fallen out. In the "After" picture he wears a very strained "hold it in" expression, and the picture rather than the man's paunch has been trimmed. The woman stands facing squarely into the camera in her "Before" picture. (Don't stand that way for even candid family shots—you'll look much wider than you are). Her arms are crossed over her chest (sometimes they hold them at the sides). In both cases there is no "air" close to the body, and the arms become part of the torso, making it look thick. Usually the "Before" woman wears flat heels, a longish, full dress and a fright wig. In the "After" picture the lady has made a quarter turn, advancing one turned-out foot. One hand is on her hip and the other out to the side, so that the torso looks slimmer whether it is or not. One can be pretty sure a girdle and an uplift bra have been added. The right shoes, much tighter (straight-line) dress and a hairdo can work wonders, but not for physical fitness.

The glamorized "health club" had its heyday around 1959, and it rode in on the first flutterings of public interest in physical fitness. Health clubs profited for a little while because people didn't know anything about *real* physical fitness. Their worst crime was that they cared so little about people that they discouraged them. No machine can look at a striving human being and say warmly, "That's better than last week—that's just great," and mean it. The clients failed to improve and they tired of the *impersonal* glittering racket. The women eventually passed up the steam baths, saunas and pools because they didn't want to get their hair wet, and what was left couldn't hold them. One by one the clubs closed and the equipment went up for sale. It's hard to calculate how many "life" memberships ended in less than a year.

In 1954 we brought out the first facts on American physical fitness, and by 1955 I had a column in *Sports Illustrated*. It was only a hop, skip and a holler to those shows with Arlene Francis and Dave Garroway, and exercise became TV's baby. One day I offered three exercises for anyone wanting to wear a bikini, and within four days I had 68,000 requests. One day on Arthur Godfrey's show he let me talk about a little Fitness Kit, complete with tests and record. It cost a quarter, and by the first of the following week we had 40,000 quarters. It showed that people were very interested, and whenever there is enough interest you can be sure someone will be sitting up late trying to figure a way to cash in on it. Within a year or so we saw the first sign of the impending flood. A company bought time on *The Today Show* to advertise a reducing pill called Regimen. The airing of that commercial always seemed to come just before or just after my spot, and I didn't like it—especially when people began to associate me with it. I asked the show not to put it so close to me, but evidently that was part of the deal. After all, what do TV people know about pills *or* fitness for that matter? My reaction was to talk about weight loss without help from pills or similar crutches. Naturally that didn't go. TV people are very sensitive about the client's feelings. We parted company, and I guess they felt better—I used to sneak in some pretty startling truths between a sit-up and a stretch-out. About six months later the commercial was proven a fake, the Food and Drug Administration went after the Regimen people and they moved on to some other product.

At that time we saw the rise of the medically prescribed reducing pill. Some doctors didn't do anything else but interview and weigh "patients," take their blood pressure, prescribe a bag full of Jack and the Bean Stalk pills—and collect twenty-five dollars. It was just about the time young people began to "turn on" with drugs, and if you check the "reducing racket" pills with the stuff that's in use to-day, you will see they are the same. Amphetamines ("up-pies"), barbiturates ("downies") and Methedrine (speed). Add to those the diuretics that kicked tired and sometimes damaged kidneys right in the kidneys, the thyroid extracts that hopped people up to jittery misery, the laxatives that hurried food along before it could settle down as fat—or provide the nutriments that keep a body going—and you've got highway robbery with aggravated assault. As far as most people knew, the medical profession was behind every one of those fake outs.

Records began to appear in great numbers. Some even had the seals of approval that make the consumer feel "safe" with the product. Some records were silly, some boring and some damaging. One such record had the poor exerciser doing the same exercise over and over for a whole band at a time, thus guaranteeing stiffness, pain and discouragement.

However not all that took place in the changing times was bad. People like Tex and Jinx McCrary, Art Linklet-ter and Mike Douglas helped me bring all kinds of physical fitness to the TV audiences. We showed them newborns exercising, and little people. We showed how parents could work with kids and we encouraged kids to help out-of-shape parents. Women did figure exercises and old people outdid young ones. Teenagers were enthusiastic and passed it on to the viewers. Arthur Godfrey and I used to scare his producer to death. When we got going, *nobody* knew what we'd say.

In 1960 President Kennedy changed the name and aim of the President's Council on Youth Fitness. It became the President's Council on *Physical* Fitness. This gave those teachers who really wanted to teach something physical the chance to try. In turn this led to the reinstatement of gymnastics, track and field and even competition for girls. Not everybody got it, but this year was the first time we have made even a ripple in gymnastics at the Olympics. *Somebody* is doing *something* right at least *somewhere*.

The biggest positive splash was made by the YMCA. The "Y"s are big business, with a long history of interest in physical, mental and spiritual fitness. As with other groups serving the public and having the physical as a part of their program, the "Y"s had started to replace active with sedentary activities. Physical fitness came to them at just the right moment, and they took to it with enthusiasm and understanding. From being a club for boys, they became *the* centers of physical fitness in their communities. While there were many men who contributed to the growth of physical fitness in the YMCAs, one stands out, Charles Swineford at the Detroit Northeastern "Y." That very much used and slightly shabby "Y" has led all the rest ever since 1954, when the "Y"s picked up our program. It was at Chuck's "Y" that we started classes for women. We hardly had that set up when he agreed that co-ed classes should start. This led to family classes in exercise the way other "Y"s had accepted family swims on Friday evenings. Next came something so outrageous, so incredible, but so enormously successful that we look back on it with amazement, "the Diaper Gym and Swim." There in the pool and gym built for boys and young men, mothers were taught to teach their little girl babies and boy babies to swim and to exercise. Pretty soon the diapers came off and they graduated to pants and "the Toddlers." At two "the Toddlers" were experts and they became "the Tiny Tots." In the meantime their mothers had been snared, as had their fathers and older sisters and brothers. The action was limited only by space and time, and waiting lists were long. This last year they added pre- and post-natal classes—might as well get them at the very beginning.

Our pre- and post-natal program has had four solid years of testing at one of Massachusett's biggest obstetrical hospitals. Four years ago I talked to a group of twelve doctors who were interested in the work I had done with mothers-to-be. They had a course that was called "Natural Child-birth," but it wasn't working out. They knew about the record I had cut for this group, and what did I suggest? The first six-week course was pretty hairy for me. I had always worked either with one woman at a time or with groups of women who had been in my regular classes, and I knew they were fit. At the hospital I got a little of everything from fit to falling apart—from two months pregnant to eight—from under- to overweight—from willing to resistant. There were a few who had been hospitalized in previous pregnancies with backache, and there were some the doctors considered three- and four-time losers (they hadn't wanted the first baby and were totally apathetic). We started off pretty gingerly, but it was no time before the mothers were out-exercising the nurses sent in to learn the system. Backaches and swollen ankles disappeared, weight was controlled, enthusiasm was high and delivery was easier. Everybody was happy and the program is still going great guns.

Another good "happening" is going on in the diet world. Years ago the only organization of any size that made overweights their business was TOPS (Take Off Pounds Sensibly). They did a fine job and were often very successful in helping people (mostly women) lose weight. One thing was certain, they had a lot of fun. For many it was the first fun ever. In the last few years we have seen the rise of the Weight Watchers. Using the New York Obesity Clinic's Diet, which brought to many their first brush with proper nutrition, they carried their program a step further than TOPS. Along with the correct and highly nutritious diet that changed the eating habits of a lifetime for most participants, they provided group therapy. The lecturers were people who had once been fat themselves (and I mean *FAT*) and been successful in reaching their weight goals. These people were trained to lecture, to encourage, and to gently scold those who could be gently scolded. Weight Watchers has caught on and spread all over the country and to other countries as well.

Weight Watchers was followed by a similar group called Diet Watchers, who put out a fairly simple book to be followed by people who can't get to meetings or who live

281

in towns where no groups have formed. Both Diet Watchers and Weight Watchers have men and teenagers in their groups.

Today my exercise teachers are getting graduates from all these groups. It isn't enough finally to be slender, they want to *do* things they have always watched other people do—and for that you need physical fitness.

It has taken fifteen years to move from complete ignorance and apathy to widespread interest in physical fitness. By today's standards, that's three generations. Once interest was aroused we saw various answers proffered. It took a while for the public to learn to discriminate between the right answers and the wrong ones, but much progress has been made. If "health" emporiums implying "instant fitness" have to offer a sixty percent reduction in their prices, they aren't on the upswing. If "Y"s with good and diversified programs have waiting lists, they *are* on the upswing. If reducing pills are called by their right names, often addicting and hallucinogenic *drugs*, people will think twice before asking for them and three times before keeping them around where kids can get at them. If people will study "real" nutrition instead of counting calories, they will have more energy, better figures and less misery. If people will accept the fact that there is no pill they can take, elixir they can drink or button they can push to give them fitness for mind, body or spirit, we will have at least a start on protecting ourselves and our families. Just what we have to fear is in the next chapter.

CHAPTER FIFTEEN

Cry havoc!

There is an ancient curse wished on all of us, *"May your children live in interesting times."* Well, the curse has come to pass, and those "interesting times" are here. *We* are the children who have been bidden to live in them and so are *our* children—and theirs. We all have to share the daily uncertainties and the often worse certainties. Face them we must, and not lying down. Even the most unaware knows there is movement in the forest, but what? It may be "friendly" and then again it may not. It may even bring mixed blessings. Education (wherever you get it) helps when it comes to sizing up the unknown, and so does the built-in drive for survival. Even kids defending a snow fort know enough to make snowballs for a defense. What seems to be the matter with us then? Is it that we do not know what is happening, or would we rather close our eyes?

For many years now the voices of the aware have cried havoc, and for as long as I can remember our answer has been to turn up the TV, light up another cigarette, drive a little faster, pour another drink and, lately, take another pill. Though none of these drown out the sound completely, they do support the illusion that the warning is for some other person, family, nation or world. Alas, it is for us.

Ten years ago the reporter Bill Longgood came to interview me about my findings concerning the physical fitness of American children. He asked questions right up to lunchtime, when I interrupted to say I was having my lunch sent in and what would he like? The change in him was instantaneous. Bill Longgood—the knowledgeable, practical, searching newspaperman of much experience and solid reputation—reared back like a scared mare. He answered so quickly I had to wait for the words to unscramble in my head. "Oh-no-thank-you-I-never-eat-lunch-but-you-go-ahead." They really *tumbled* out.

The words were natural enough; it was the tone that disturbed me. I felt as if I were a cannibal and had offered him a nice slice of Albert Schweitzer. A little later, when my secretary set down my tray containing a jar of yogurt, an apple and a cup of tea, Bill looked at that apple as if it were fresh out of Eden. If he'd looked that way at the yogurt I would have understood. Ten years ago people were very skeptical about "food faddists," and if you ate yogurt, sunflower seeds, the skins on the potatoes or drank buttermilk, you had to be a food faddist. I felt that it was unwise to be more than one "fanatic" at a time, so I only had *them* at home or at the office. But what was with the *apple?* The answer was fast in coming. Shocking as my story sounded when I talked about the low fitness level of Americans and what these low levels meant in terms of emotional stability, energy for study or drive for productive work, his was much worse. Bill Longgood's story was about the mass poisoning of you, me and our children. After all, muscles you can always improve, but slow poisoning is often irreversible.

Bill had been sent by his paper to look into some food additives the Cassandras were wailing about—certainly a routine and unexciting assignment for the foreign correspondent who had covered the Middle East for Scripps-Howard. He certainly hadn't expected to find himself exposed to a war here at home that was to change his life. I knew just what he meant when he told me how he felt as each new day of investigation brought him closer to that broiling, coiling thing, the truth.

At the close of the First World War in 1919, when I was five, I used to ride down the block on the high seat of Mr. Bloom's produce market wagon. He got the fresh vegetables (in season) from a farm near our town. Winters they came from further away, and I guess we were stuck with a limited variety, but it had always been that way.

Life did change some between the two world wars but it was after the second one that things really picked up. Suddenly supermarkets and shopping centers erupted, and the thousands of little produce markets that belonged to thousands of Mr. Blooms everywhere simply faded away. Miles of shelves had to be stocked for the millions of people who passed through like sea creatures moved along by currents and tides, darting from side to side to snatch bits and pieces of food from crevices. No "farm near town" was near enough and big enough to supply even one of them as they vied with each other to entice the passing stream. Enticing the public gave rise to the packaging industry, and many foods became like records and paperbacks—the cover was sensational, the contents from Dullsville. That wasn't all. New products had to come out blaring greater and greater advantages, even if the only change from the old was in the color. People didn't shop every day either, so foods that wouldn't spoil had to be either treated or invented, and the frozen food industry skyrocketed.

Bill Longgood discovered that when this new economic pattern took over, we as a nation (for the pattern is now part of the national scene) became the victims of overwhelming ignorance, greed and complete disregard for human beings. Anyone who feels distress at the plight of wounded, diseased or even starved Vietnamese need not send concern so far—just look around your own dinner table.

"Since World War Two a torrent of chemicals has poured into food in the form of dyes, bleaches, emulsifiers, antioxidants, preservatives, flavorings, buffers, acidifiers, alkalizers, moisteners, drying agents, extenders, thickeners, defoliants, fungicides, insecticides, neutralizers, sweeteners, anti-caking and anti-foaming agents, conditioners, curers, hydrolizers, hydrogenators, maturers, fortifiers, and many others. Virtually everything we eat has been treated with chemicals somewhere along the line." That unsettling paragraph is on the dust jacket of the book Bill finally wrote, *The Poisons in Your Food,** and if you care about your family, I think you should read it.

---

* New York: Ronald Press Co., 1960.

We have placed great faith in government agencies that do their best to ride herd on new products, but it is almost impossible to prevent at least some time from elapsing from the day a product makes its debut (often with thousands of dollars' worth of TV advertising behind it) to the day it is thoroughly checked out (remember Regimen Tablets?). By that time the company is probably ready to launch a *new* and *improved* product serving the same purpose, and checking the old one becomes useless in the face of the onrushing wave of still newer ones. *We don't have the right* to place that responsibility on someone else's shoulders. It rightly rests with us.

There *is*, if not a big watchdog, then at least a very noisy, protective, agitated little fox terrier in Washington. It's a lobbying group (the one that discovered that peanut butter had a twenty percent hardened oil base) and they really put their time and hearts to work. There are roughly 5,000 nonpaid members in The Federation of Homemakers (927 North Stuart Street, Arlington, Va. 22203), and if you ever wonder about something, ask them. Very few of the millions and millions of products we use ever get to the government labs for testing. The Industry is supposed to "police itself." Their policing is often influenced by what they take for granted (most of you take for granted that aspirin is absolutely harmless—but it isn't, especially if you take a lot of it) and the condition of the company's balance sheet. If you really care about your family's health, *you* find out what's going into your food. *You* read about the problem and then buy a magnifying glass. Don't go to the supermarket without it. Armed with the knowledge you need to pass up chemicals that will cause nerve disease, cancer and a host of unwelcome woes, *read the ingredients list*. You need the magnifying glass because you're not *supposed* to read it. If the manufacturer could write it in Japanese, he would. Start paying attention to articles on food rather than the menus in the paper and in magazines. Keep track of the companies that the government does catch up with. If *you* know the facts, there are enough of you to force the industries to ask themselves, not "Will it sell?" but "Will they buy it?" Read the

Longgood book. It may scare you to death and save your life.

Frank works with the soil. He plants, waters, fertilizes, prunes and picks—and he used to spray. At the end of a day, when spraying was done, the muscles of his arms and sometimes his legs would jump and twitch and "pain" at night. Sometimes he felt sick for a few days afterward, sometimes even longer. No, he didn't read what was in the spray. (Do you?) He only knew it would "kill pests," and that was enough. It killed the pests all right, and over the years it half killed him. It and others of its kind killed the birds in the sprayed trees, the fish swimming in pesticide-polluted waters. It coated the crops, cows ate it and it got into the milk. It was in the meat of animals, on the skins of fruit—*and it is in us.*

Back in 1962, a very aware and concerned woman by the name of Rachel Carson raised her voice in warning when she wrote *Silent Spring.** She, like Bill, was appalled by what she saw happening around her. Nature is so terribly important to our happiness and to our health that its potential destruction—and therefore our destruction—must be prevented. Now, in the papers, you are beginning to hear these things discussed. Even government is alarmed. Suddenly, because the danger to it is so apparent, environment is being studied. What impression have the Longgoods and the Carsons and a host of others made on you to this moment? Have you heard them? If you *ever* let your frozen vegetables thaw before you cook them or if you buy an apple in a store and don't peel it, *you have not heard them.*

Last year when I was doing a TV series in Toronto, most of my guests were doctors. One told me that the cigarette that follows breakfast wipes out the Vitamin C provided by your orange or orange juice. I wonder, how many of you have any idea what Vitamin C does for you? First of all, it prevents toxicity in a world swarming with toxic substances. Lots of people use saccharin or other sweeteners in spite of repeated warnings from the government. Vitamin C nullifies the toxicity of those sweeteners —and also that of fluorine, lead, benzine, carbon tetra-

---

* New York: Fawcett Crest (paperback), 1964.

chloride (and to think I used to like that smell!) and drugs. Don't think for a moment that if you are given a drug for a specific problem that it is harmless. I can remember many times when I had to choose between the discomfort of a bad cold and the absolute misery caused by antibiotics. When you take drugs, such as estrogen (attention, menopausers), barbiturates (you might not need or want those if your diet was adequate), stilbestrol (you didn't know you were already getting it in your food), adrenalin, sulfonamides, ammonium chloride, antihistamines, thiouricil, thyroid, atropine, Benzedrine, mercurial diuretics, procaine, Dilantin and even aspirin, Vitamin C (whatever supply you *do* have) moves in to fight the resulting toxicity. The bigger the fight, the more C is used in the battle, and you can continue to lose Vitamin C for six weeks after you have stopped taking the drug in question.

Vitamin C brings down blood pressure and cholesterol levels, and it is a staunch backup in times of stress. Since it is deadly to all bacteria and viruses and yet not toxic itself, it is better to have too much C than too little. Pity the poor soul with not enough—and who has enough? I was having my hair done about six weeks ago, and the lady in the next chair said she felt like she was coming down with the flu. Great. I needed that badly. I told her about Vitamin C and she said she'd get some. I forgot about it till I saw her last week. "Say, you remember telling me to get Vitamin C for my cold?" I'd forgotten, but then I tell everybody to take C for a cold. "Well, you know it cleared up my bleeding gums. I've had that condition for years." Bleeding gums or mouth sores are often the first sign of a lack of C. Bruising is, too. Vitamin C is a help for people who have arthritis, especially those who take aspirin for pain. If you wonder how much C to take, figure that the aspirin will nullify a lot of C even after you don't take it—and you need some left over for the arthritis. Back to that breakfast cigarette—how much Vitamin C do you think is in the body of an inveterate smoker?

Another doctor said that the only thing keeping the tobacco people in business was the filter. He also said that while the filter did check the nicotine that contributes to hypertension, it did *not* check the *eight* carcinogens that are liberated like so many evil spirits the minute you light up. Still another doctor was more than descriptive about lung cancer, which doesn't take kindly to any form of cure and generally wins the fight hands down. "But," he said, "while people know at least something about lung cancer danger, they don't know that cigarettes also cause cancer of the bladder. One doesn't hear much about that particular problem, but the patient must submit to a complete rearrangement of the excretory setup, which then permits life for a little while—if you can call complete exhaustion, and feeling lousy all the time, living."

I never even heard the word "emphysema" until ten years ago. Today it is boisterously pushing its way up the ladder as a killer. That's the only boisterous thing about emphysema, however. As all too many of us breathe and rebreathe the poisonous air around us, we slowly ruin the delicate air sacs in the lungs. You can see the shroud of death if you look at New York from just across the river, or Los Angeles as you fly in over the Pacific, or Denver (already a mile in the sky) from its burgeoning suburbs. Death in the form of emphysema is a slow one. The little sacs lose their elasticity and efficiency. Air gets into the lungs, *but it can't get out.* If you notice that you are suddenly tired by things that never used to bother you, the stairs or a walk in the country for example, or puff on almost no provocation, see your doctor. You will need exercise to develop the healthy part of your lungs, but you may need oxygen at first, since the limited areas will require help for the building.

Emphysema can attack anybody exposed to pollution long enough, but the welcome mat lies across the mouth of the smoker. If that smoker also has a history of bronchial distress, asthma, pneumonia and other respiratory problems, don't bother making snowballs—the opposition is using napalm.

"Pollution" is a nine-letter word that is much dirtier than all the four-letter words, much more shocking and much more dangerous. The gray, strained faces and slumped shoulders we see around us don't just belong to other people, but to people with pollution sickness, which mirrors the pollution sickness in ourselves. Many people fortunate enough to have lived in "clean" areas (there are a few) who move to the cities are disturbed by the blackheads and whiteheads that show up in suddenly clogged pores. They rarely translate that into terms of breathing, or of the oxygen supply to the entire body, fatigue and even the "blahs." The people who have always lived in cities or close enough for contamination, rarely *know* there is anything different. There is *knowing* and *knowing*. People have called cigarettes "coffin nails" for years and gone right on smoking. But today that knowledge has been pounded through into the survival mechanism of the brain—and people are actually giving smoking up.

If you are used to breathing air from a sailboat standing well out to sea, you can smell the difference in the air. If you have ever backpacked on skis deep into a white wilderness, you can *see* the difference. If you have ever climbed a 14,000-foot peak, you can *feel* the difference. But the city dweller who does such things is rare. For him and his family it's bumper to bumper through a haze of gas-floated filth. He may make an occasional sortie into strange and unaccustomed country, but far more often he travels highways more deadly than a fever swamp (if pollution doesn't get you the other car will) from his own patch to someone else's. The air isn't cleaner there, just different. Try driving through the towns in the industrial part of New Jersey with the top down.

Then there's water. Once upon a time you could swim almost anywhere if you were able to swim. Now in many places the waters ooze instead of flow. Garbage floats in the once-sparkling bays, and the water skier never knows into what foulness he may fall. Big public swimming pools are more predictable. They are mobbed as never before, and constant checks must be made to see that the disinfectant level is kept at "Safe." If it is, your eyes will look like red jellyfish and you may even have a headache. Disinfectant isn't so innocuous, either. If you *must* swim there to swim at all, remember that Vitamin C is an antitoxicity agent. If there is room, you might use mask, fins and snorkel for your laps—then at least your innards obey the mother's injunction, "But don't go near the water."

Don't stop now, there's more, lots more. In 1924 I was known as a "holy terror," and I was, too. With trouble at home in small and large doses, plus at least two or three dietary deficiencies (we weren't "poor" either, but then you don't have to be poor to be hungry any more), I lived up to the name. Like many another "bad" child, I had a sibling that was a "good" child, and nobody let me forget it. To quell my craving for sweets, I stole money. When I had money left over, I bought cigarettes. Being a "holy terror" didn't net me any friends amongst the citizenry. There were "nice" kids who weren't allowed to play with me, and they didn't—when their mothers could see them. I quickly learned that if I couldn't make it with the parents I could sure scare them, and that is what a whole generation is up to now. The only difference between them and me is that I was through that phase before my teens and these kids don't start until they get there.

Smoking got me lots of attention. I smoked like a chimney and hated the taste, the smell and my parched throat. I was only too glad when the YMCA swim coach said to the team, "Swim or smoke, it's all the same to me. You choose." I quit. In those days adults weren't kidding, it was swim or smoke.

When my children came along they too wanted to stir up the adults, feel a little wicked, be one of the gang. By that time it wasn't a way of getting back (after all parents smoked and teachers smoked and all the "real" athletes smoked), it was a matter of belonging. Would we let the kids have their wicked little moment? I should say not. Freud had taught us about guilt, and we knew that the worst thing that could happen to children was guilt. "If you are going to smoke anywhere, do it here," we said pompously, our only adverse comment being about tobacco stunting their growth. This we dared to say to kids growing so fast we could hardly keep them in clothes— and told them so often. My mother lied to me, to the folks she told she wasn't going to be home, to my father about small, unimportant matters, to my teachers about why I'd been absent, but I survived it. I told my kids tobacco would stunt them, and that was as bad, but I also took away their chance to be a little wicked, and that was worse. If you condone small sins, you encourage bigger ones. I am grateful that they are grown up, married and mothers before what ultimately happened, happened.

Last winter two boys in a boarding school near here wanted to be wicked enough to have something to talk about and enterprising enough to get a thrill or a kick by mixing up a batch of glue or some other chemical with hallucinogenic properties. They were fifteen and thirteen. Well, while minds under the influence of these drugs or chemicals are highly unpredictable, chemicals follow an inexorable law. Expose highly flammable ingredients to flame and you get fire. One of the boys lit a match *to see by,* and the whole works blew up. It took the younger boy two days to die, and one hopes that the one who survived did not light that match. But who really lit that match?

In my day they said aspirin and coke would make you pass out—we all tried it. Today kids even bypass liquor (or include it) for more exciting things. Let the grown-ups get bombed on gin, vodka, Scotch or whatever their "bag" is, let them act like idiots, vomit by the club pool and fall down in the garage—the kids were for higher "highs." They didn't want to be sloppy, they wanted out of this world—and they got it.

Since the Establishment smokes tobacco and drinks liquor, both must be square—but if you smoke pot, which shocks them, you get something "real" and you belong. There's even a dividend—you can feel "brave" because it's against the law. Of course, you only have to be brave in theory, as even the Establishment is smart enough to know they can't arrest *everybody.*

Today's children are children whose parents tried to be "close" to them and gave up being parents. Can you blame them for having something to say on every subject when their parents have asked them what they thought about everything from the adequacy of their allowance to whether or not the family should move to Peoria? Worse, the parents not only asked, they obeyed.

Disillusioned by a setup that not only won't let them study what they want to study, but often provides graduate students instead of professors as teachers, youngsters start fuming from the first moment they hit the college campus. Barred from many subjects that interest them and forced to "serve time" in something completely unrelated, the formless fuming takes shape. Forty-one percent of today's high school graduates go on to college, but fifty-one percent will drop out. Any manufacturer knows that when fifty-one percent of the total production of a machine must be discarded, there's something wrong with that machine. Only education has gone on year after year using up kids as though no bill was ever going to be presented. That bill is being presented now. The drug scene has hit the campus like you can't believe.

It will probably be years before we really know what marijuana, LSD, DMT, STP, amphetamines, methamphetamines (much stronger), barbiturates or any of the other hallucinogenic substances really do. Over a hundred are available, with at least that many promised for the next decade. By that time it may be too late for even those who only "turn on" socially (that's the one who thinks he can take it or leave it alone) to backtrack. On the other hand, except in the case of the "freakouts" (kids who "crash" and end up in institutions, do themselves in or simply get scared out of their heads) many of these new "escapes" may turn out to be no worse than tobacco or alcohol. But I have the uneasy feeling that I have just said it is no worse to be attacked by a shark than a barracuda.

Alcohol isn't used much by today's young—it isn't "in." However, the need to "escape" is just as strong as ever, and the same unstable types that used to be carried gagging into the showers, still clutching a quart of bourbon, now boast loudly of "the trip." He doesn't need alcohol—he has drugs or marijuana, and "they aren't one bit more harmful than liquor." He may be right, so how harmful *is* alcohol?

Alcohol, like drugs, is absolutely harmless until someone takes it. There are some people who can drink a little and there are some who think they can drink a lot. They mistake "holding your liquor" for drinking safely. Then there is the addictive group—they can't drink at all. Sooner or later, and sometimes with the first drink, they become alcoholics. There are about 6,000,000 of them in the United States. We who are "after thirty" have often felt like the kids do about drugs—"taken in moderation it can't hurt you"—and the "you" you mean is yourself. The drug "freakout" running naked down the street is always going to be someone from the next dorm, just as the disheveled man or woman swaying into the driver's seat couldn't ever be you either. Maybe so, but listen once.

Alcohol robs the body of the B vitamin, folic acid. You don't have to be a drunk to suffer this loss, just the usual run-of-the-mill drinker. As a nation we have poor eating habits, partly from ignorance and partly because of our economy, and we often are Vitamin B hungry. Add to this the "relaxing" cocktail hour and you can get "large cell" anemia. Anyone who has been to a beer party knows that there will be considerable tripping to the john. This doesn't seem very menacing unless one understands that if enough magnesium goes down the drain with the water, there will be a whale of a hangover next morning.

Not long ago I watched an MC on TV doing a coffee commercial. If I hadn't already known where he'd spent the days just prior to that unhappy rendition, I'd have known when he came on the air. Tense, nervous and with shaking hands, he got through it somehow—and this was a fellow who tosses off commercials like a chef tosses a pizza, only this time with a magnesium shortage. A hearty eater, our MC was really living dangerously, because magnesium is all-important in preventing blood clots, both in heart and brain. If you tie that in with alcohol's facility to change without hindrance into saturated fat plus the fact that it slows circulation, which in turn encourages clots, alcohol isn't all that harmless.

Everybody knows alcoholics get liver trouble, but not everybody knows that "social" drinkers do too, and that even before liver trouble shows up they may have damaged their kidneys. Alcohol has an absolute aversion to vitamins and is especially destructive to the B vitamin choline. Hemorrhages develop, fat and cholesterol deposits begin to settle in and, instead of having to "go" all evening, you can't. Circulation slows down and water accumulates in the tissues. I once saw a woman swollen to almost twice her normal size with huge, immovable, elephantine legs.

We've all seen people with "just a touch" of this bloating. Have you checked your ankles and under your eyes lately?

The liver (hardworking and indispensable) resents anything toxic. As you think of Bill Longgood's report, and Rachel Carson's, you know that every one of us is loaded with toxic substances we can't avoid any more than miners can avoid coal dust. Our liver has to be on the job twenty-four hours a day, cleaning us up to keep us going. If we add the extra burden of alcohol, is that fair?

A sick liver gives off vague miseries like the now-famous "blahs." Digestion is always off a little and energy is low. You think what you feel is your age, but more than likely it's twenty to thirty years of toxicity taking pot-shots at your liver. And speaking of pot—that "harmless" marijuana so highly recommended by the intelligentsia has a great affinity for the liver. *Fifty percent of it settles there at the outset* (and it's highly toxic). *Five days later* it slowly wends its way via the bile to the intestines and is then excreted. What do you suppose the chances are for a healthy liver in a young person who smokes marijuana daily, eats poorly and only occasionally, lies around watching the days slip by and makes up for dietary lacks, as well as the intake of marijuana, by munching candy bars?

CHAPTER SIXTEEN

Tomorrow

Go back to your Take Stock Chart and do a write-up on what you remember of your food habits from as far back as you can go. List the drugs you have been on and why you were on them. Your "binges" will be important. Are they beer, vodka or chocolate-covered cherries? What are your drinking habits and drug habits? Ask yourself if the kids are right when they say, "The grown-ups drink and take drugs, why shouldn't we?" Do you really need those sleeping pills, or would a good exercise workout and the calcium in milk do the job? I've put a good relaxation section in my record *Keep Fit—Be Happy, Vol. 1*. It puts kids to sleep—why don't you try it?

Go through your medicine cabinet and write down a list of what is *actually* there—not the brand names, the chemicals. Check with Adelle Davis's book, *Let's Get Well,** to find out what those things can do to you. While you are reading that book, pick up some pointers on what things are good for you, and why. If you are a man you will get the *whys* answered in the books I've suggested. If you are a woman and want to open your mouth on the subject, you'd better have the whys down pat, especially if you want to get through to your youngsters. There are two examples you can set—*must* set. One is the example of how you use your energy to make an enjoyable life. This is particularly important now when so many people are against so much and don't seem to know what to be for.

---

* New York: Harcourt, Brace & World, 1965.

The second is the means by which you gather your energy and drive. You can't tell a young person he is wasting his life if you are wasting yours. You can't say drugs are bad if you take them every night. You can't say people are slovenly if you are careless about yourself—and you can't say "Eat decently" as you whip up an "instant" dinner.

We live in "interesting times," so let it be said of you that, whatever else, you are interesting. To be interesting you have to believe in something fully. At least be interested in *you*.

EXERCISE INDEX

(All exercises in the book are numbered and the following references are to exercise numbers except where page numbers are clearly indicated.)

GENERAL INDEX